Landscape Detailing

Landscape Detailing

Michael Littlewood

The Architectural Press : London

First published in 1984 by the Architectural Press Ltd,
9 Queen Anne's Gate, London SW1H 9BY

British Library Cataloguing in Publication Data

Littlewood, Michael
Landscape detailing.
1. Landscape architecture
I. Title
712 SB472.3

ISBN 0 85139 859 6

Typeset by Phoenix Photosetting, Chatham
Printed in Great Britain by
Biddles Ltd, Guildford, Surrey

Contents

Foreword

Many landscape architects, architects and other professionals responsible for the production of drawn details for landscape construction works, have need of a ready reference. This Handbook has been produced to meet that need and can be extended by additional sheets. It has been arranged for ease of reference, removal and copying of sheets, and is sufficiently flexible for designers to use it for their specific requirements.

There are, of course, as many elements to be detailed as are found in site development for landscape architectural projects, and there can be no definitive list of detail requirements in landscape design, nor of the details that supplement other contract documents. These must be specified, with precise regard to each element, by the landscape architect, architect or designer based on his or her experience and the needs of the contractor. Site conditions must be the final arbiter of the detail required.

Design information has been excluded; many other publications deal with this subject more adequately than could be achieved in this Handbook.

Acknowledgements

I must give particular thanks to my draughtsman, Derek Perkins, who has produced such excellent work from my rough sketches. He has at times, because of the pressure of work, been assisted by Ros Norman and I am grateful to her for coming to my aid. I would also like to thank Bill Ambridge and Michele Lovelle, who have worked with me on projects in the past and who have given me tremendous support especially during difficult times, also Manny Stefanikis, and Chris Blandford, all landscape architects.

Special thanks are also due to Maritz Vandenberg, Managing Editor of the Architectural Press, for his continued support and enthusiasm, and to Keith Kneebone, Production Manager, for a fine job of printing.

Last, but certainly not least, to my wife, Joan, who always gave me tremendous support and encouragement even when severely ill, and who died before I could show her a finished copy of this book.

Introduction

These landscape detail sheets have been produced in an effort to eliminate needless repetition in detailing landscape works covering hard elements. It is possible to use them without alteration, but in some cases, minor modifications and additions to dimensions or specification may be necessary. Lettering has been standardised by the use of a stencil (italic 3.5 mm).
When a detail is required which is not available on a detail sheet the new detail can be drawn by the designer using the standardised format which will enable it to be added to the original collection of details and to be easily re-used on other projects. Readers are invited to send the publishers copies of their own details which they think would merit inclusion in future editions of this book. Appropriate acknowledgement will be made.
Each sheet portrays a detail without reference to its surroundings. This approach has been adopted because it affords to each detail the maximum number of possibilities for re-use. No attempt has been made to recommend a particular detail for a particular situation. This remains the responsibility of the landscape architect, architect or designer.
The construction notes which precede each section are intended to give only the briefest outline of main points. For more detailed guidance the publications listed at the end of the notes should be consulted. Details should not be used without a knowledge of the content of the British Standards contained in the specification. Some British Standards contain alternative specifications which may prove more suitable in a particular case.
There are, of course, a great many other details which might be included on specific projects or in specific situations. In some cases, the detailing of site elements and site structures can be co-ordinated very carefully with the architect or building designer in order to ensure a uniformity of form and material. In yet other instances, various agencies and organisations may have standard details which must be used on their particular projects.

Use of the detail sheets

The collection of detail sheets, as purchased, may if users wish be broken down into individual leaves, punched, and stored in a ring binder. The detail sheets have been bound in such a way as to facilitate this operation. In the form of individual leaves the details can easily be photocopied or traced or copy negatives can be made.
The sheets must be used in conjunction with a site layout drawing, preferably at 1:200. There may be more than one sheet depending upon the size of the project. The layout drawing will convey all information on levels, directions of falls, setting-out dimensions for walls and paths, and location of posts, piers and construction joints. The layout drawing will also indicate the location of the selected details and the deployment of surface finishes. (See Figure 1)

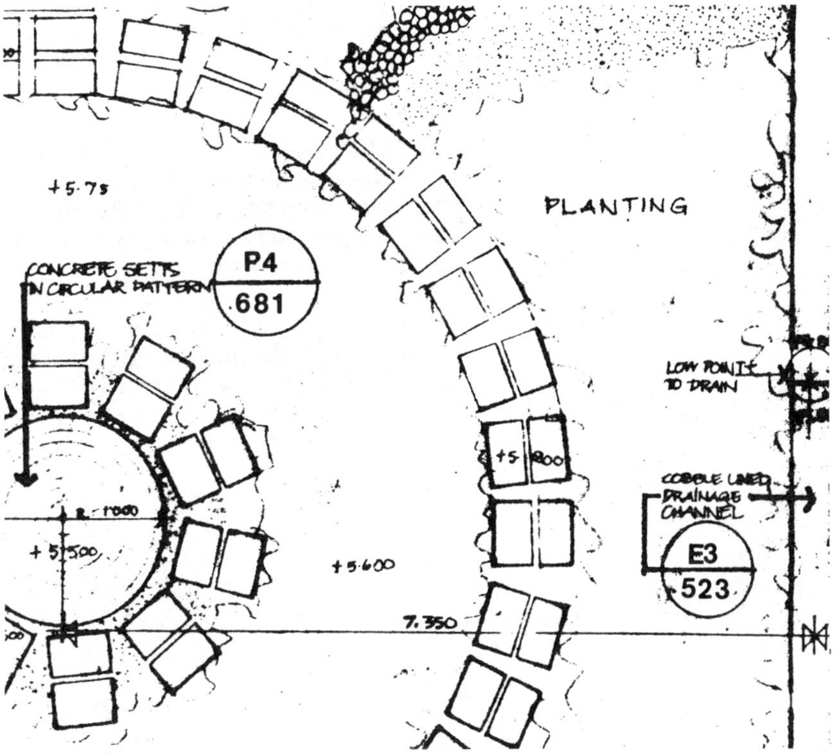

Figure 1

Simple conjunction of details, for example a wall and a mowing strip, can be indicated by the drawing of the two relevant section lines in close proximity. (See Figure 2)

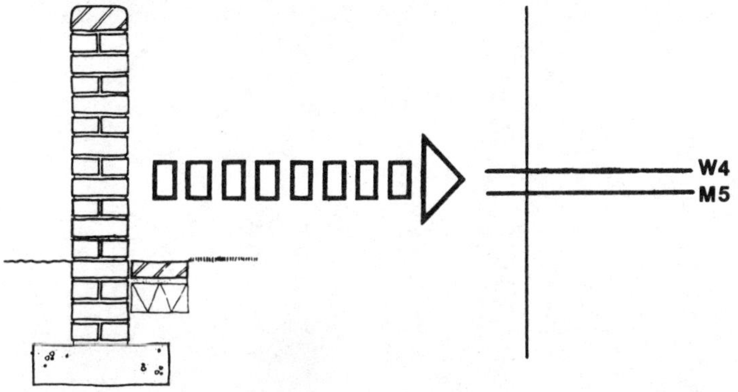

Figure 2

Standards

British Standards and Codes of Practice are referred to where necessary. Users of this book living in countries where British Standards are not used should delete the reference to the British Standard and, if they feel it necessary, either insert a reference to an equivalent national standard or describe what is required in empirical terms.

Production of new detail sheets

Where the use of a detail not included in the original collection of Detail Sheets is required, the new detail is produced on A4 tracing paper using a standard format. This enables it to be added to the original collection and to be easily re-used. New details are assigned a reference number by the Design Office using their own reference system. The title of the new detail as shown in the centre label at the foot of the drawing, is then added to the contents list prefacing each section.

Issue of detail sheets

Detail sheets can be used in two ways. A set of photocopies can be issued to the contractor of the selected details, after completion of the title panel reference, and number-stamping each detail with the office stamp.
The second method is to trace or copy a batch of details, grouped according to type and identified with key numbers onto an A1 sheet of tracing paper and include the drawing with the contract set in the normal way.

Chapter 1

Free-standing walls

The stability of a free-standing wall can be improved by adding piers, staggering the wall in bays, or by increasing the thickness of the wall. The thickness of a free-standing wall can be estimated by reference to appropriate publications given at the end of these Notes.
All walls over 2000 mm high should be referred to a structural engineer for checking. Stability calculations for such walls may also be required by the district surveyor or building inspector. Only in the Inner London area is approval required from the local authority when the height exceeds 1800 mm above ground level.

Choice of bricks and blocks

Bricks used in free-standing external walls, being exposed on both sides, are more prone to deterioration through frost action than the same bricks used, for example, in the external walls of a building.
Frost-resistant bricks are generally those with low water absorbencies. However, certain types of stock bricks with absorbencies of up to 20% are frost-resistant because their highly-porous structure allows ice to expand within the brick without causing damage. Users should contact the manufacturers to confirm that their bricks are suitable for the degree of exposure intended.
External free-standing brick walls are also subject to deterioration following the reaction of soluble sulphates present in the bricks with the tricalcium aluminate constituent in ordinary Portland cement. The reaction is accompanied by expansion of the mortar and subsequent cracking. Sulphate attack can be avoided by the use of a 'special' quality brick as defined by BS 3921:1974. The BS limits the soluble salt content of bricks of 'special' quality, but not those or 'ordinary' quality. Alternatively, use a richer mortar mix, e.g. 1:3 or a sulphate-resisting cement.
Concrete blocks used in free-standing external walls should be Type A, as defined in BS 2028, 1364:1968. A rough surface texture helps reduce weather staining. Special pierced concrete blocks are also available. Calcium silicate bricks should be Class 3 or higher as defined in BS 187:Part 2:1978.

Copings and cappings

Their purpose is first to prevent water seepage into the wall from the top, and secondly to shed water clear of the face of the wall, both as effectively as possible.

Copings

Reference should be made to BS 3798:1964 for copings of clayware, concrete or stone. A minimum weight of 1.5kN/m^2 is preferred for copings with concrete or stone units.
The overhang, if any, of any coping or capping should include a throating recess or a drip not less than 13 mm wide, with the outer drip edge at least 40 mm from the face of the brickwork.

Cappings

The usual practice of using a brick on edge coping is acceptable because it is the damp proof course under the coping that is functioning as a coping and not the brick on edge. Because of the presence of the damp proof course, brick on edge copings tend to become saturated and are particularly susceptible to frost damage and movement.
End bricks of brick copings should be held in position by metal cramps. Cramps can also be built into the top of the wall at a spacing of 900 mm to secure the coping bricks along the length of the wall.

Mortars

It is essential that there be a permanent flexural tensile bond between the bricks and the mortar to ensure that free-standing walls resist lateral pressure.
In sulphate-free conditions use a relatively weak mortar, e.g. 1:1:6 with clay bricks. If sulphates are present in the bricks a sulphate-resisting cement or a stronger mix should be used, as recommended under 'Choice of bricks'. Calcium silicate bricks are generally laid in a weaker gauge than clay bricks. Brickwork below ground level and up to 150 mm above ground level, should be laid in a 1:3 cement mortar mix.

Damp proof courses

A damp proof course, 150 mm from ground level, is required. The use of any damp proof course near ground level must provide the necessary adhesion across the joint. Only two methods meet this requirement:
1 Two courses of (engineering) bricks, to

BS 3921 : 1974 or BS 743 : 1970, having a water absorption of not more than 7% laid in 1 : ¼ : 3 mortar.
2 Two courses of 5 mm slates fully half-lapped and bedded in 1 : ¼ : 3 mortar to BS 743 : 1970.
In certain situations where walls are constructed of frost-resistant bricks a damp proof course near ground level may not be necessary.
A damp proof course is also necessary at the top of the wall under the coping if the coping is of a porous material such as brick on edge. If the coping is of an impermeable material such as metal, PVC or engineering bricks, no damp proof course is required. Although natural slate or clay tile is the best damp proof course in this position, a lead core bituminous damp proof course can also be used.
If a damp and mossy appearance to the lower parts of a wall is not objected to, the damp proof course may be omitted provided that the bricks be of 'special' quality and a strong mortar mix (e.g. 1 : 3) is used. The same applies to the damp proof course under the coping.

Expansion joints

Expansion or movement joints are necessary to accommodate thermal and moisture expansion. They must be constructed in such a way as to ensure a complete separation over the full height of the wall including the damp proof course and coping/capping, but not the foundations. A 10 mm joint should be provided every 12 m for clay, bricks and concrete blocks and every 6 m for calcium silicate (sand lime) bricks.

Foundations

The depth and width of a foundation will vary according to the type of subsoil. On average subsoils a depth of 450–600 mm is usually sufficient; on shrinkable clay the depth may have to be 900 mm or greater. A maximum width of 525 mm for unreinforced concrete foundations for 225 mm wide walls is advised, but site conditions will determine a final size after consultation with an engineer. A concrete mix of 1 : 6 is used in all the details although other mixes may be equally suitable.
Where a wall is below 500 mm in height, foundations can be omitted altogether. The topsoil should be removed and the brick-work built off the top of the subsoil which should be thoroughly compacted. Where more than 150 mm of topsoil has to be removed, the level of the excavation can be made up with well consolidated clinker.
The depth of brickwork below ground should not exceed 200 mm.

References

The Architectural Press Ltd, London
M Gage and T Kirkbride
Design in Blockwork, 2nd Ed, 1976

C C Handisyde
Hard Landscape in Brick, Chap 11, 1976

E Beazley
Design and Detail of the Space between Buildings, 1960

Brick Development Association
The Design of Free-standing Brick Walls, February 1983
Mortars for Brickwork, September 1973

Building Research Establishment Digests
65, 66 The selection of clay building bricks
89 Sulphate attack on brickwork
77 Damp proof courses

HMSO
C W Newberry and K J Eaton
Wind Loading Handbook Building Research Establishment Report, 1974

E & F N Spon Ltd
M F Downing
Landscape Construction, 1977

British Standards Institute
BS 3921 : 1974 Clay bricks and blocks
BS 2028, 1364 : 1968 Pre-cast concrete blocks
BS 187 : Part 2 1978 Calcium silicate (sand lime and flint lime) bricks
BS 3798 : 1964 Coping units
BS 4729 : 1971 Shapes and dimensions of special bricks
BS 743 : 1970 Material for damp proof courses
BS 5628 : 1978 The structural use of masonry : Part 1 Unreinforced masonry
CP 3 : Chap V : Part 2 : 1972 Wind loads
CP 111 : 1970 Structural recommendations for loadbearing walls

British Ceramic Research Association
SP 91 : 1977 Design guide for reinforced and pre-stressed clay brickwork.

Detail sheets

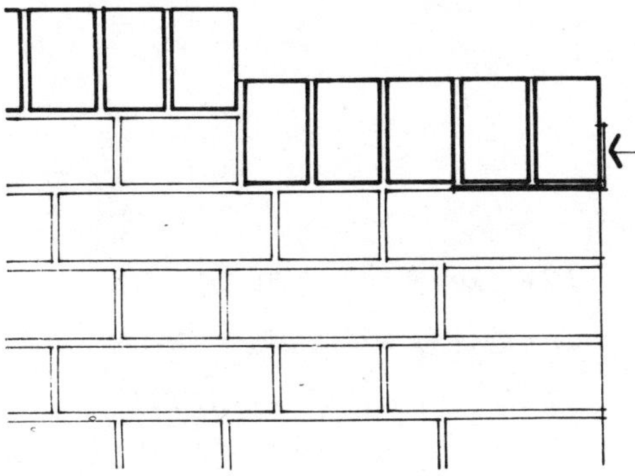

ELEVATION

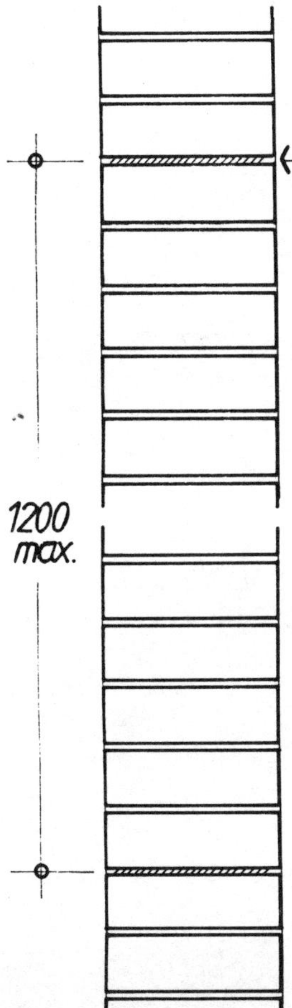

1200 max.

PLAN

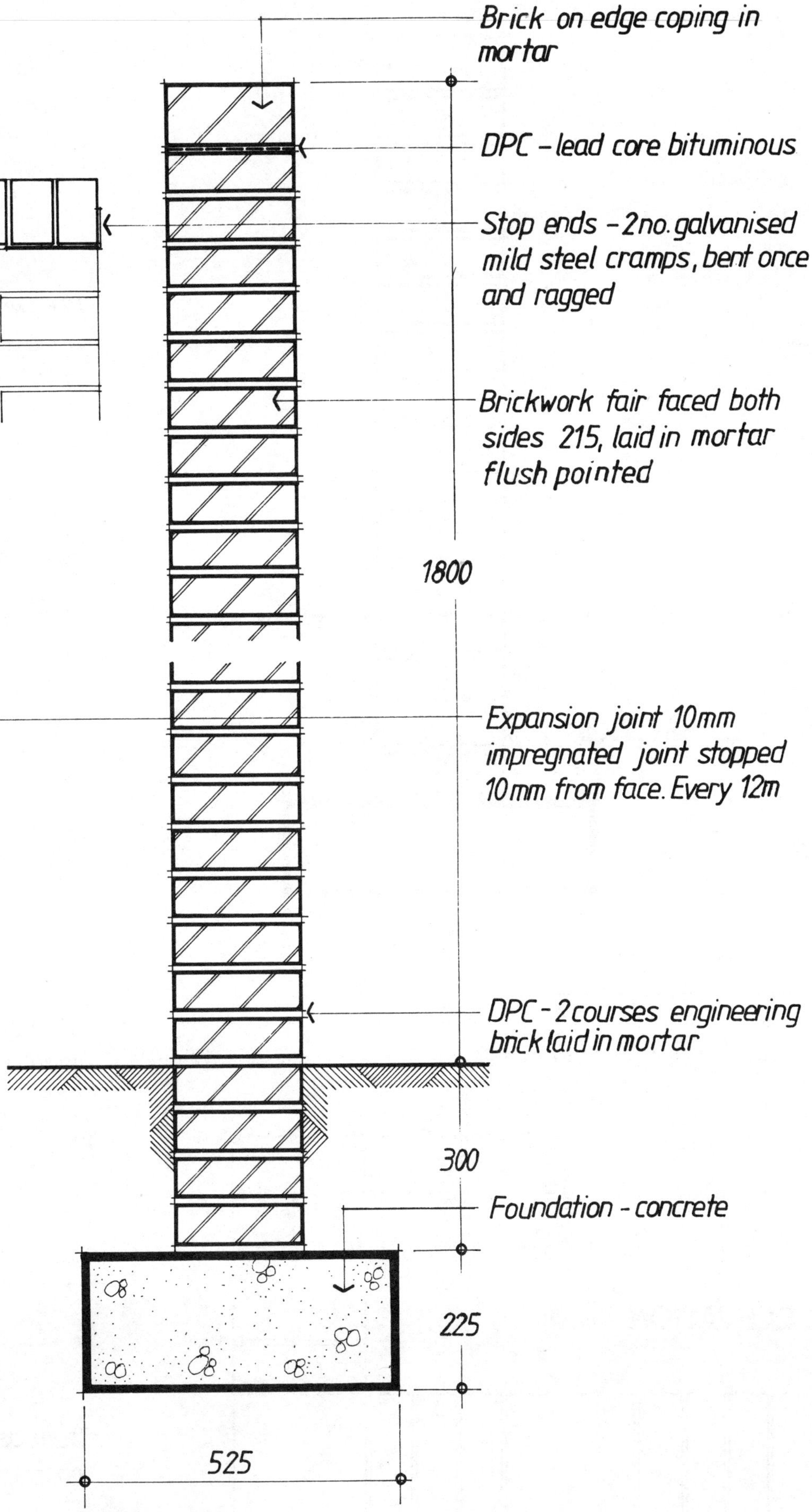

Brick on edge coping in mortar
DPC – lead core bituminous
Stop ends – 2no. galvanised mild steel cramps, bent once and ragged
Brickwork fair faced both sides 215, laid in mortar flush pointed
1800
Expansion joint 10mm impregnated joint stopped 10mm from face. Every 12m
DPC – 2 courses engineering brick laid in mortar
300
Foundation – concrete
225
525

SECTION

Scale 1:10

WALL
brick (high)

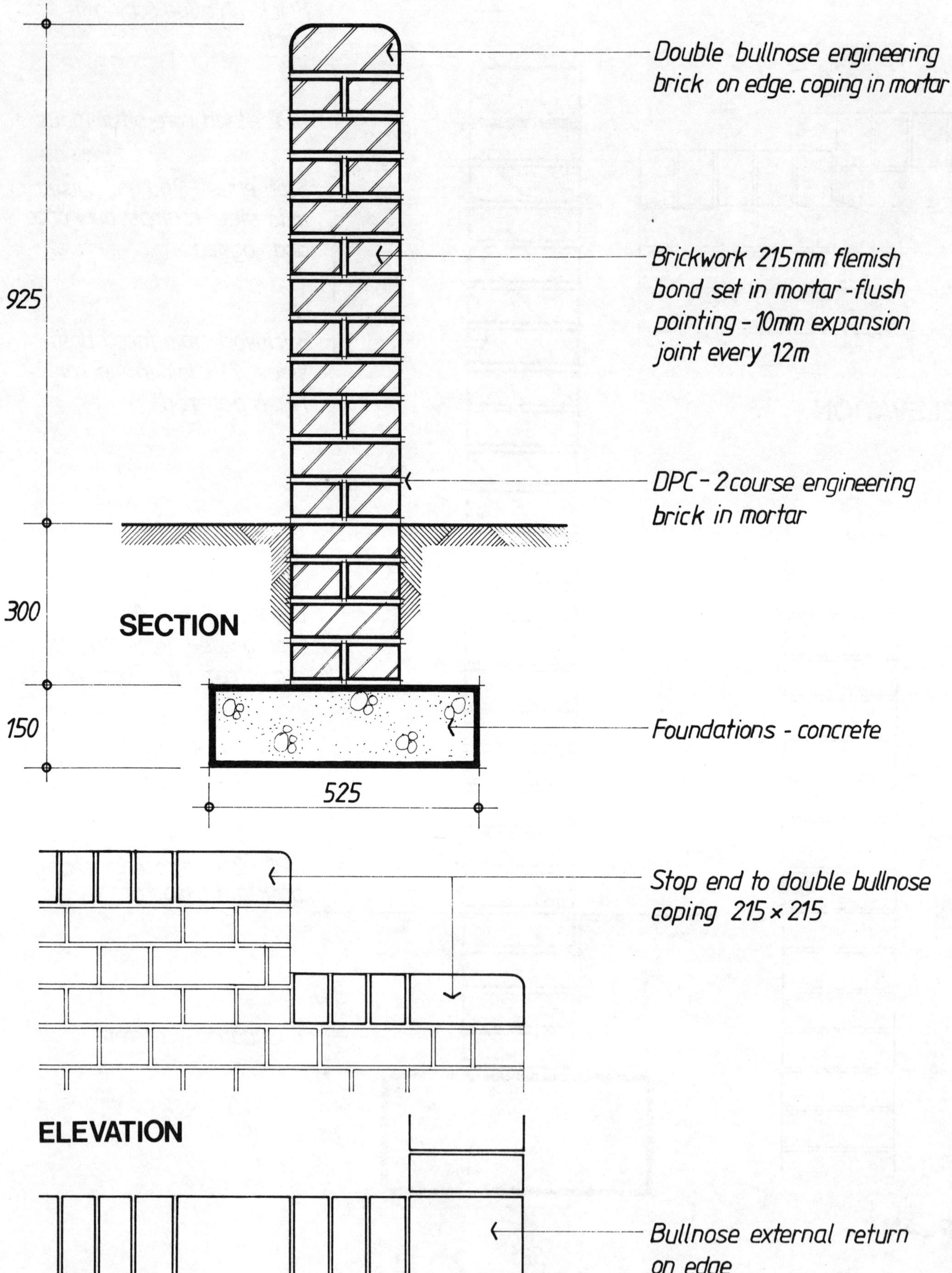
925
300
150
525
SECTION
Double bullnose engineering brick on edge. coping in mortar
Brickwork 215mm flemish bond set in mortar - flush pointing - 10mm expansion joint every 12m
DPC - 2 course engineering brick in mortar
Foundations - concrete
ELEVATION
Stop end to double bullnose coping 215 × 215
PLAN
Bullnose external return on edge

Scale 1:10

WALL
brick (medium)

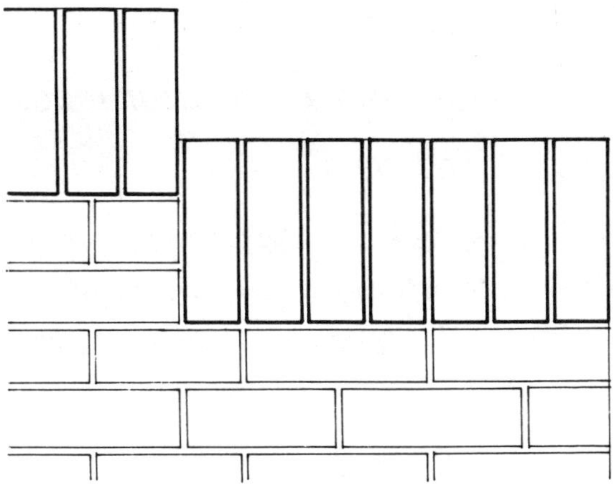

ELEVATION *(step coping)*

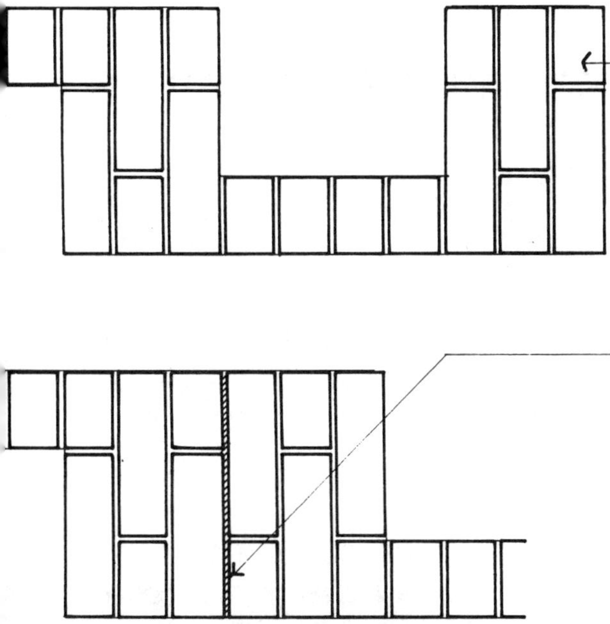

PLANS

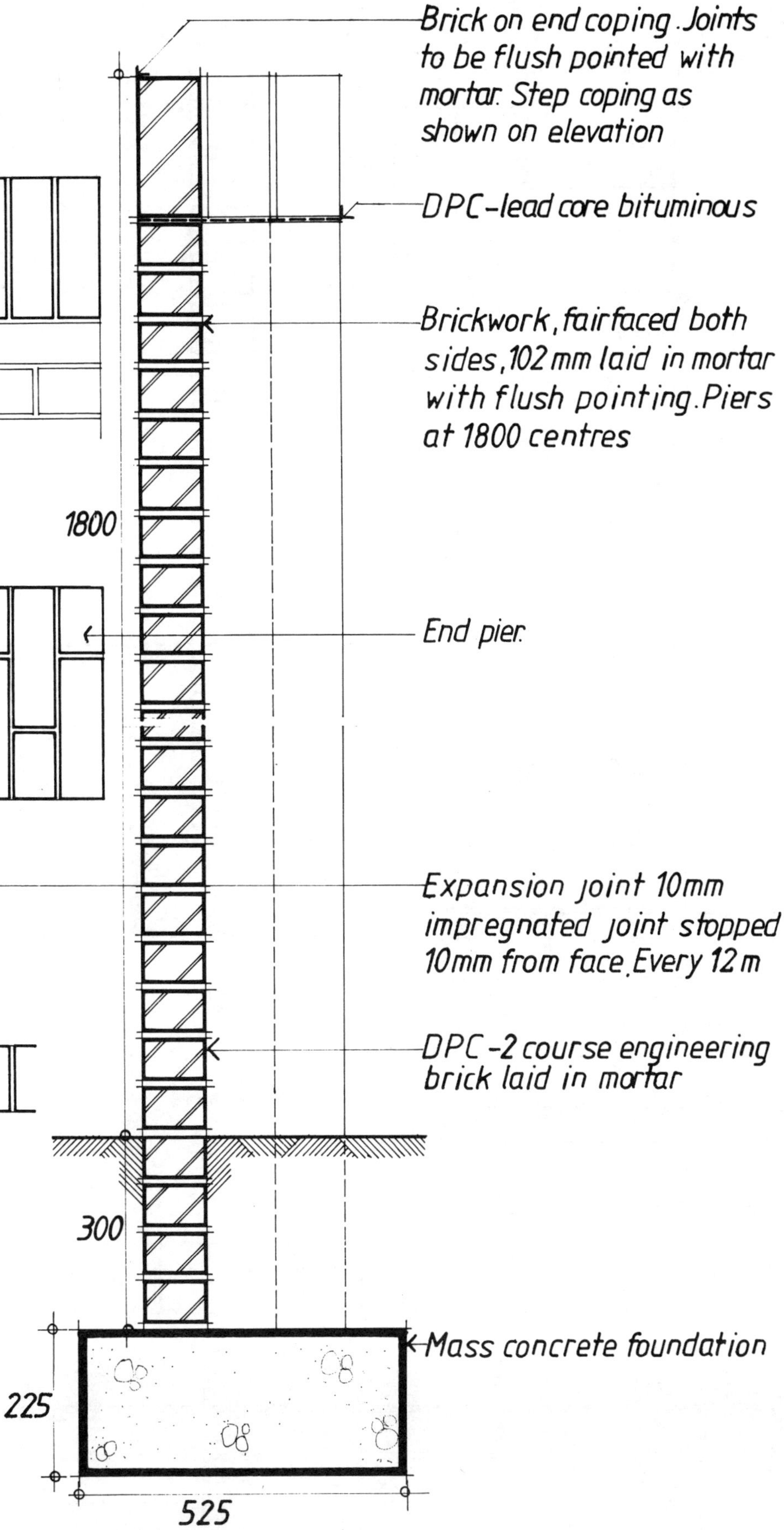
Brick on end coping. Joints to be flush pointed with mortar. Step coping as shown on elevation
DPC–lead core bituminous
Brickwork, fairfaced both sides, 102 mm laid in mortar with flush pointing. Piers at 1800 centres
1800
End pier
Expansion joint 10mm impregnated joint stopped 10mm from face. Every 12 m
DPC–2 course engineering brick laid in mortar
300
Mass concrete foundation
225
525

SECTION

Scale 1:10

WALL
brick (high)

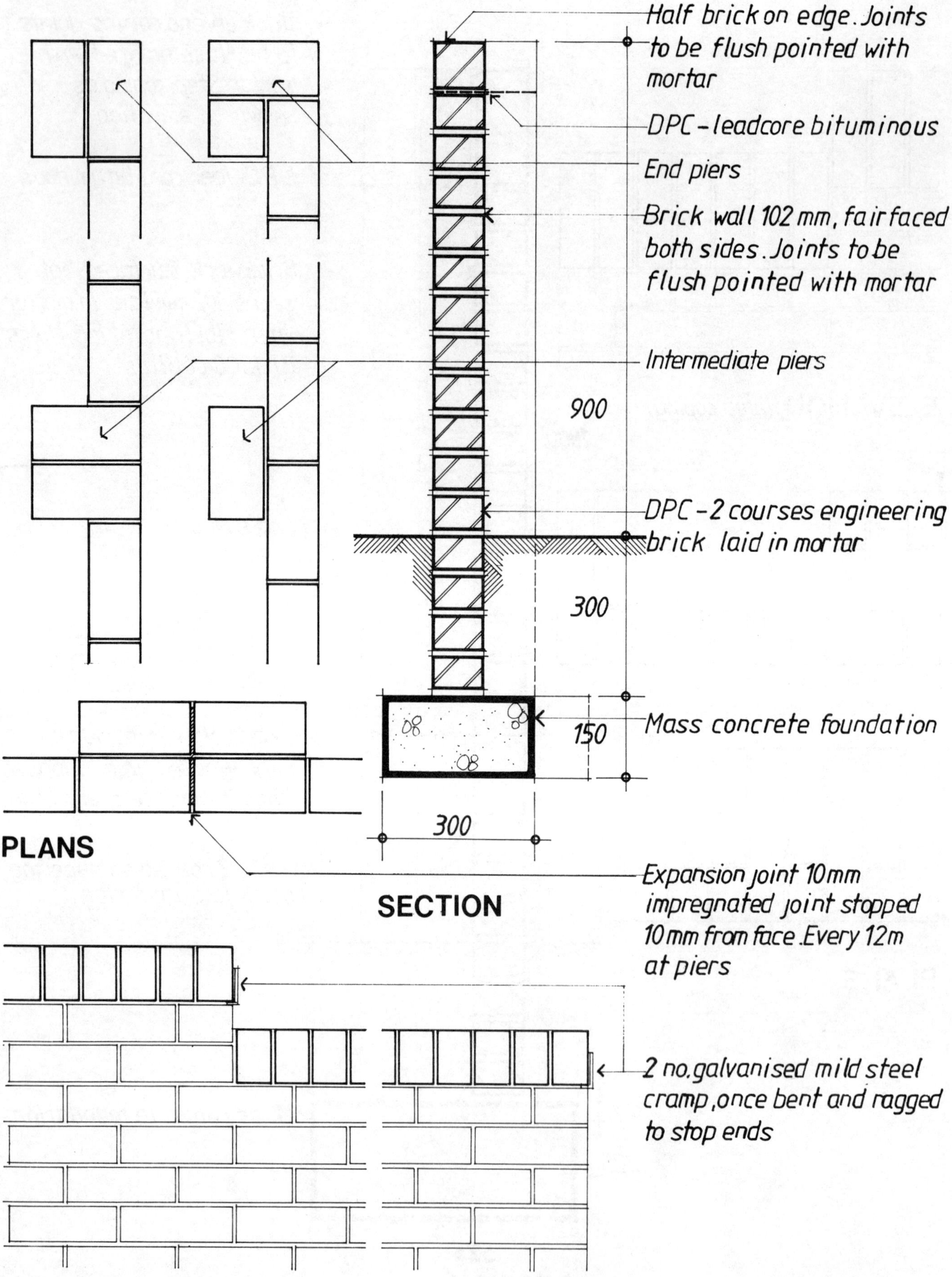
Half brick on edge. Joints to be flush pointed with mortar
DPC - leadcore bituminous
End piers
Brick wall 102 mm, fairfaced both sides. Joints to be flush pointed with mortar
Intermediate piers
900
DPC - 2 courses engineering brick laid in mortar
300
Mass concrete foundation
150
300
PLANS
Expansion joint 10 mm impregnated joint stopped 10 mm from face. Every 12 m at piers
SECTION
2 no. galvanised mild steel cramp, once bent and ragged to stop ends
ELEVATION

Scale 1:10

WALL
brick (medium)

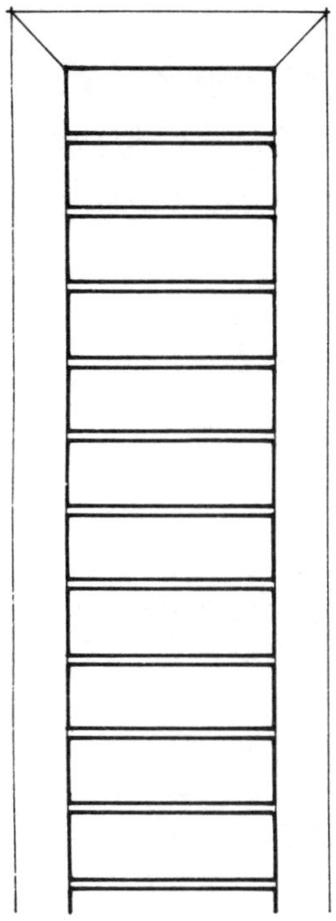

PLAN

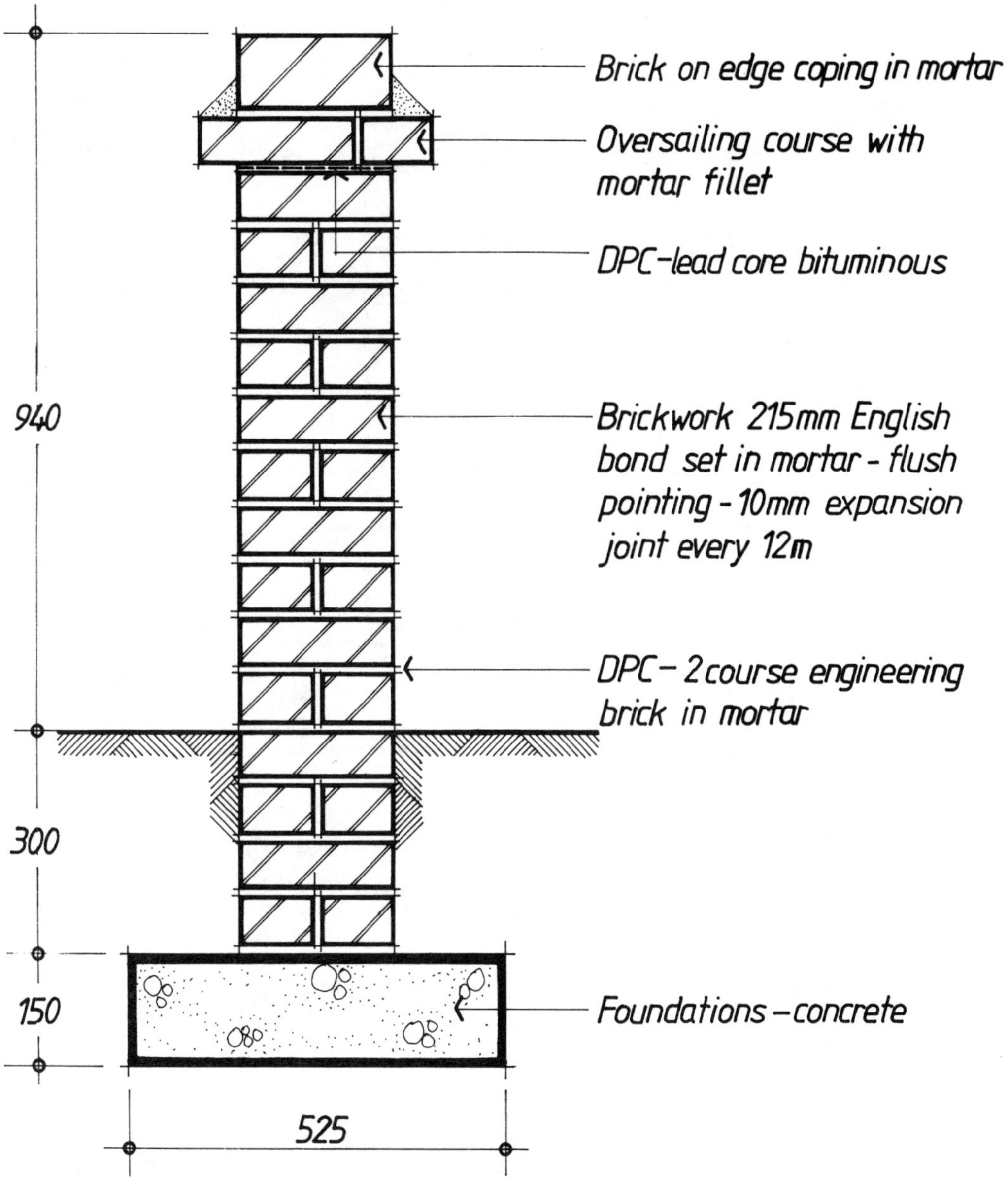
Brick on edge coping in mortar
Oversailing course with mortar fillet
DPC-lead core bituminous
Brickwork 215mm English bond set in mortar - flush pointing - 10mm expansion joint every 12m
DPC – 2 course engineering brick in mortar
Foundations – concrete
940
300
150
525

SECTION

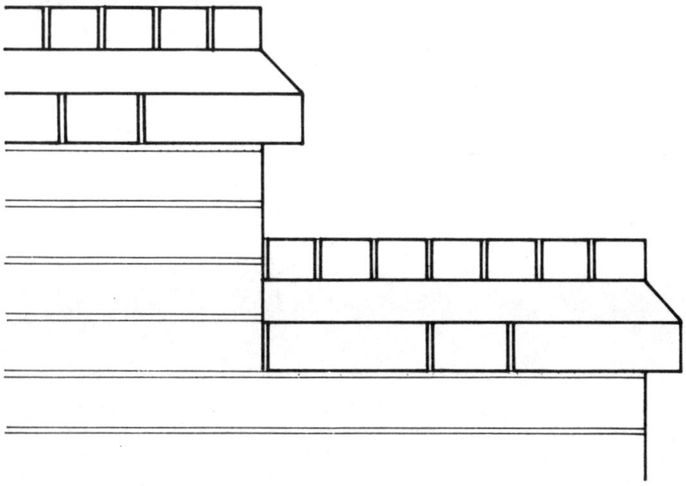

ELEVATION

Scale 1:10

WALL
brick (medium)

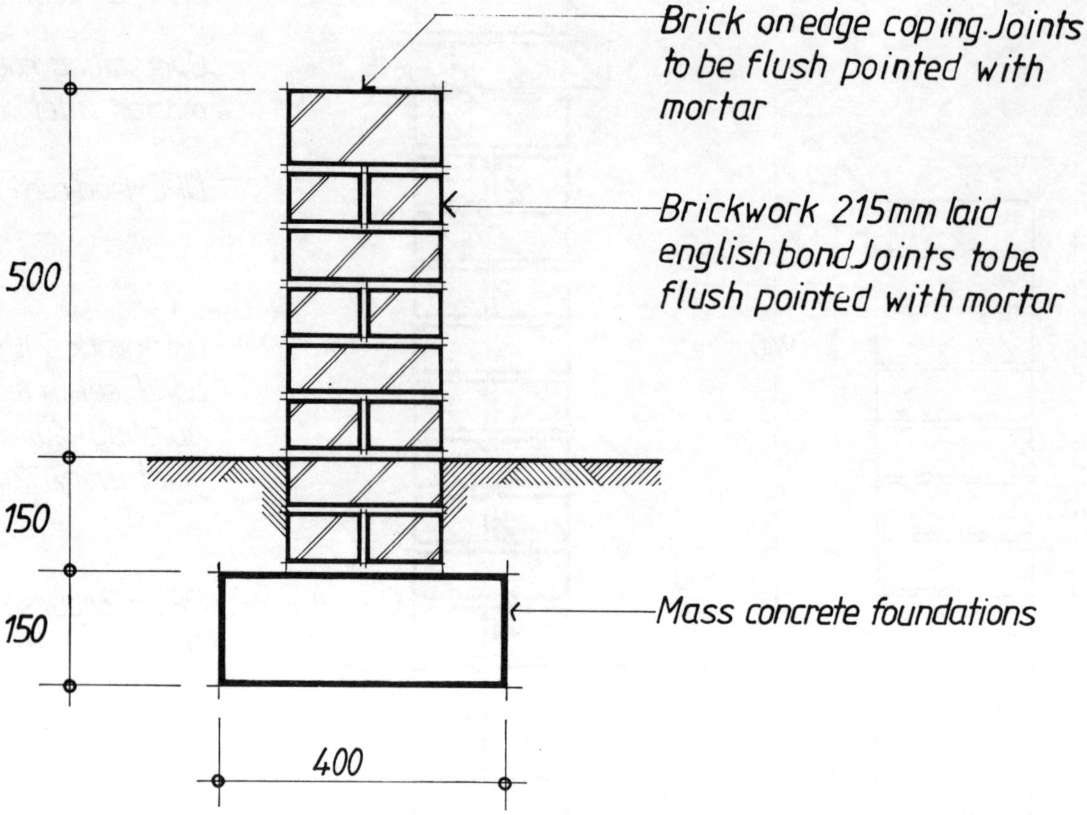

SECTION

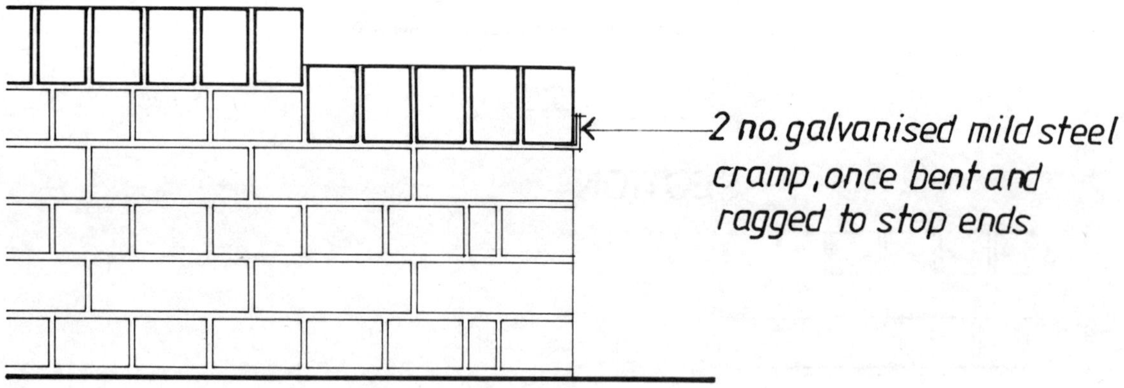

ELEVATION

Scale 1:10

WALL
brick (low)

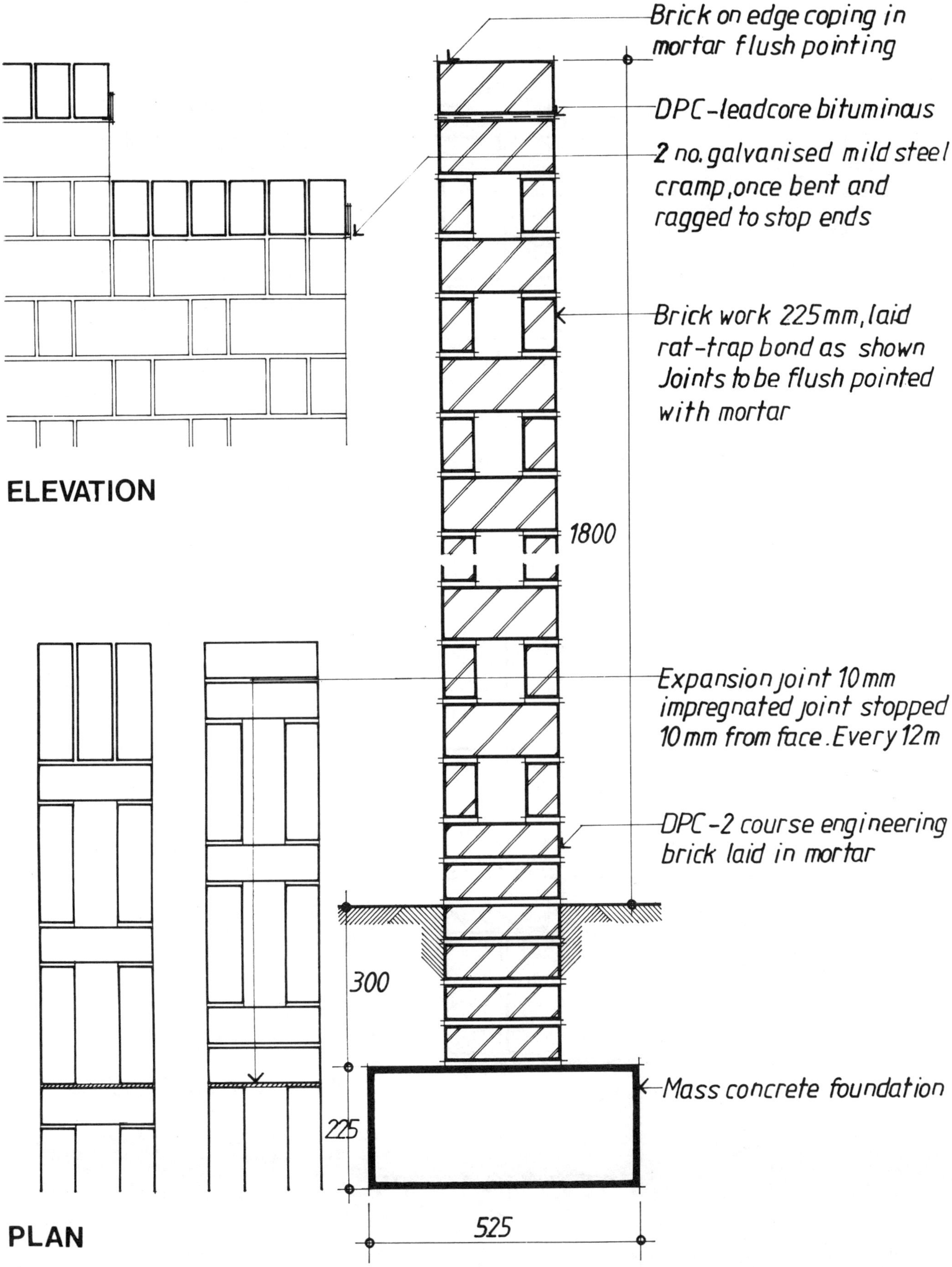
Brick on edge coping in mortar flush pointing
DPC-leadcore bituminous
2 no. galvanised mild steel cramp, once bent and ragged to stop ends
Brick work 225mm, laid rat-trap bond as shown Joints to be flush pointed with mortar
1800
Expansion joint 10mm impregnated joint stopped 10mm from face. Every 12m
DPC-2 course engineering brick laid in mortar
300
225
Mass concrete foundation
525
ELEVATION
PLAN

SECTION

Scale 1:10

WALL

brick rat trap bond

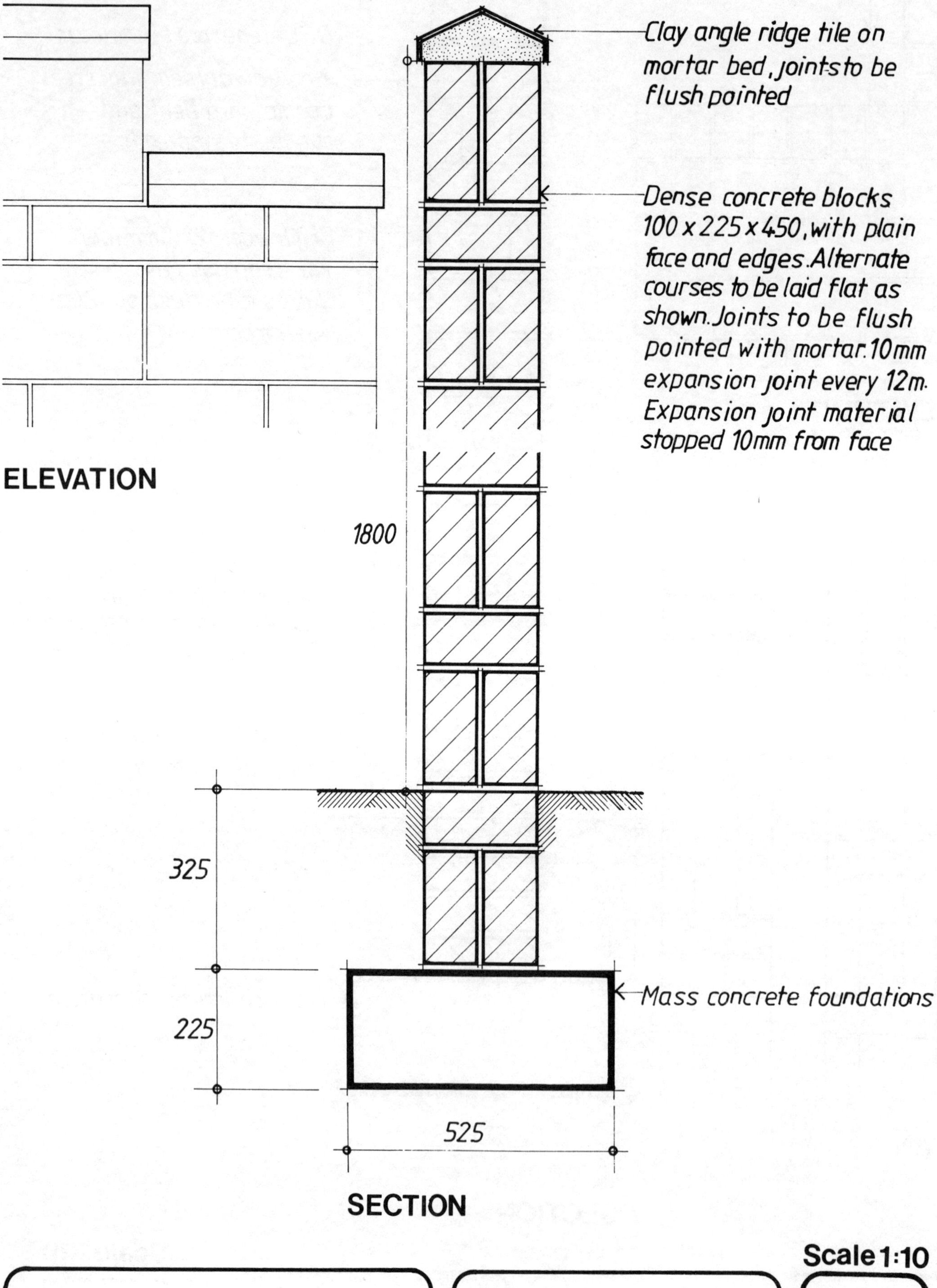
Clay angle ridge tile on mortar bed, joints to be flush pointed
Dense concrete blocks 100 x 225 x 450, with plain face and edges. Alternate courses to be laid flat as shown. Joints to be flush pointed with mortar. 10mm expansion joint every 12m. Expansion joint material stopped 10mm from face
ELEVATION
1800
325
225
Mass concrete foundations
525
SECTION

Scale 1:10

WALL
concrete block (high)

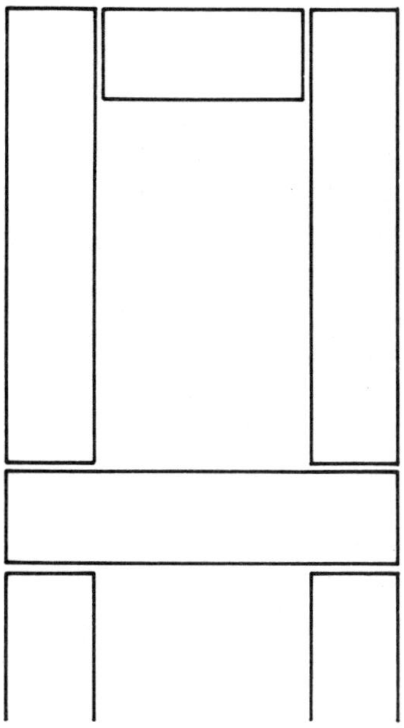

PLAN

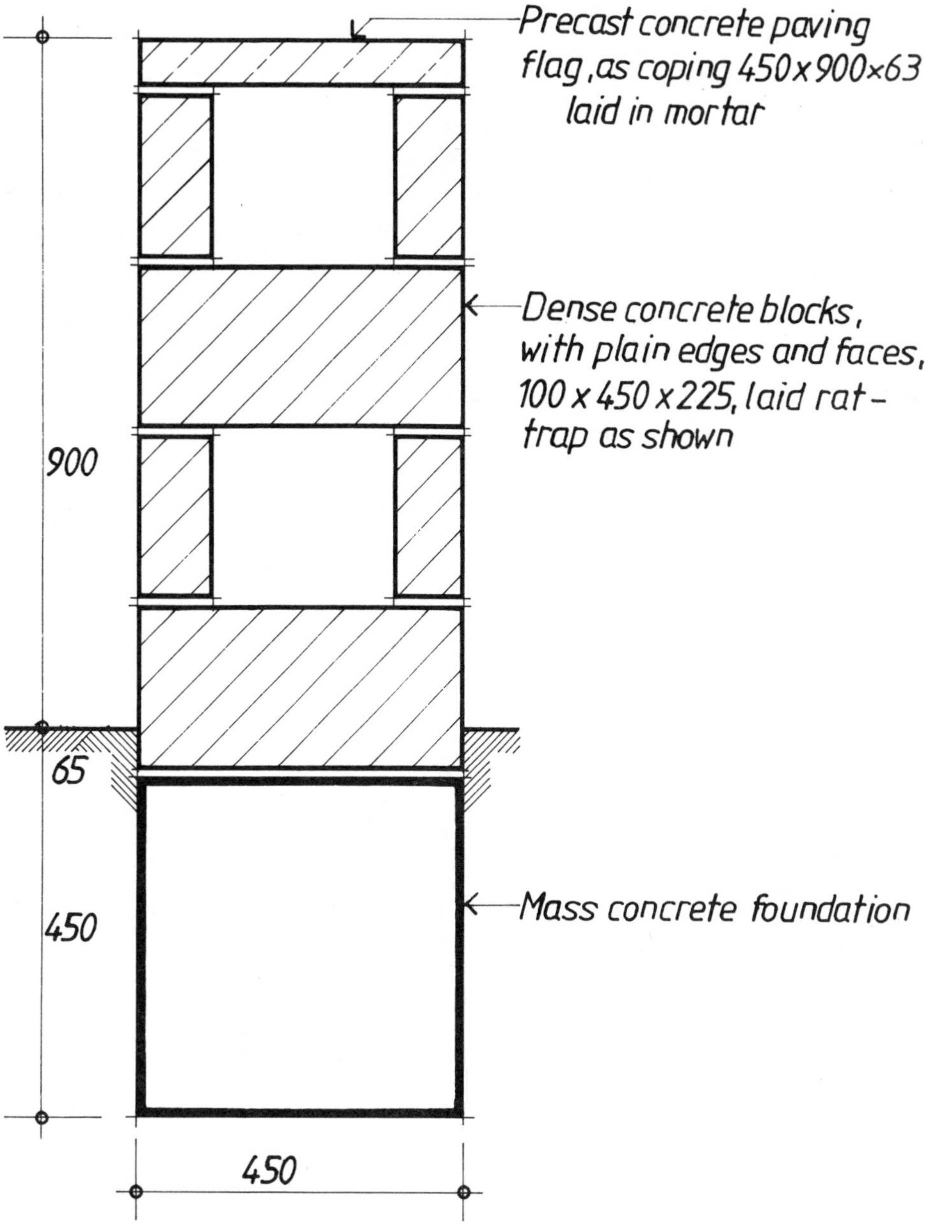
Precast concrete paving flag, as coping 450 x 900 x 63 laid in mortar
Dense concrete blocks, with plain edges and faces, 100 x 450 x 225, laid rat-trap as shown
Mass concrete foundation
900
65
450
450

SECTION

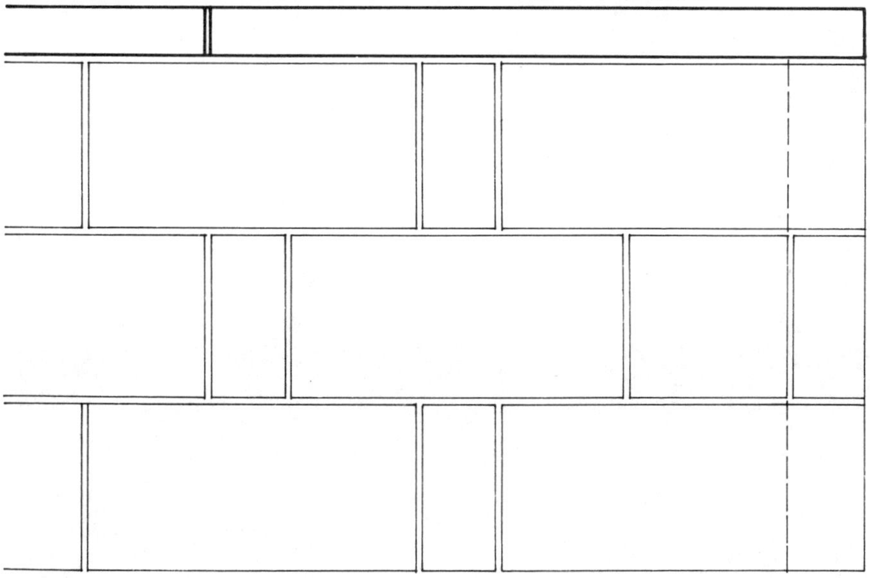

ELEVATION

Scale 1:10

WALL

concrete block

Chapter 2

Screen walls

This type of walling is quite easy to erect and reinforcement is not usually necessary. Concrete blocks are available in several standard designs, but in general they are approximately 300 mm square, and 90 mm thick. Colour and finish vary according to the manufacturer. Alternatively, a screen wall can be achieved with perforated bricks.

Foundations

Screen blocks can be mortared directly onto the concrete foundations of 1 : 6 mix. They should be 200 mm wider than the wall (100 mm each side) and at least 200 mm deep depending upon the wall height and ground conditions. Soft ground may necessitate thicker foundations. Alternatively, lay two courses of ordinary concrete blocks on a hardcore bed, with a flat coping stone on top.

Mortar

This should be workable, but not too sloppy. Prevent spillage on to the block faces. A mix of one (1) of cement to five (5) parts of sand should be used.

Joints

These should be 9 mm throughout.

Piers

Pilaster or pier blocks are needed at each end of a free standing wall and at 3000 mm centres depending upon the height of the wall. Walls above four (4) courses high should be reinforced with rods set into the foundations. The cavity must then be filled with mortar and capped with a special capping block.

Coping

A special coping block should be placed on top of the screen blocks to provide a suitable finish.

References

Cement And Concrete Association
Concrete Block Walls, 1966
Screen Walls of Pierced Concrete

Detail sheets

2.1 Perforated Brickwork
2.2 Decorative Concrete Block

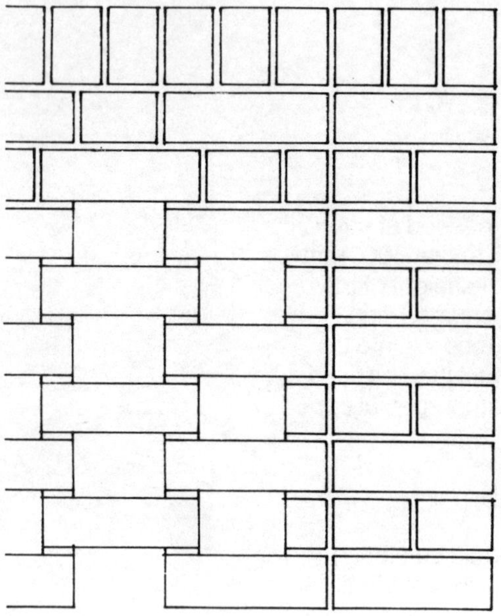

ELEVATION

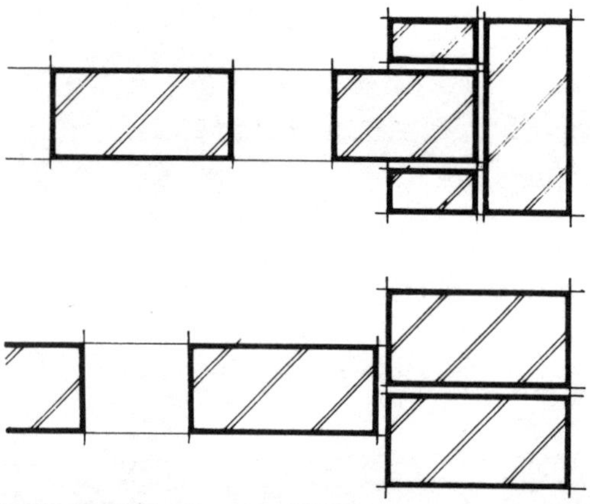

PLANS bonding

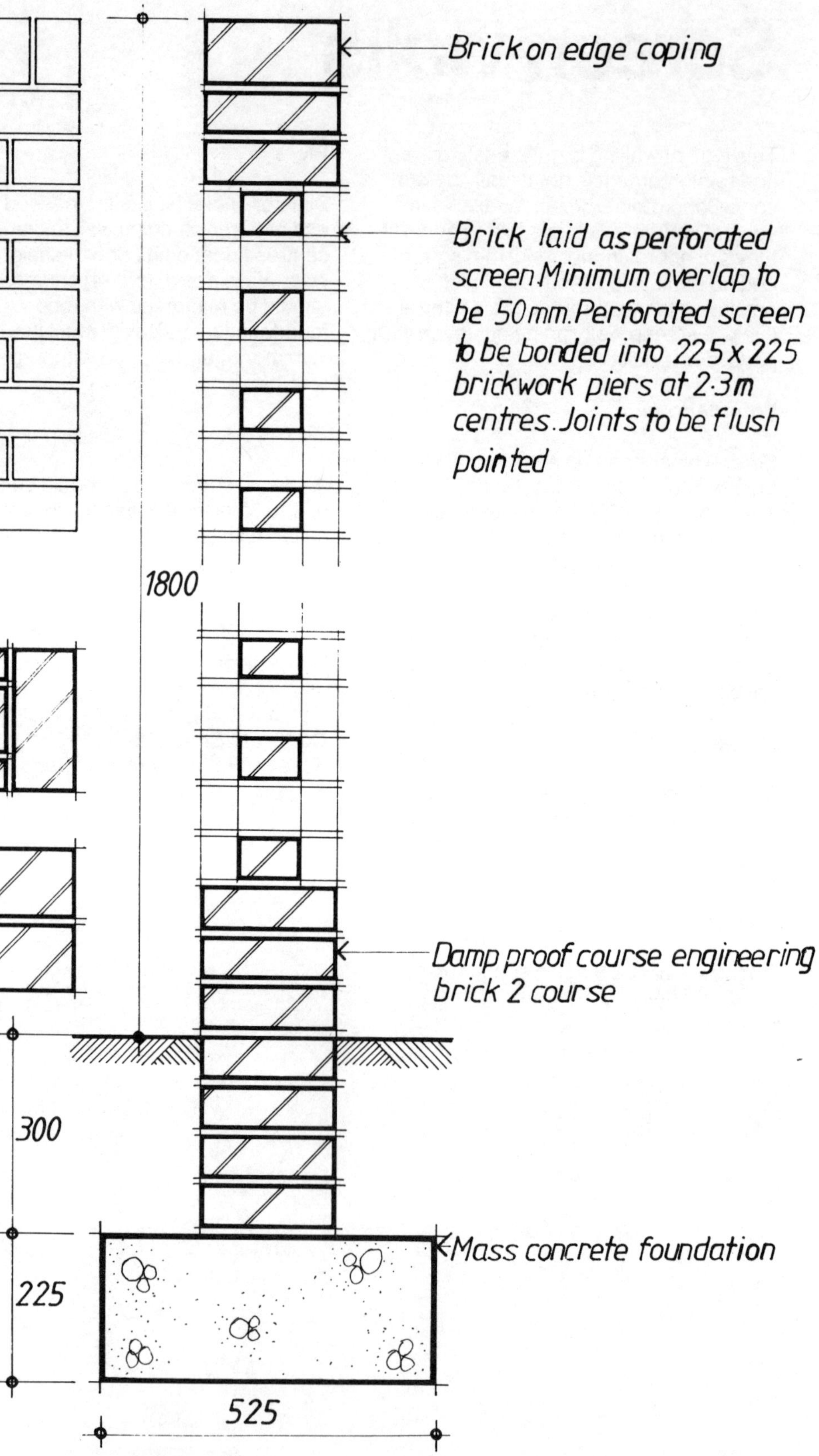
Brick on edge coping
Brick laid as perforated screen. Minimum overlap to be 50mm. Perforated screen to be bonded into 225 x 225 brickwork piers at 2·3m centres. Joints to be flush pointed
1800
Damp proof course engineering brick 2 course
300
225
Mass concrete foundation
525

SECTION

Scale 1:10

WALL
perforated screen

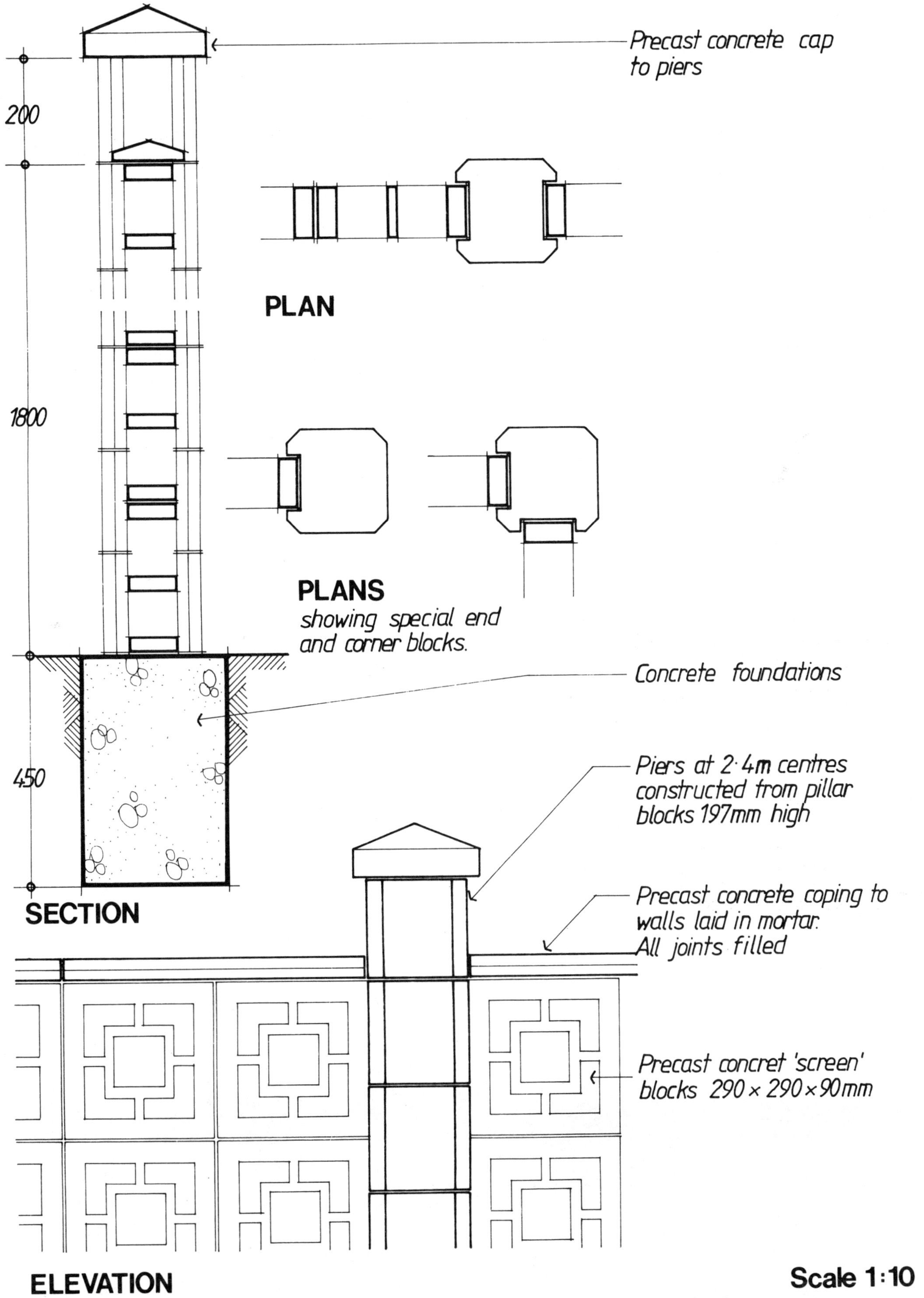
Precast concrete cap to piers
200
1800
450
PLAN
PLANS
showing special end and corner blocks.
Concrete foundations
Piers at 2·4m centres constructed from pillar blocks 197mm high
SECTION
Precast concrete coping to walls laid in mortar. All joints filled
Precast concret 'screen' blocks 290 × 290 × 90mm
ELEVATION
Scale 1:10

WALL

concrete block screen

Chapter 3

Retaining walls

Retaining walls can be constructed of a wide choice of materials such as brick, block, concrete, stone and timber. Combinations of these materials are used in some instances, but in the interests of simplicity these have not been included.

Brick retaining walls

Choice of bricks

Retaining walls can be constructed of ordinary clay bricks BS 3921 : 1974 or calcium silicate bricks of Class 3 or stronger to BS 187 : Part 2 : 1978. If there is any likelihood of the brickwork becoming frozen after being saturated by high rainfall, either frost-resistant clay bricks (special quality) or calcium silicate bricks of Class 4 or stronger should be used. Where ordinary clay bricks are proposed, the manufacturer's advice should be sought.

Copings/cappings

The comments in Chapter 1 'Free-standing walls' apply equally to brick retaining walls. The coping selected should be effective in throwing the water clear of the exposed surfaces of the wall.

Mortars

Sulphate-resisting cement in a mortar of 1 : ¼ : 3 (cement : lime : sand) should be used up to and including the ground damp proof course, and above if the retaining face is not effectively waterproofed where aggressive sulphate ground conditions are found. When clay bricks of ordinary quality are used in high rainfall areas, mortar with sulphate-resisting cement should be used for the whole wall. It is advisable to use the same mortar for brickwork below the damp proof course.

Expansion joints

Retaining walls are less susceptible to horizontal movement than other walls, and although CP 121 suggests that vertical joints be provided at 12 m centres in long runs of clay brickwork walling, and at 7.5 m – 9.0 m centres in calcium brickwork, these could be extended to 15 m and 12 m respectively. A water bar included in the joint will prevent staining of the face. When brick on edge cappings are used, expansion or movement joints should be provided at about half the normal spacing.

Drainage

To prevent the build up of water pressure behind a retaining wall, a land drain should be provided near the base on the retaining side. The size will depend on ground conditions, but an average of 100 mm – 150 mm diameter is generally used. The drain must be surrounded by granular sulphate-free material extending to the surface where possible. Weep-holes should discharge at least 150 mm above ground level and at intermediate levels if necessary. Care should be taken to ensure that the drainage is not allowed to become blocked through siltation.

Reinforcement

In grouted cavity retaining walls the maximum size for reinforcement bars is 25 mm diameter and the maximum and minimum spacings are 500 mm and 25 mm respectively.

Cover to reinforcement

Grouted cavity walls: minimum cover to all reinforcement = 10 mm. Pocket walls: minimum cover to all reinforcement = 40 mm. Quetta bond: minimum cover to all reinforcement = 10 mm. Buttressed wall, or other wall with reinforcement positioned in the joints: minimum cover to main reinforcement = 25 mm; nominal cover above and below reinforcement positioned in bed joints = 3 mm. All reinforcement within 100 mm of either face of the wall to be galvanised to BS 729 : Part 13 : 1971, be of stainless steel, or have a similar degree of protection. For details see Figure 3.

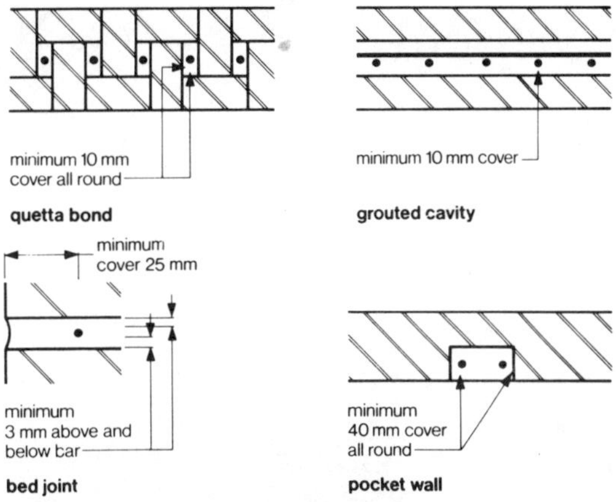

Figure 3 Cover to reinforcement

The above recommendations are in accordance with SP 91(8), to which reference should be made for further information.

Concrete retaining walls

These are either cast in situ or pre-cast. If above 2.0 m in height, in-situ reinforced concrete retaining walls should generally be designed by a structural engineer.
Pre-cast concrete retaining wall units are available either as L-shaped units or as small units which are interlocked to form a lattice 'crib' then filled with gravel or topsoil and established by planting.
In-situ mass concrete walls without reinforcment are double the thickness of reinforced walls. Only in exceptional circumstances will it pay not to use reinforcement, but there are occasions when a heavy structure is required.

Foundations

To simplify the shuttering of the wall the bottom 150 mm should be constructed with the foundations. Reinforcement using 9 mm starter rods at 300 mm centres should be placed in the foundations and run up into the wall. A damp proof course will be necessary.

Expansion joints

A 12 mm open joint should be provided at 5.0 m intervals in un-reinforced walls and at 10.0 m intervals in reinforced walls. Except in battered walls, joints should form an integral pattern in un-reinforced walls to avoid cracks caused by shrinkage.

Timber retaining walls

Little guidance exists in this country on the use of timber outdoors. Retaining walls of timber should be built of hardwood or naturally resistant wood (redwood or cedar). All timbers should still be treated with fungicidal and insect-repellent preservatives. Softwood when used must be pressure impregnated with preservative by a vacuum process. Consideration should be given to the shrinkage of timbers especially where joints are used.

References

The Architectural Press Ltd, London
M Gage and M Vandenberg
Hard Landscape in Concrete 1975

E Beazley
Design and Detail of the Space between Buildings, 1960

Brick Development Association
Brickwork Retaining Walls, August 1981
External Walls: Design for Wind Loads

E & F N Spon Ltd
M F Downing
Landscape Construction, 1977

British Standards Institute
BS 3921 : 1974 Clay bricks and blocks
BS 5628 : 1978 The Structural Use of masonry: Party 1
Unreinforced masonry
BS 187 : Party 2 : 1978 Calcium silicate (sand lime and flint lime) bricks
BS 729 : 1971 Hot dip galvanised coatings on iron and steel articles
CP 111 : 1970 Structural recommendations for loadbearing walls
CP 121 : Part 1 : 1973 Walling: Brick and block masonry
CP 110 : 1972 The structural use of concrete
Civil Engineering CP 2 : 1951 Earth retaining structures

British Ceramic Research Association
SP 91 : Design guide for reinforced and pre-stressed clay brickwork

Detail sheets

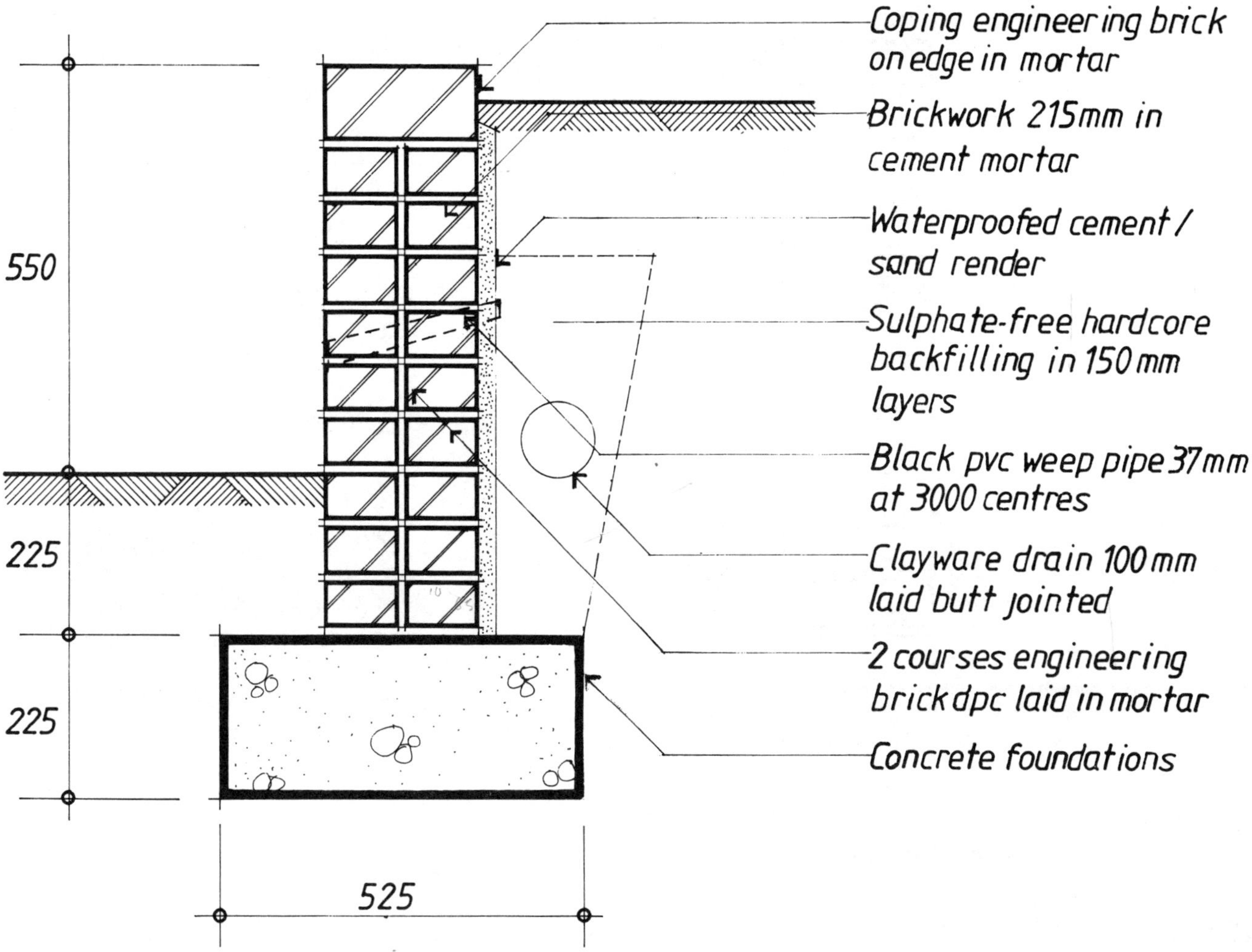

SECTION

Scale 1:10

RETAINING WALL
brick

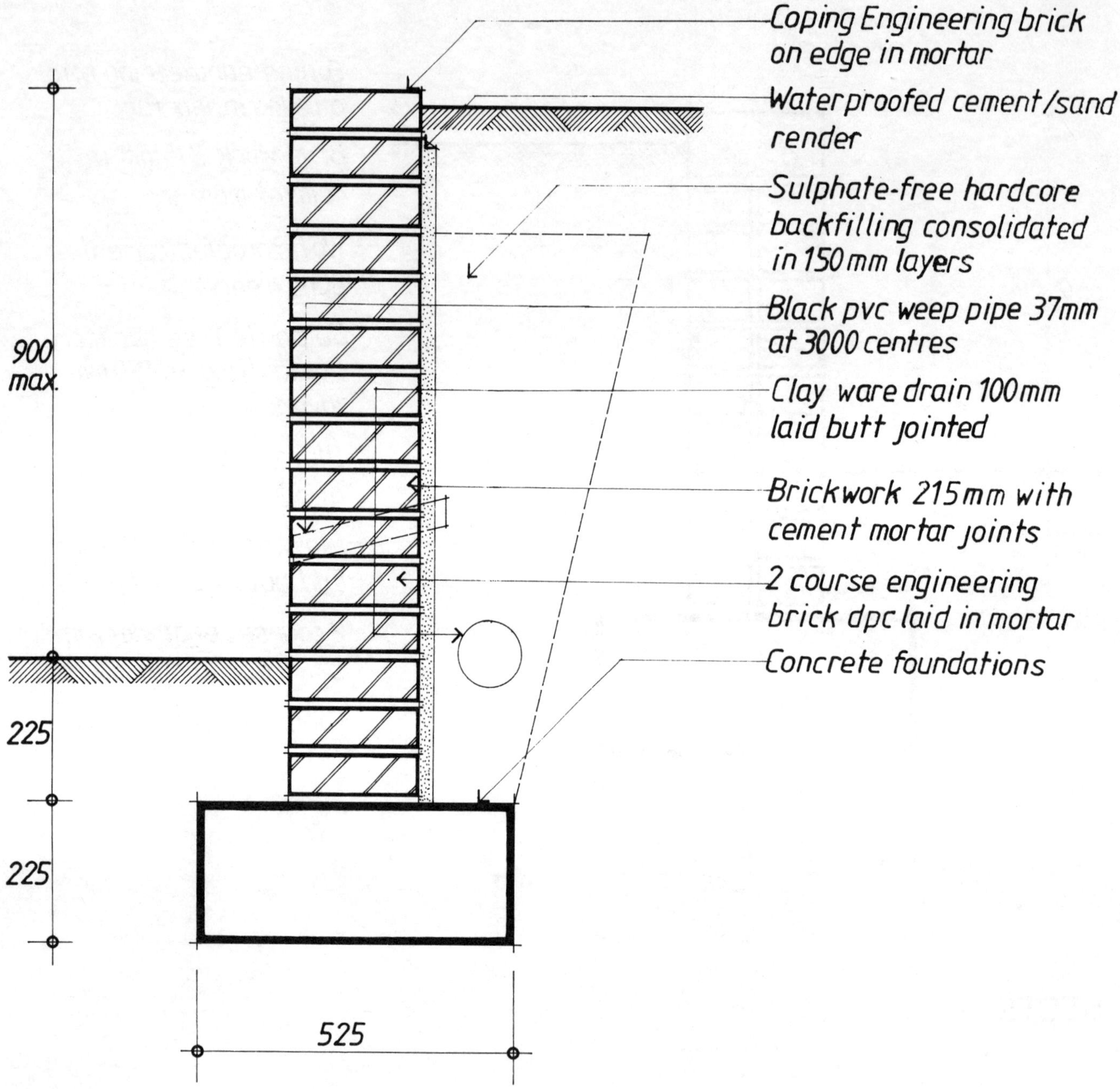

SECTION

Scale 1:10

RETAINING WALL
brick

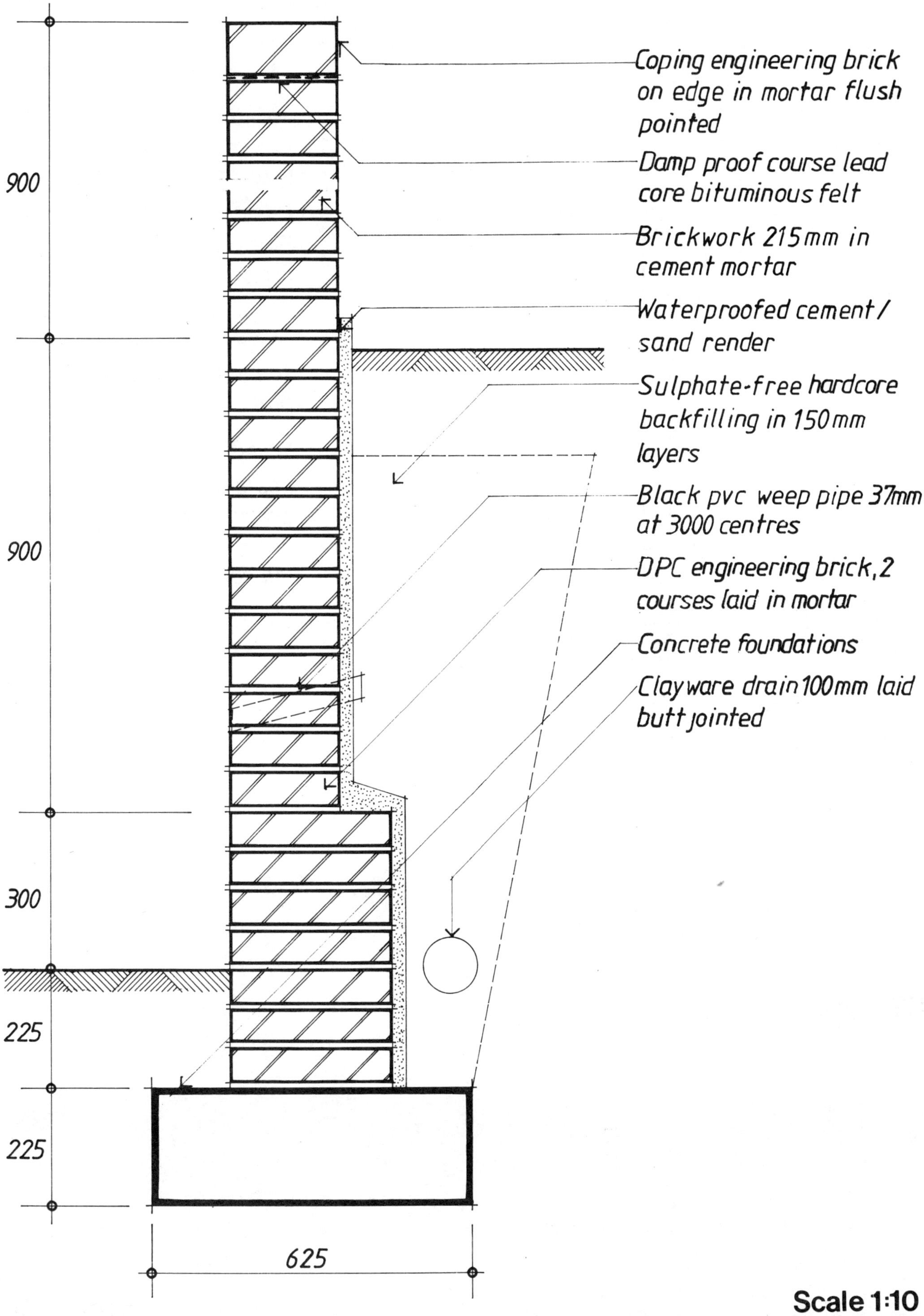
Coping engineering brick on edge in mortar flush pointed
Damp proof course lead core bituminous felt
Brickwork 215mm in cement mortar
Waterproofed cement / sand render
Sulphate-free hardcore backfilling in 150mm layers
Black pvc weep pipe 37mm at 3000 centres
DPC engineering brick, 2 courses laid in mortar
Concrete foundations
Clayware drain 100mm laid butt jointed
900
900
300
225
225
625

Scale 1:10

RETAINING WALL

brick

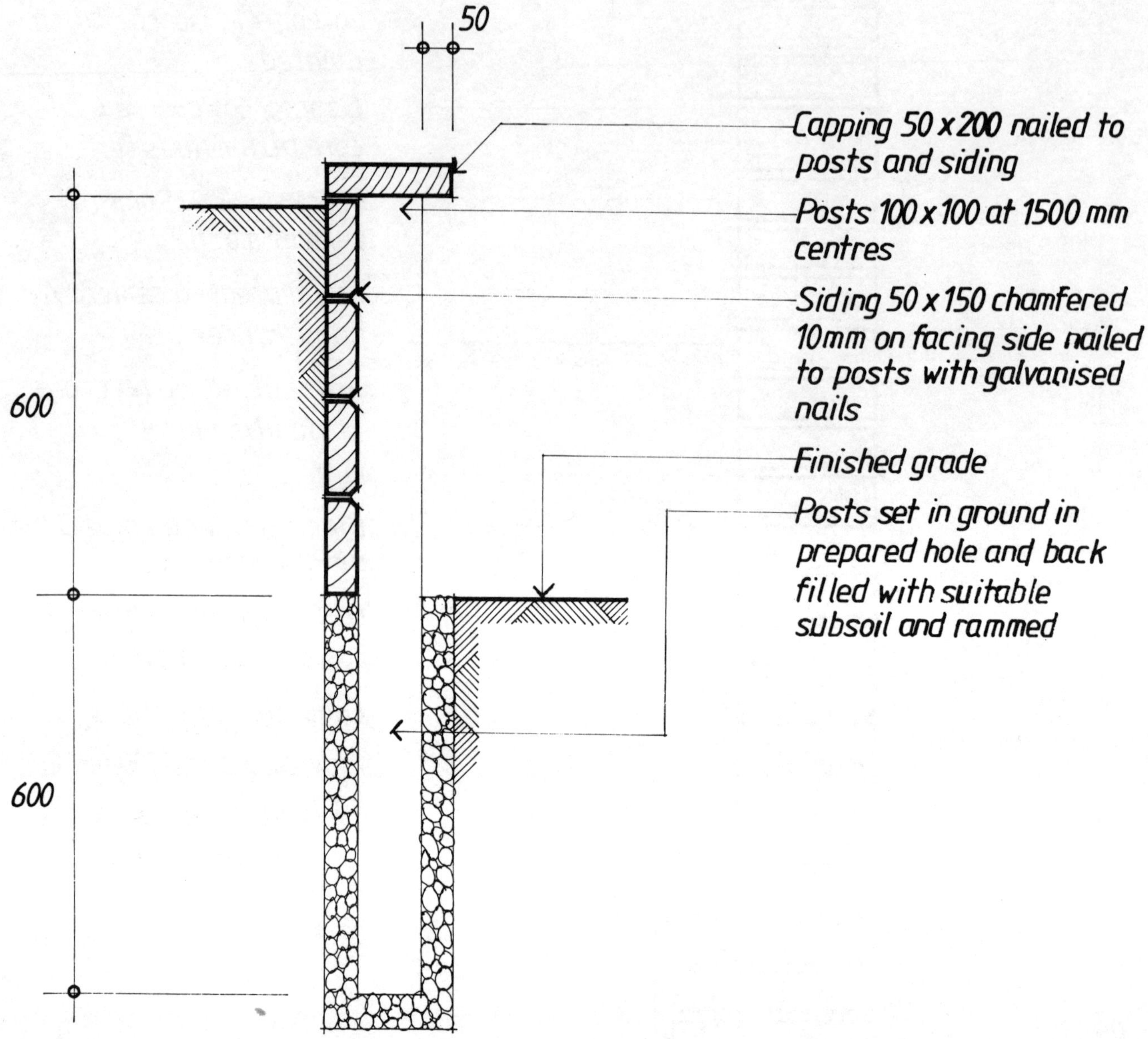

50
600
600
Capping 50 x 200 nailed to posts and siding
Posts 100 x 100 at 1500 mm centres
Siding 50 x 150 chamfered 10mm on facing side nailed to posts with galvanised nails
Finished grade
Posts set in ground in prepared hole and back filled with suitable subsoil and rammed

SECTION

Scale 1:10

RETAINING WALL

timber

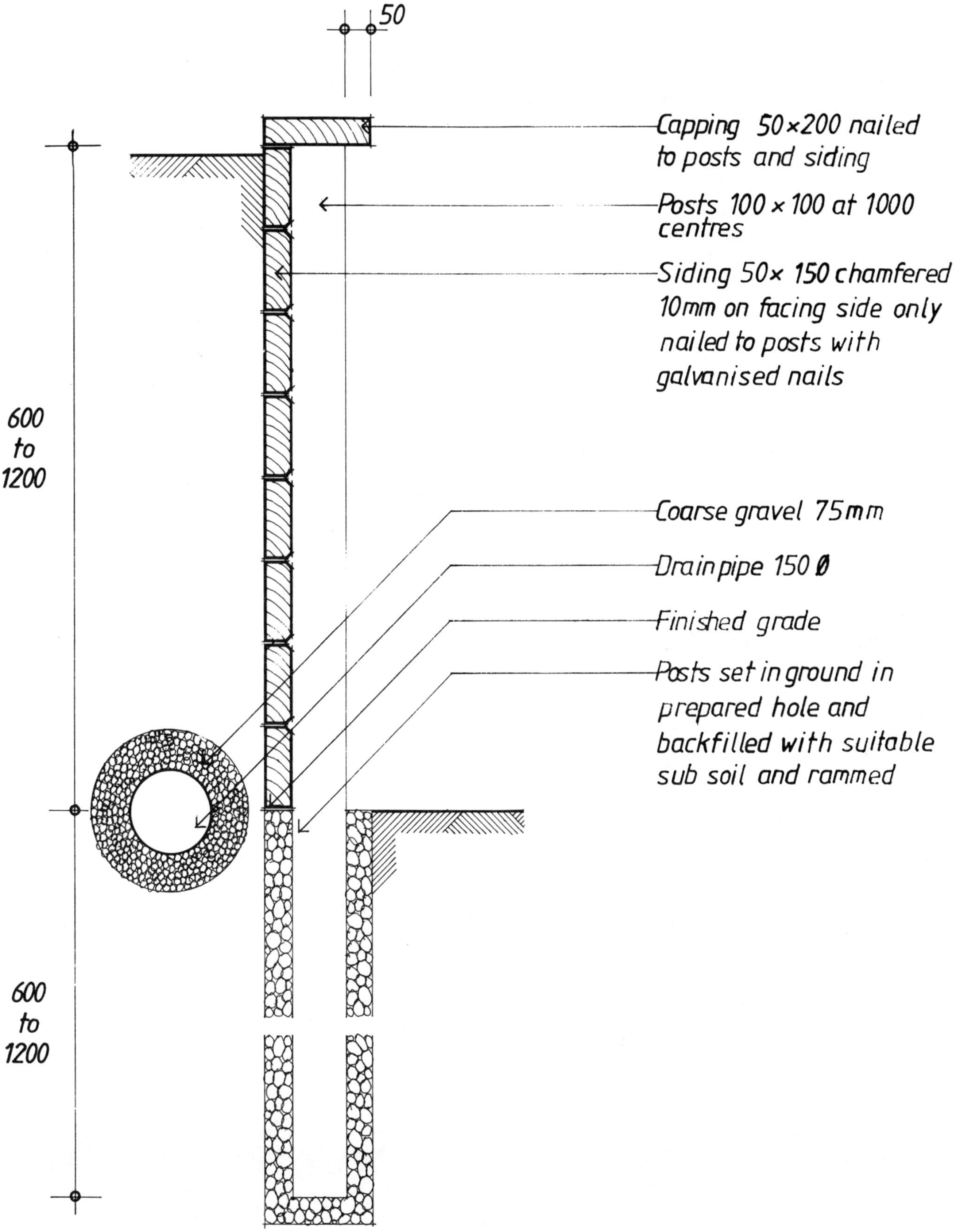

SECTION

Scale 1:10

RETAINING WALL
timber

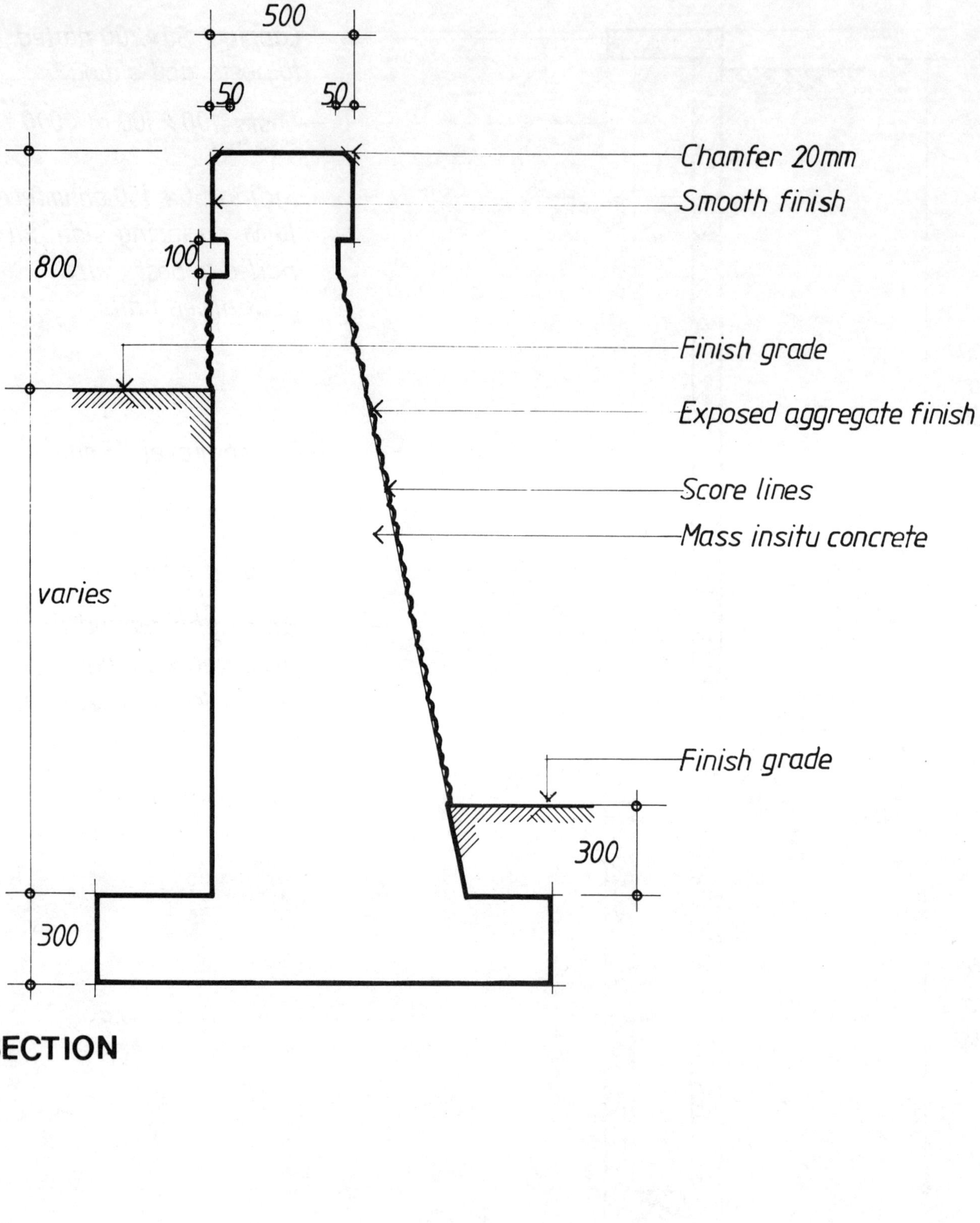
500
50
50
Chamfer 20mm
Smooth finish
800
100
Finish grade
Exposed aggregate finish
Score lines
Mass insitu concrete
varies
Finish grade
300
300

SECTION

Scale 1:10

RETAINING WALL
battered concrete

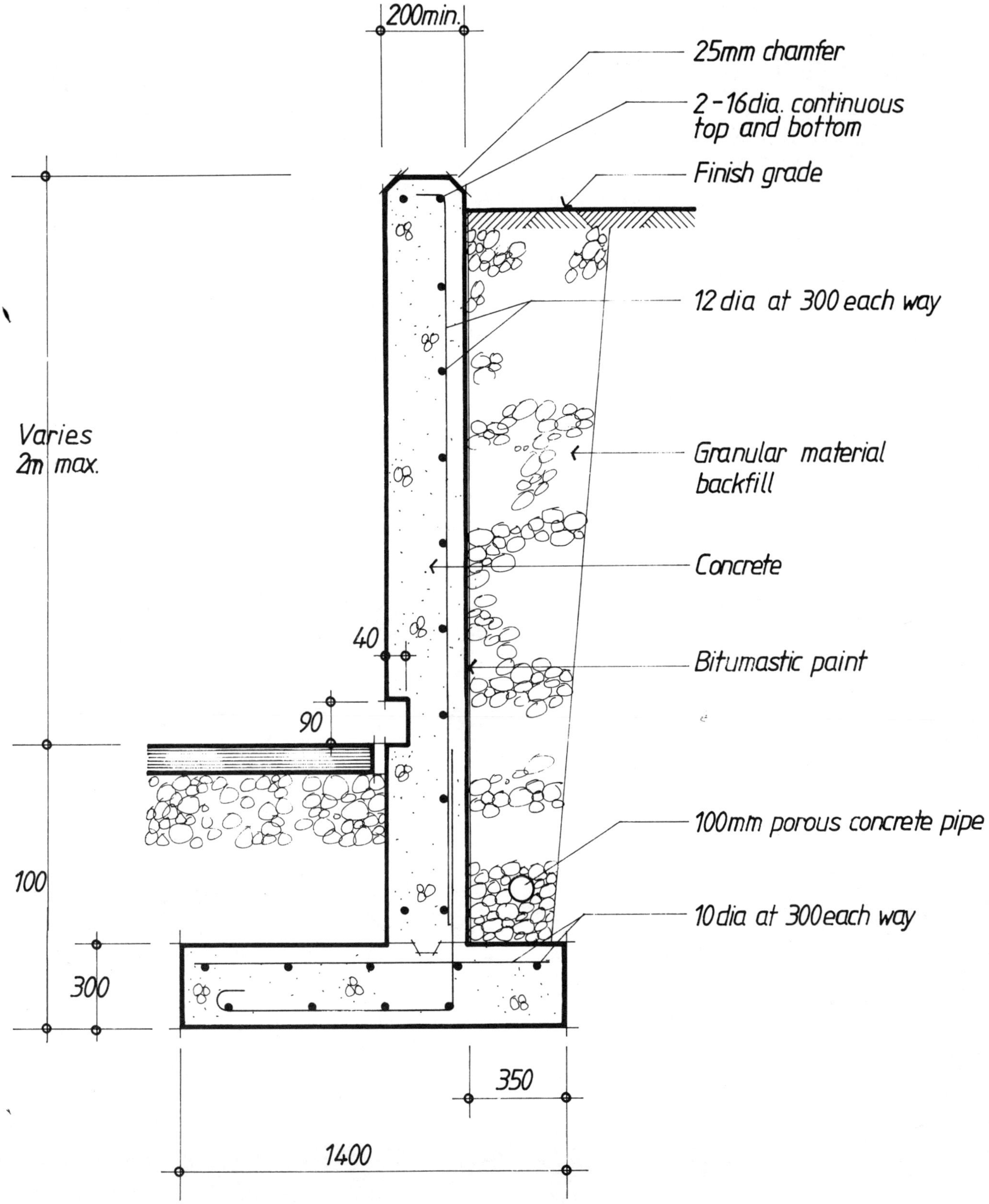

SECTION

Scale 1:20

RETAINING WALL
reinforced concrete

Chapter 4
Fencing

BS 1722 covers many kinds of fencing. Each part of the Standard specifies in detail not only the materials required, but also the method of erection. Fences are also classified according to variable characteristics, e.g., height, number of wires or rails, post material.

Types

These are listed in Table 1 in each part of the Standard, together with examples of typical uses of each type. There are, of course, many other types of fencing, not yet covered by the Britsh Standard, such as wattle, interwoven, etc.

Preservation

The most common fencing timbers are oak, sweet chestnut and cedar. These need no preservation when used above ground. Where these timbers are used as posts, the ends should be impregnated with creosote. All softwood used in fencing should be preservative impregnated by a vacuum process.

Post spacing

Posts should be spaced at 2700 mm maximum centres for mortised fencing and 1800 mm maximum centres for nailed fencing.

Depth of Insertion
Under normal exposure conditions a post insertion depth of 500 mm is sufficient for a 1.0 m high fence, and 750 mm for a 1.8 m high fence. If a concrete surround is used these dimensions can be reduced to 400 mm and 650 mm respectively because of the greater face area given by the concrete in certain locations.

Fixings

All fixings for fencing should be galvanised. In public areas, drive screws or wood screws should be used. Where bolts are used the nuts should be recessed into the post or the projecting threads should be burred over.

Finish

Suitable timbers, such as oak, cedar, sweet chestnut or larch, can be left unfinished. Otherwise use a two-coat application of wood dye or a coloured preservative, e.g. 'cuprinol'. Some brush-applied preservatives are not compatible with vacuum preservation processes which include water repellents.
Opaque oil paint systems can be satisfactorily used on vacuum impregnated timber provided that the preservative does not contain a water repellent. Where a water repellent has been used, loss of adhesion of the paint film may result unless a special primer is used. The paint manufacturer should be consulted.

Changes in level

These are accommodated by stepping each panel when using fences made from prefabricated panels. Posts at the steps will have to be increased in length. Where post and rail fencing is used, changes in level are accommodated by inclining the rails in the mortises, while keeping the posts vertical.

Metal fencing

Sizes of members

The materials used almost exclusively for metal fencing are wrought iron and mild steel. BS 1722 : Parts 8 and 9 can be used as a guide for sizes and spacing of members. Space between vertical members should not be less than 100 mm or more than 120 mm.

Standards

An insertion depth of 600 mm is suitable for a fence up to 1.8 m high. Spacing should be 2.7 m maximum. A wing plate parallel to the fence line should be welded to each standard. Standards should have a bearing plate welded to the base. Standards for fences incorporating strained wire should have stays fixed at 60° to horizontal at corners and ends. Because of the small face dimension of metal members, a concrete surround to the standard should always by used.

Preservation and finish

BS 1722 : Part 8 specifies a range of ex-works finishes, the usual finish being a red-oxide primer or hot-dip galvanising after fabrication. The finish coating should be paint, applied as two undercoats and one gloss top coat.

Changes in level

Prefabricated metal fencing is accommodated to changes in level by stepping the panels or fabricating special inclined panels. With either method, the profile of the ground must be known in advance of fabrication.

References

The Architectural Press Ltd, London
E Beazley
Design and Detail of the Space between Buildings, 1960

E and F N Spon Ltd
Spon's Landscape Handbook

Monmouthshire County Council
Fences in the Countryside, 1974

Central Electricity Generating Board
Design Memorandum on the Use of Fences, January 1966

Greater London Council
Development and Materials Bulletin 79, October/November 1974
Use of Pigmented Water-repellant Finishes for External Softwood Joinery: A Warning

Forestry Commission
Forest Fencing
NBA 'Building' Commodity File, Components (90) Section 02: Fencing

Timber Research and Development Association
Timber Fencing and Gates

British Standards Institute
BS : 1722 Fences
Part 1 : 1963 Chain link fences
Supplement 1 : 1974 Gates and gateposts used in connection with chain link fences
Part 2 : 1963 Woven wire fences
Part 3 : 1963 Strained wire fences
Part 4 : 1963 Cleft chestnut pale fences
Part 5 : 1963 Close-boarded fences including oak pale fences
Part 6 : 1963 Wooden palisade fences
Part 7 : 1963 Wooden post and rail fences
Part 8 : 1951 Mild steel or wrought iron continuous bar fences
Part 9 1963 Mild steel or wrought iron unclimbable fences with round or square verticals and flat standards and horizontals
Part 10 : 1963 Anti-intruder chain link fences
Part 11 : 1965 Woven wood fences
Part 12 : 1979 Steel palisade fences
Part 13 : 1978 Chain link fences for tennis court surrounds
BS 4102 : 1971 Steel wire for fences
BS 5589 : 1976 Code of practice for the preservation of timber

Detail sheets

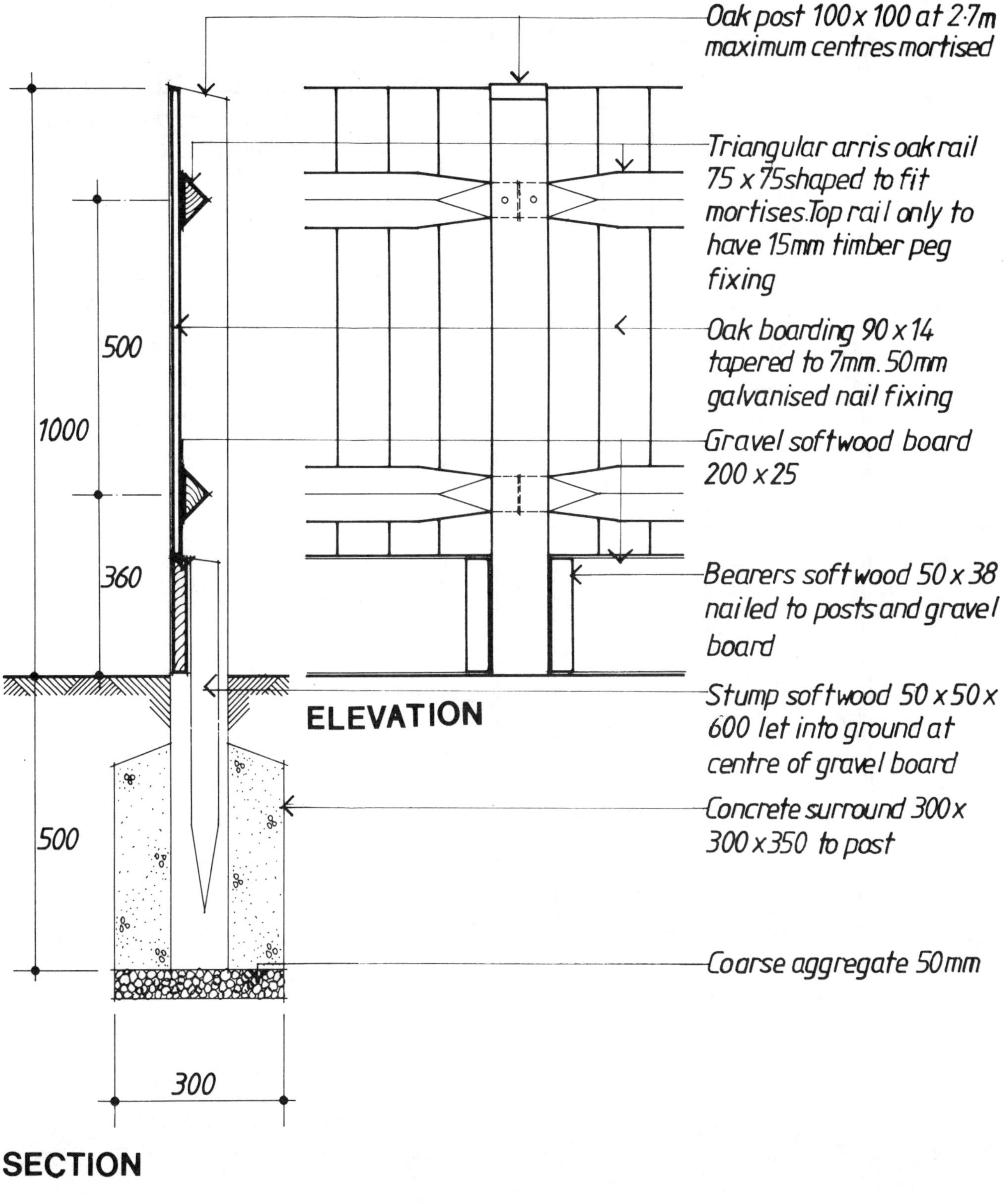
Oak post 100 x 100 at 2·7m maximum centres mortised
Triangular arris oak rail 75 x 75 shaped to fit mortises. Top rail only to have 15mm timber peg fixing
Oak boarding 90 x 14 tapered to 7mm. 50mm galvanised nail fixing
Gravel softwood board 200 x 25
Bearers softwood 50 x 38 nailed to posts and gravel board
Stump softwood 50 x 50 x 600 let into ground at centre of gravel board
Concrete surround 300 x 300 x 350 to post
Coarse aggregate 50mm
500
1000
360
500
300
ELEVATION
SECTION

Scale 1:20

FENCE
close board

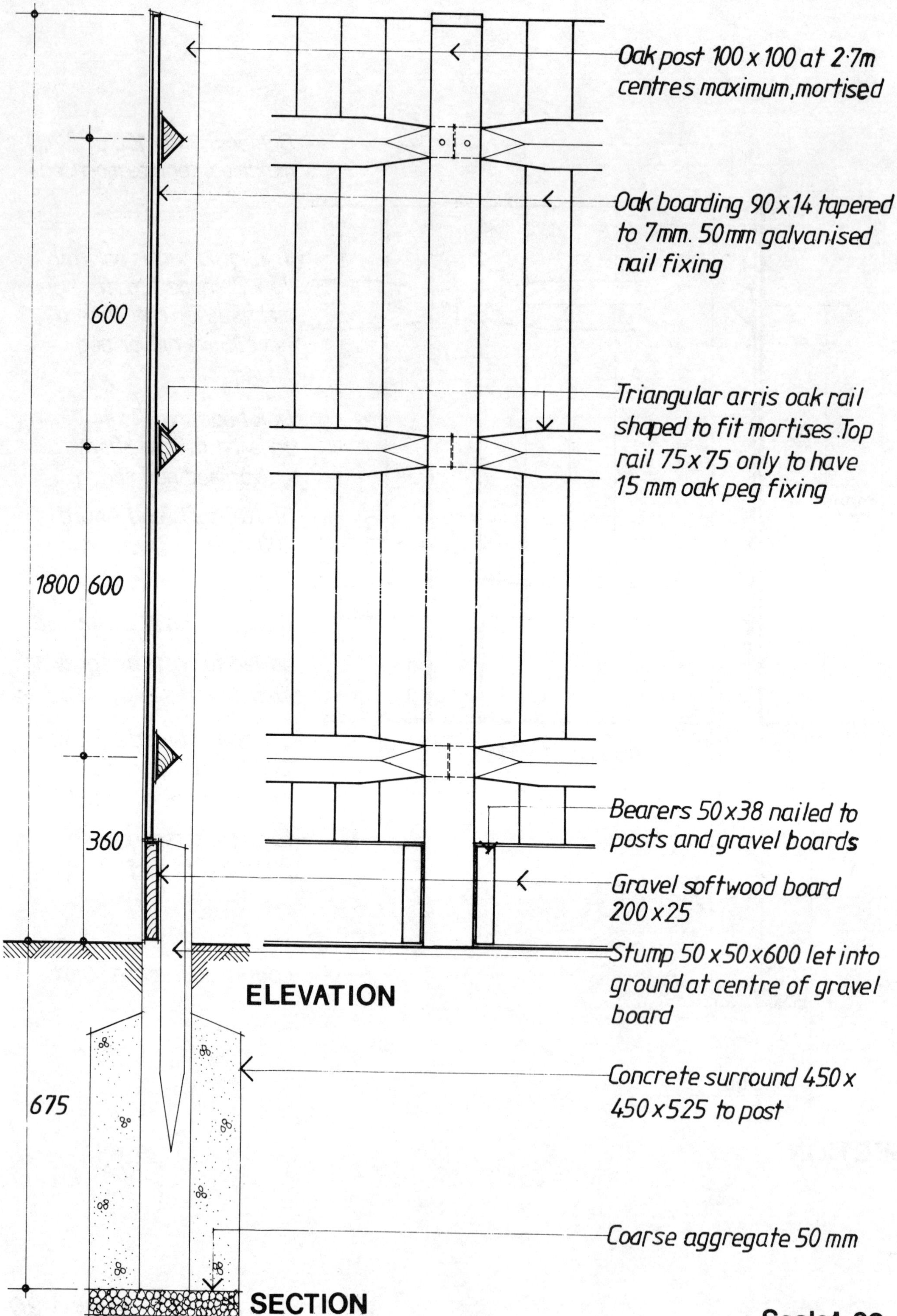
Oak post 100 x 100 at 2·7m centres maximum, mortised
Oak boarding 90 x 14 tapered to 7mm. 50mm galvanised nail fixing
Triangular arris oak rail shaped to fit mortises. Top rail 75 x 75 only to have 15 mm oak peg fixing
Bearers 50 x 38 nailed to posts and gravel boards
Gravel softwood board 200 x 25
Stump 50 x 50 x 600 let into ground at centre of gravel board
Concrete surround 450 x 450 x 525 to post
Coarse aggregate 50 mm
600
1800
600
360
675
ELEVATION
SECTION

Scale 1:20

FENCE
close board

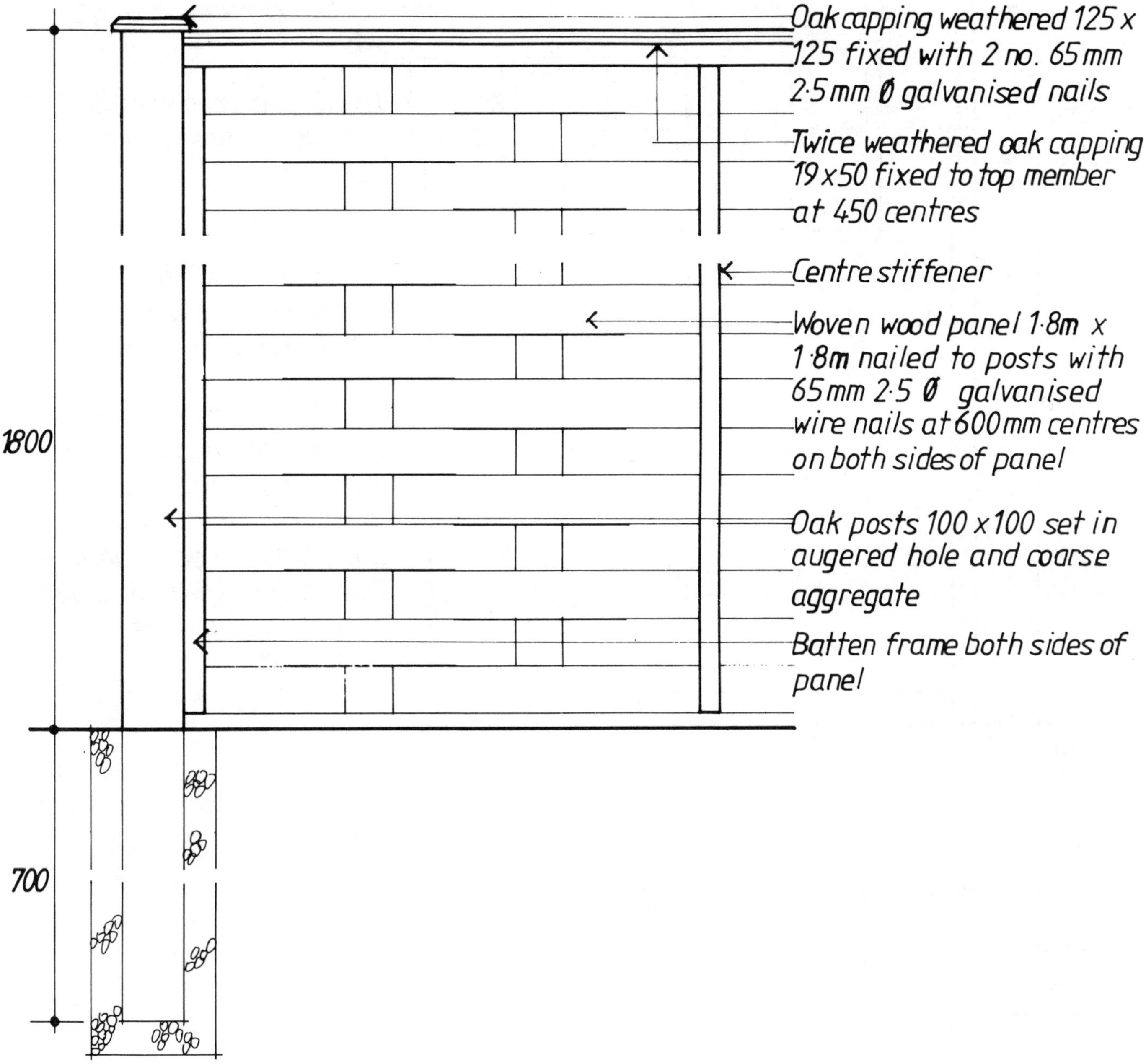

Oak capping weathered 125 x 125 fixed with 2 no. 65 mm 2·5 mm Ø galvanised nails
Twice weathered oak capping 19 x 50 fixed to top member at 450 centres
Centre stiffener
Woven wood panel 1·8m x 1·8m nailed to posts with 65 mm 2·5 Ø galvanised wire nails at 600 mm centres on both sides of panel
Oak posts 100 x 100 set in augered hole and coarse aggregate
Batten frame both sides of panel
1800
700

ELEVATION

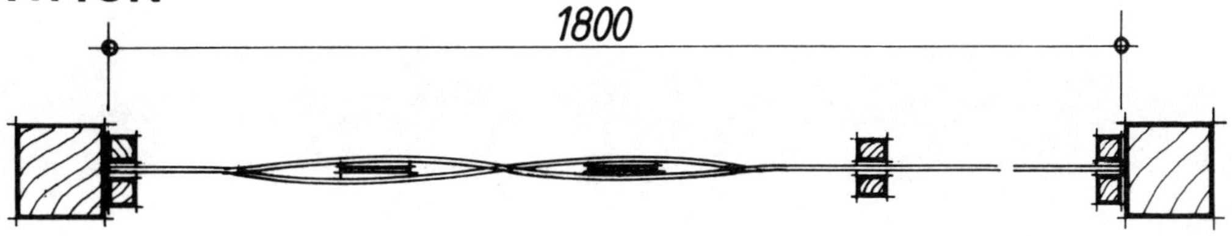

1800

PLAN

Scale 1:10

FENCE
woven wood

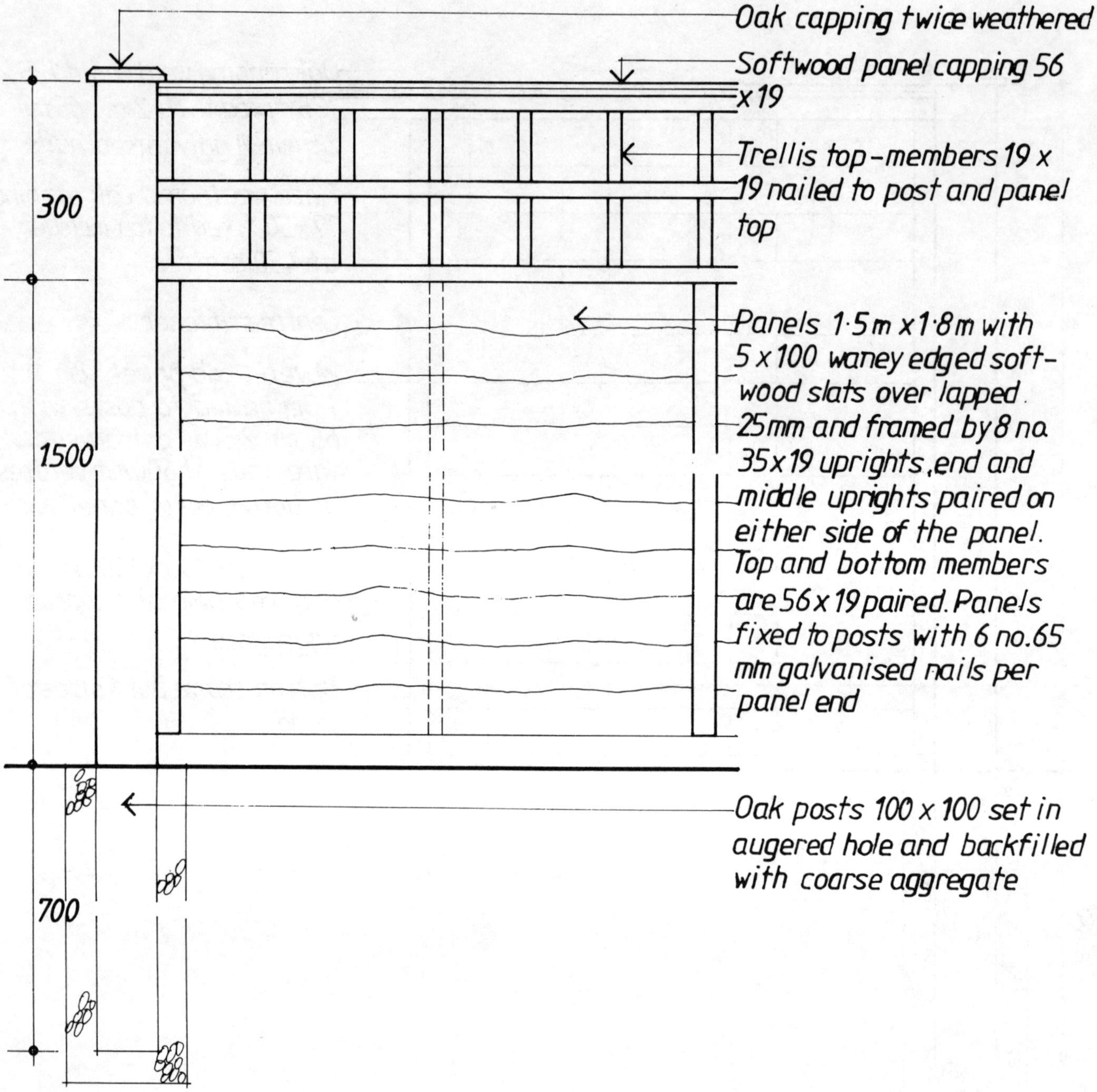

ELEVATION

Scale 1:10

FENCE

waney edge board

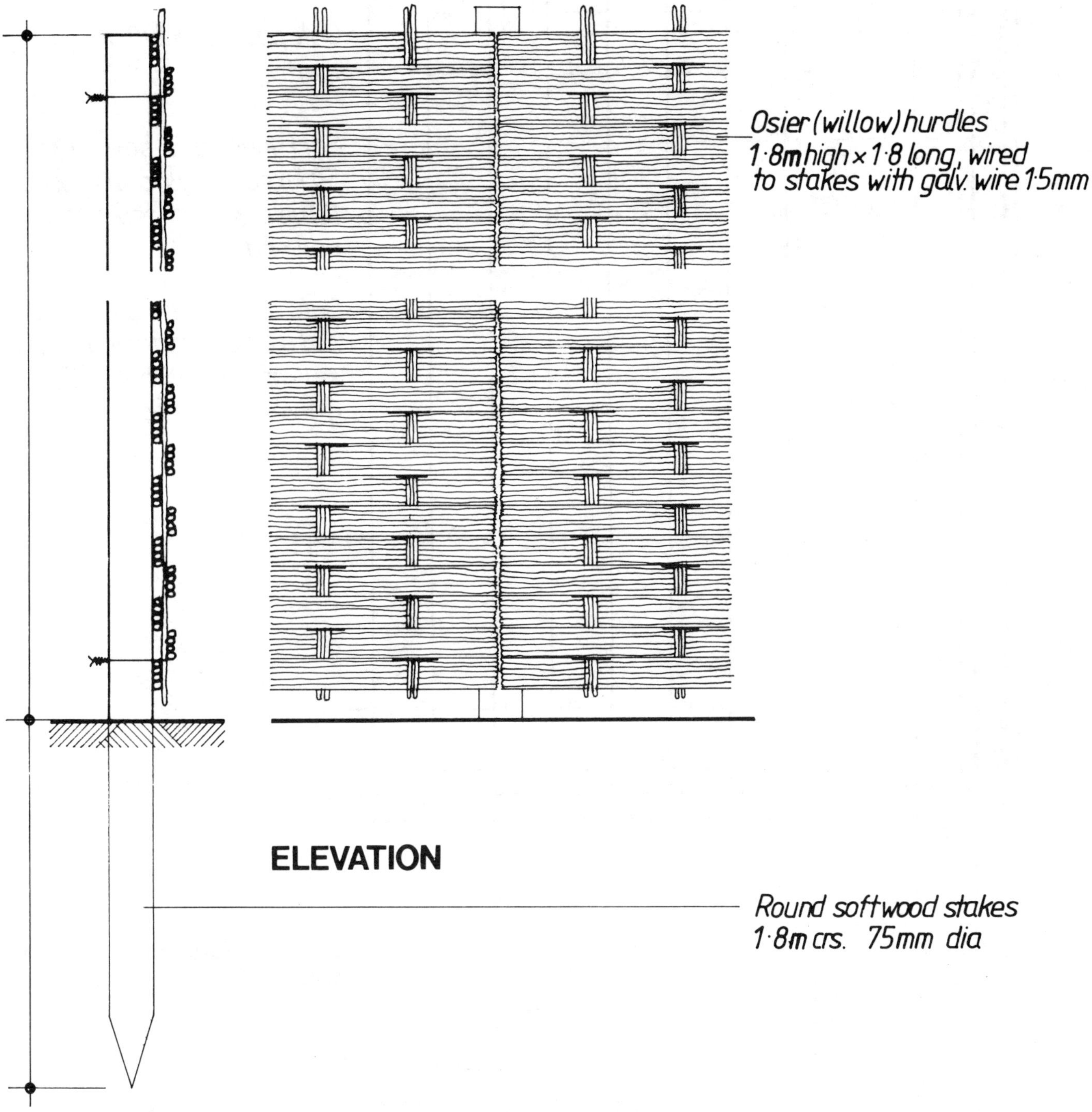
Osier (willow) hurdles
1·8m high × 1·8 long, wired
to stakes with galv. wire 1·5mm
ELEVATION
Round softwood stakes
1·8m crs. 75mm dia

SECTION

Scale 1:20

FENCE
osier hurdles

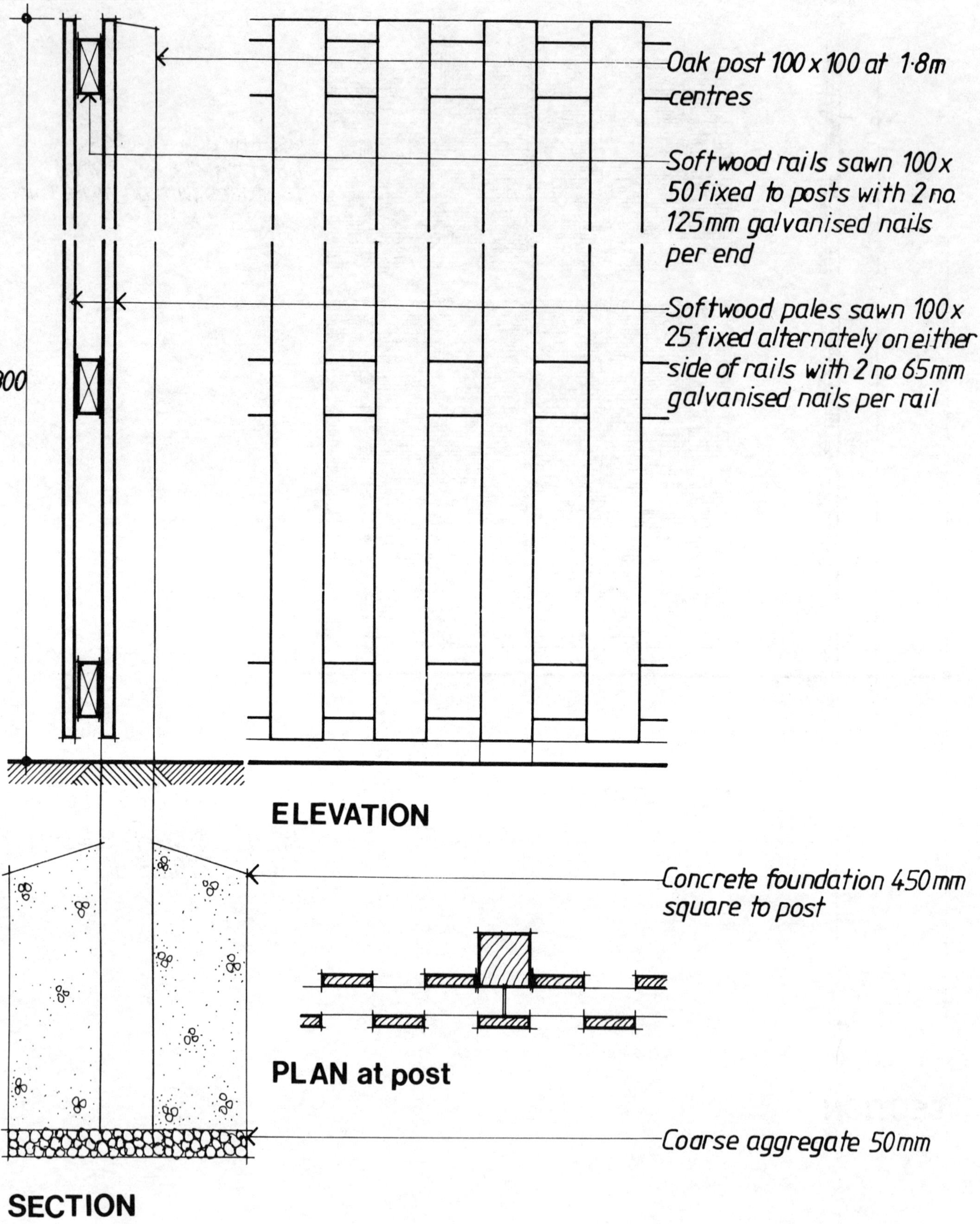
1800
Oak post 100 x 100 at 1·8m centres
Softwood rails sawn 100 x 50 fixed to posts with 2 no. 125mm galvanised nails per end
Softwood pales sawn 100 x 25 fixed alternately on either side of rails with 2 no 65mm galvanised nails per rail
ELEVATION
Concrete foundation 450mm square to post
PLAN at post
Coarse aggregate 50mm
SECTION

Scale 1:10

FENCE
double sided palisade

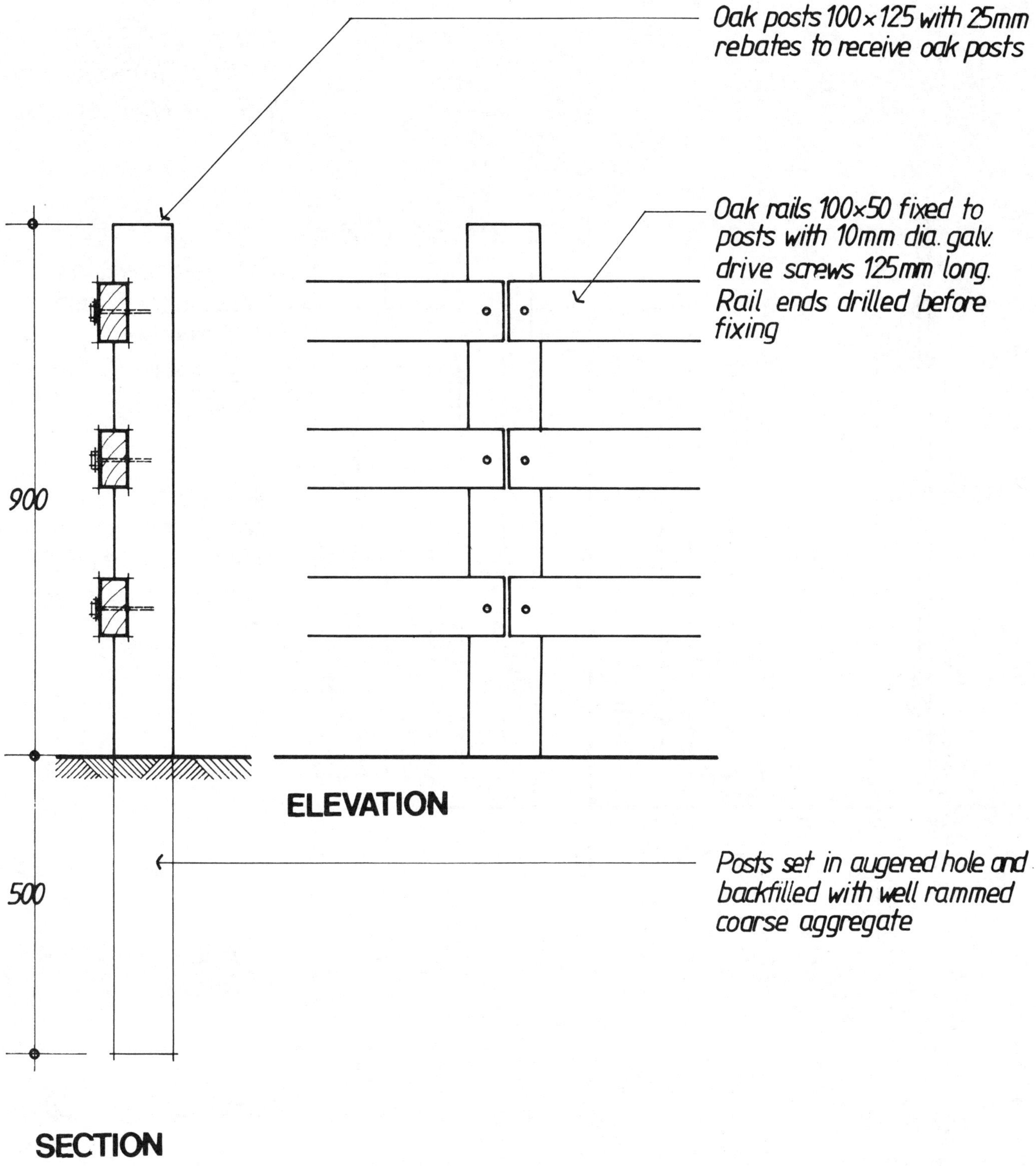
Oak posts 100×125 with 25mm rebates to receive oak posts
Oak rails 100×50 fixed to posts with 10mm dia. galv. drive screws 125mm long. Rail ends drilled before fixing
900
500
ELEVATION
Posts set in augered hole and backfilled with well rammed coarse aggregate
SECTION

Scale 1 : 10

FENCE
Timber post & rail

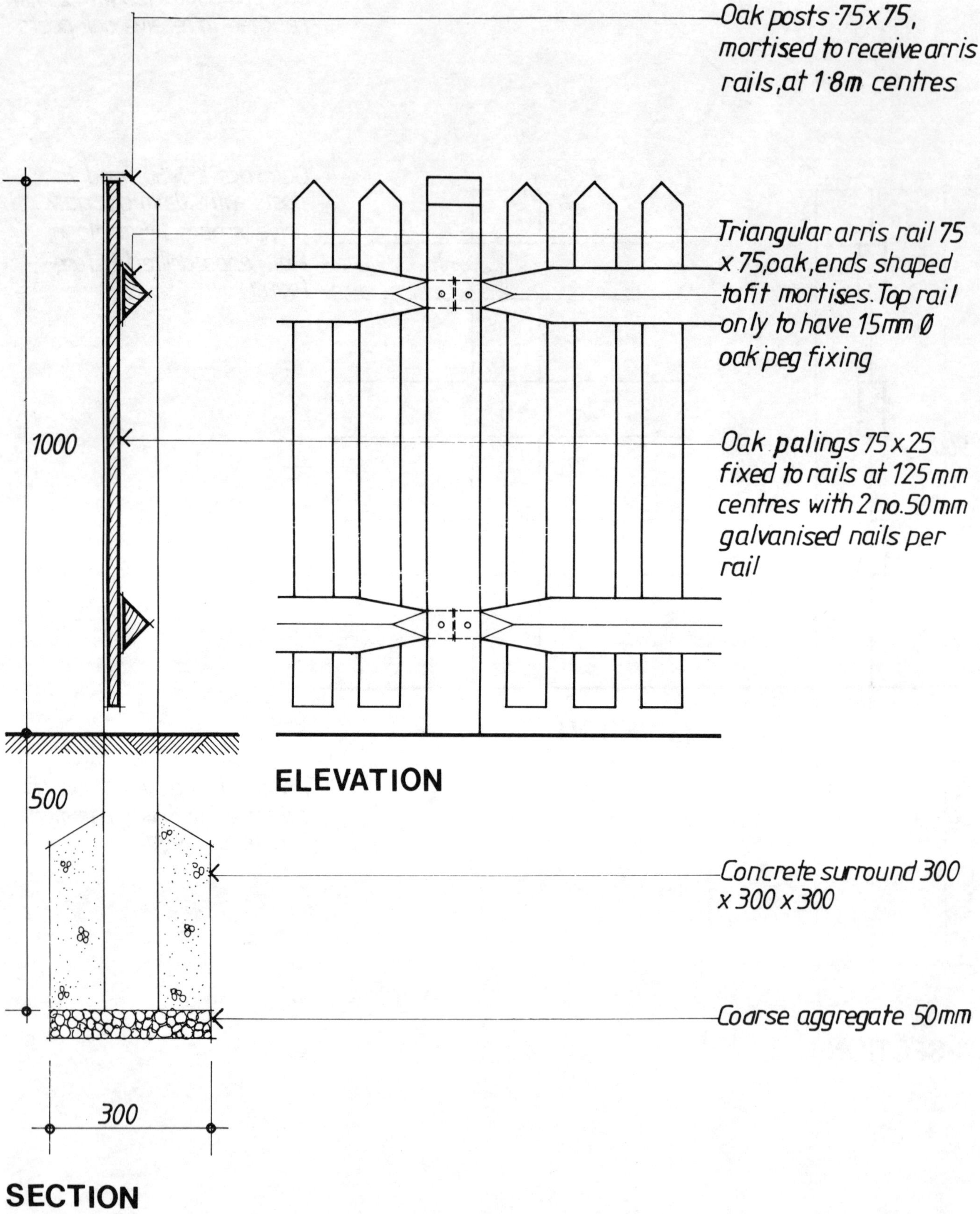
Oak posts 75x75, mortised to receive arris rails, at 1·8m centres
Triangular arris rail 75 x 75, oak, ends shaped to fit mortises. Top rail only to have 15mm Ø oak peg fixing
Oak palings 75x25 fixed to rails at 125mm centres with 2 no. 50mm galvanised nails per rail
Concrete surround 300 x 300 x 300
Coarse aggregate 50mm
1000
500
300
ELEVATION
SECTION

Scale 1:10

FENCE
timber palisade

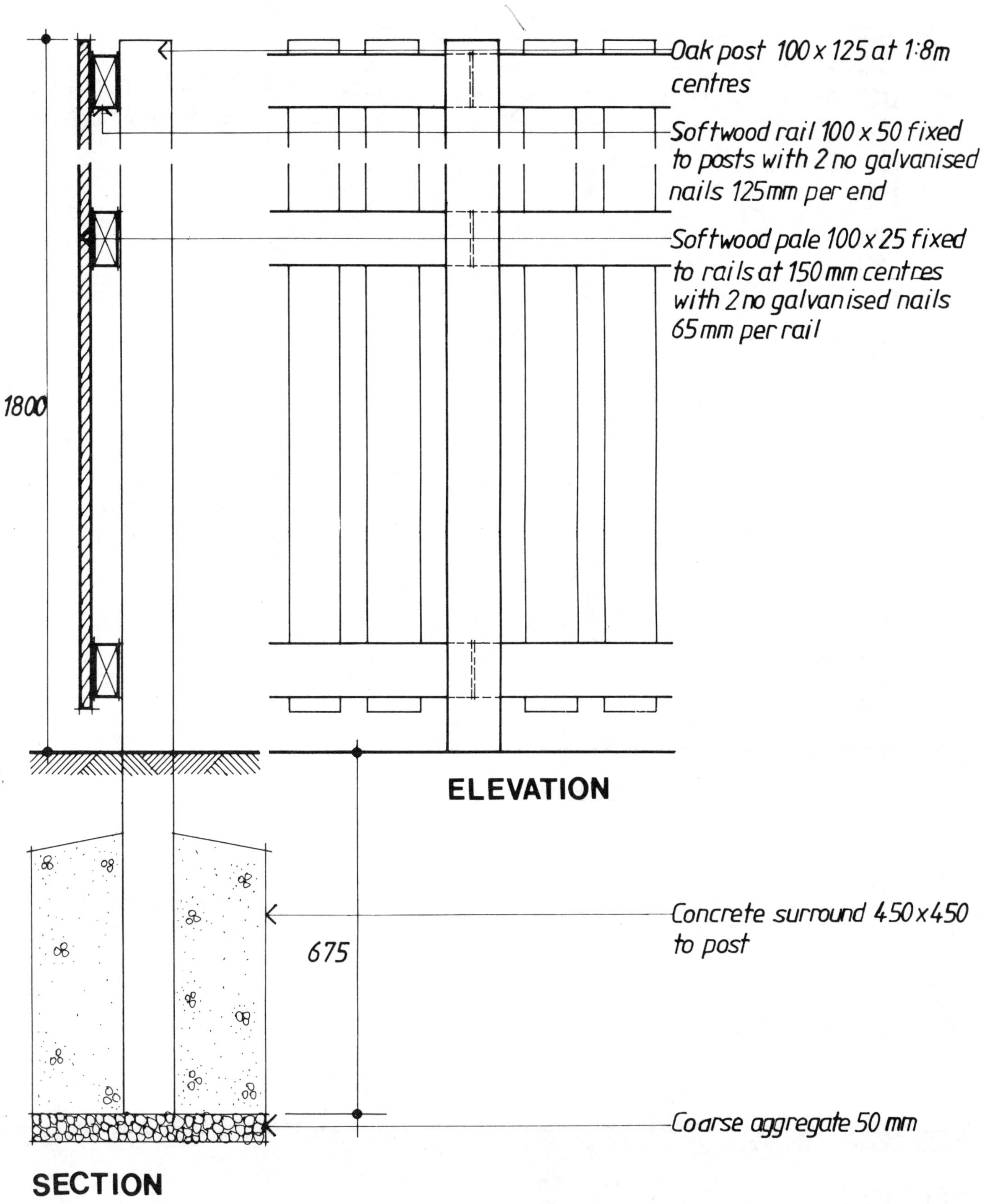

Oak post 100 x 125 at 1:8m centres
Softwood rail 100 x 50 fixed to posts with 2 no galvanised nails 125mm per end
Softwood pale 100 x 25 fixed to rails at 150 mm centres with 2 no galvanised nails 65mm per rail
1800
ELEVATION
675
Concrete surround 450 x 450 to post
Coarse aggregate 50 mm
SECTION

Scale 1:10

FENCE
timber palisade

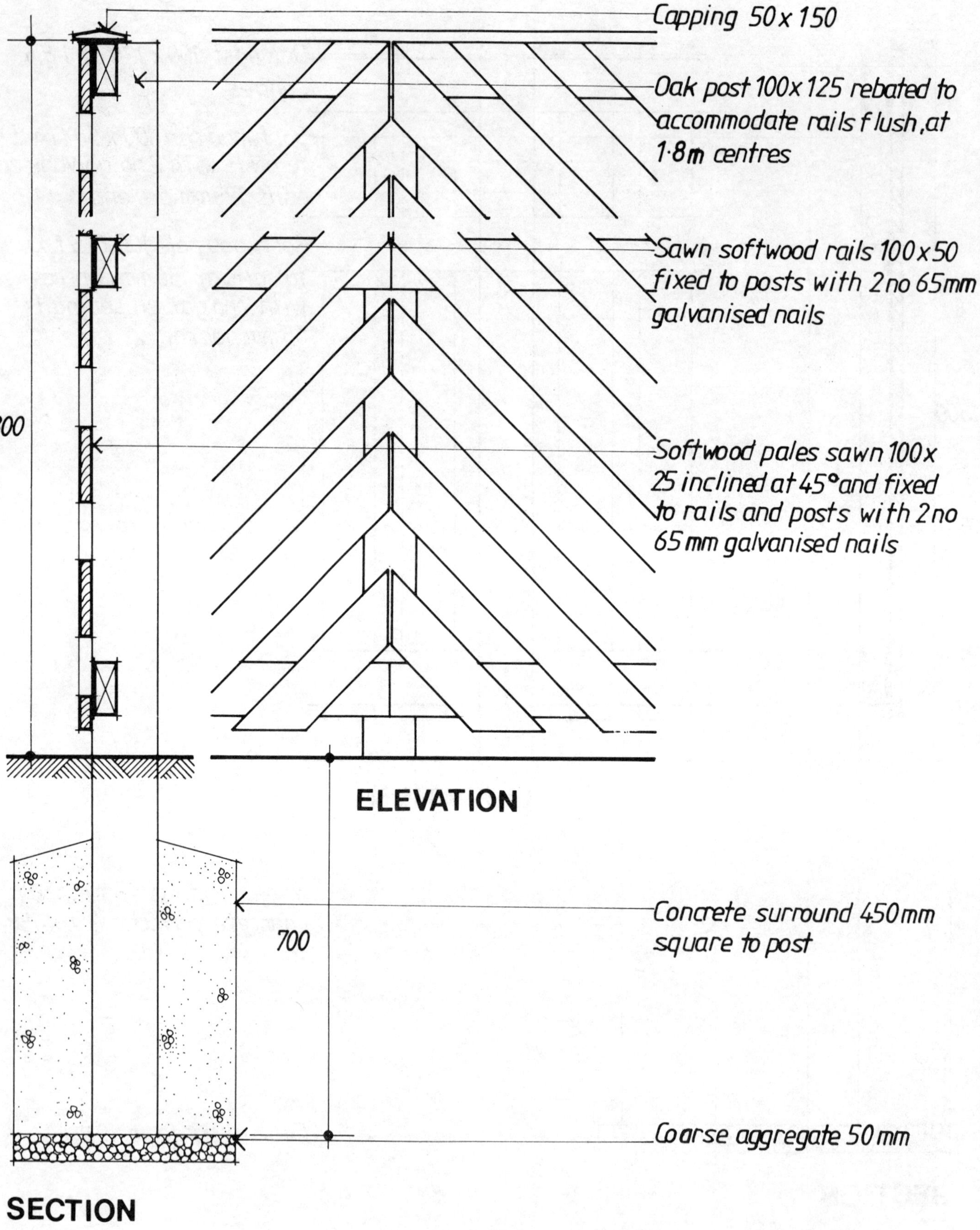
Capping 50 x 150
Oak post 100 x 125 rebated to accommodate rails flush, at 1·8 m centres
Sawn softwood rails 100 x 50 fixed to posts with 2 no 65 mm galvanised nails
Softwood pales sawn 100 x 25 inclined at 45° and fixed to rails and posts with 2 no 65 mm galvanised nails
800
ELEVATION
700
Concrete surround 450 mm square to post
Coarse aggregate 50 mm
SECTION

Scale 1:10

FENCE
diagonal board

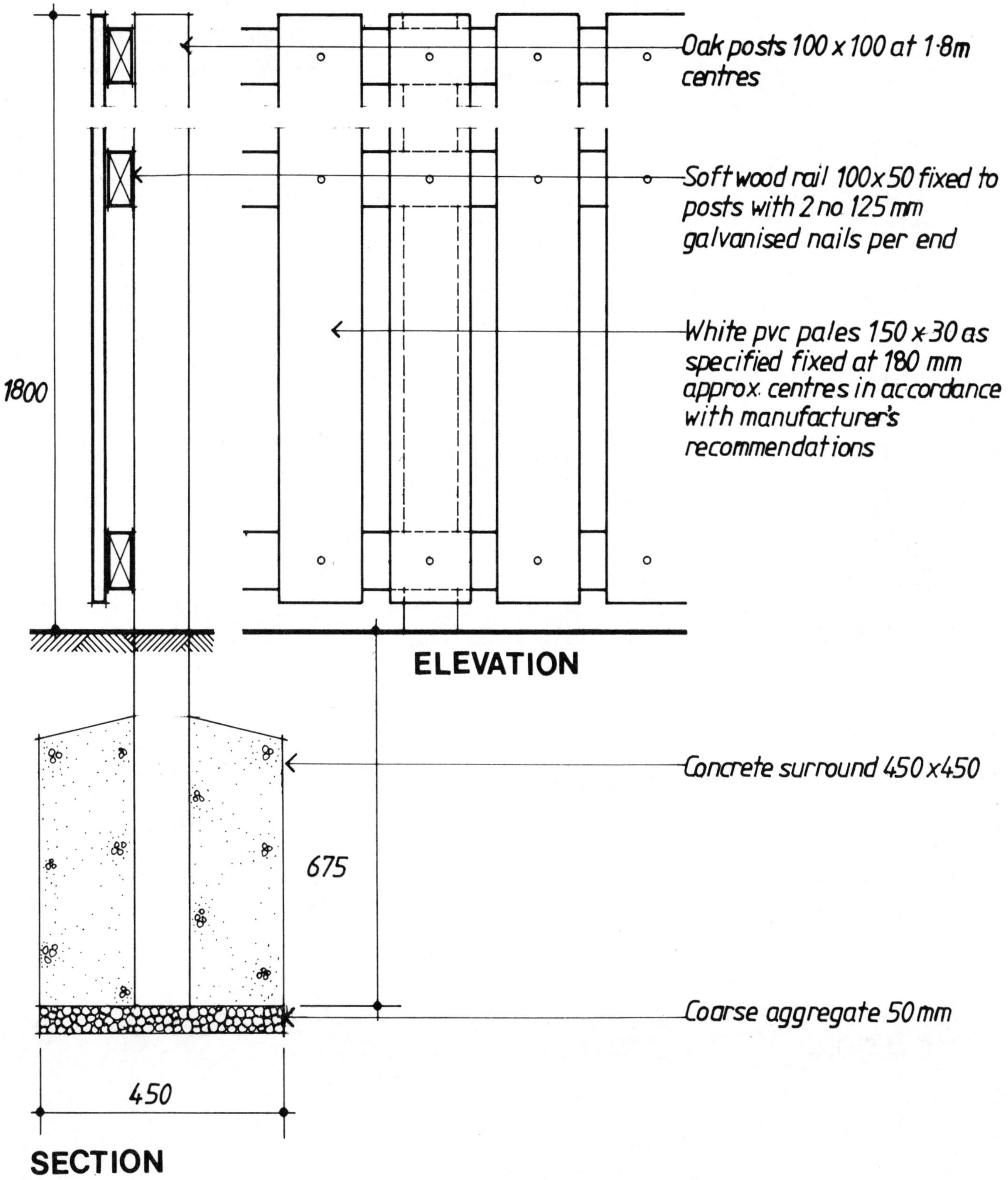

1800
Oak posts 100 x 100 at 1·8m centres
Soft wood rail 100x50 fixed to posts with 2 no. 125 mm galvanised nails per end
White pvc pales 150 x 30 as specified fixed at 180 mm approx. centres in accordance with manufacturer's recommendations
ELEVATION
Concrete surround 450 x 450
675
Coarse aggregate 50 mm
450
SECTION

Scale 1:10

FENCE
timber & pvc palisade

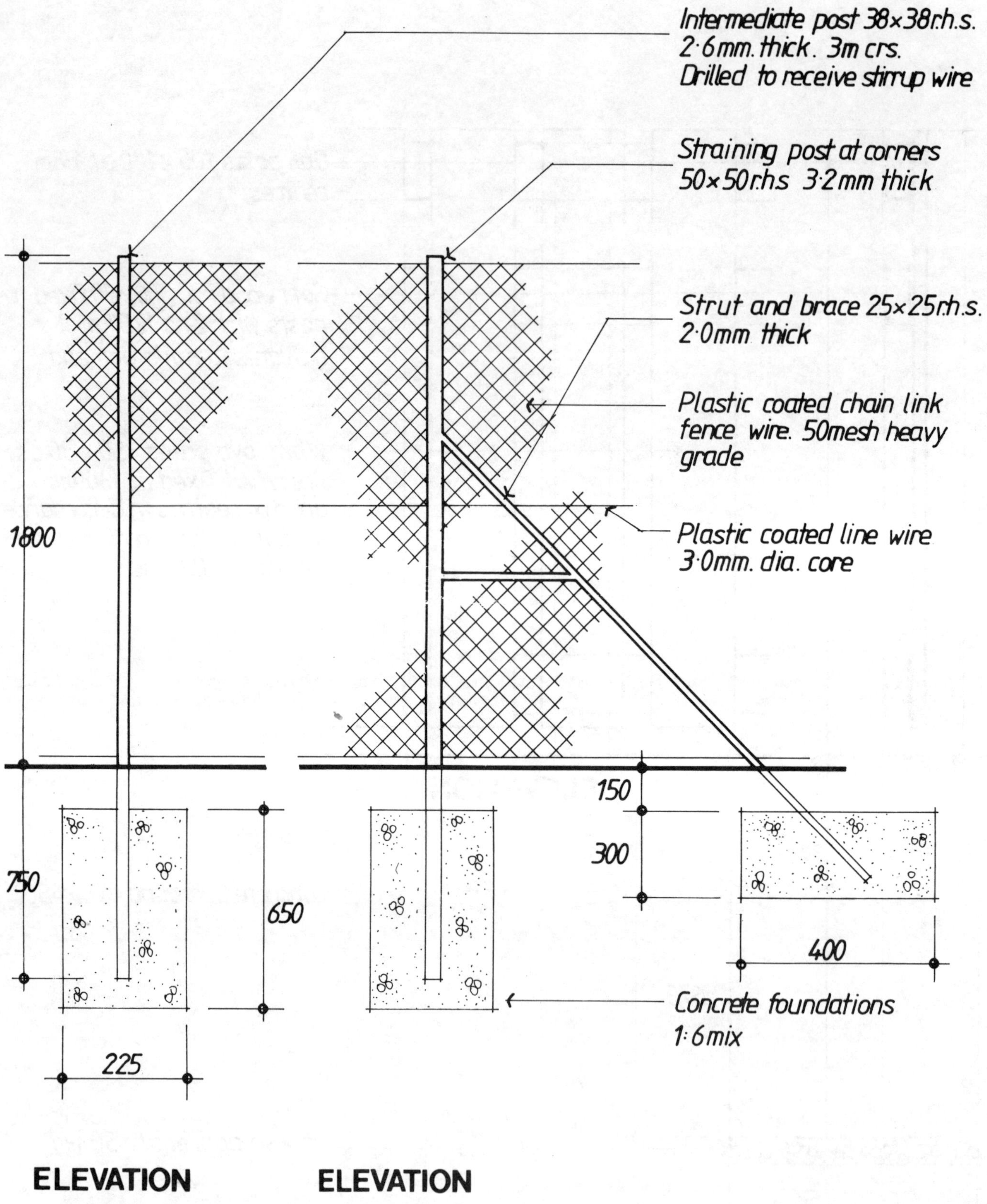
Intermediate post 38×38r.h.s.
2·6mm. thick. 3m crs.
Drilled to receive stirrup wire
Straining post at corners
50×50r.h.s 3·2mm thick
Strut and brace 25×25r.h.s.
2·0mm thick
Plastic coated chain link
fence wire. 50mesh heavy
grade
Plastic coated line wire
3·0mm. dia. core
1800
750
650
225
150
300
400
Concrete foundations
1:6mix
ELEVATION
ELEVATION

Scale 1:20

FENCE
chain link

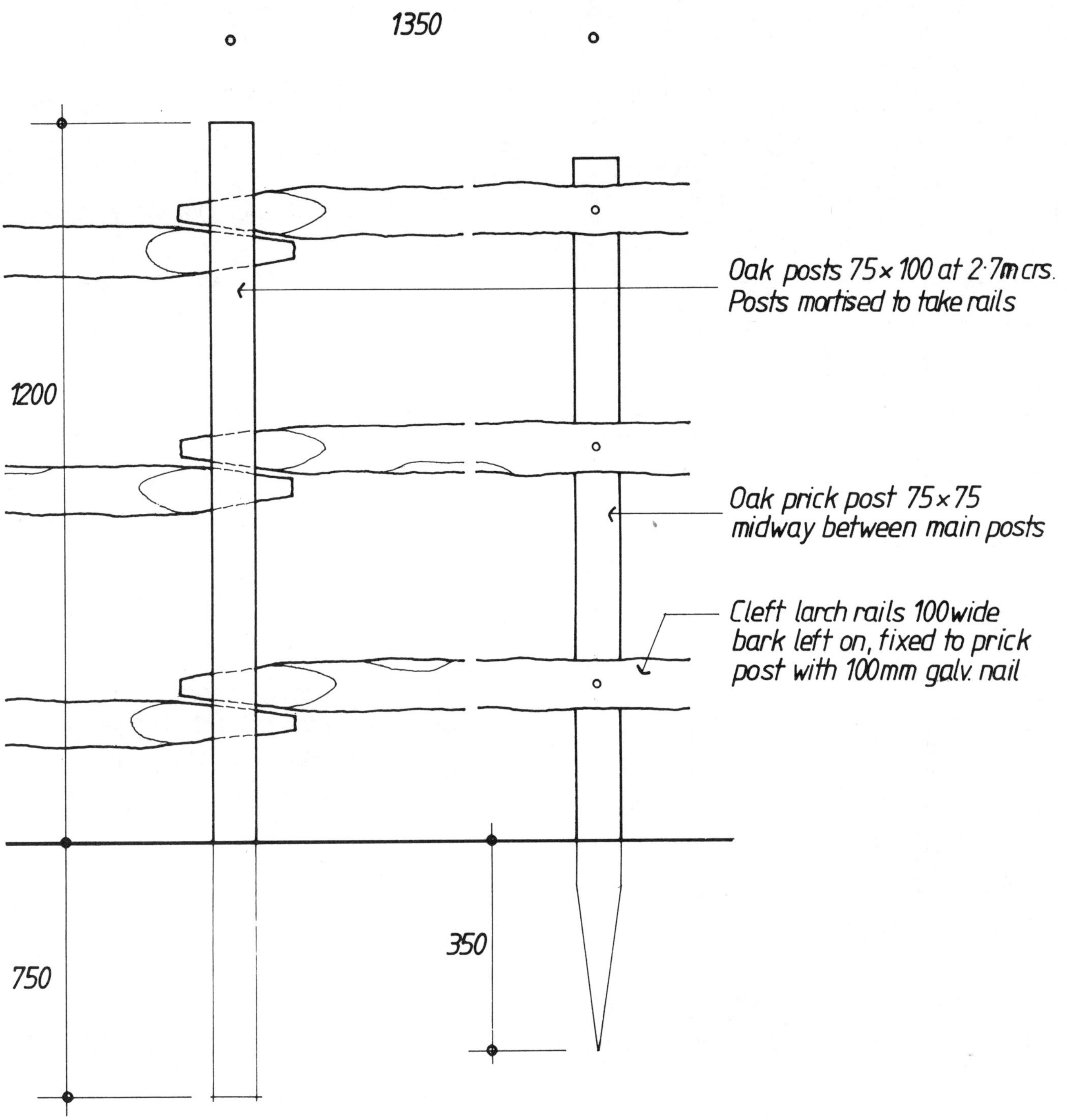
1350
1200
750
350
Oak posts 75×100 at 2·7m crs.
Posts mortised to take rails
Oak prick post 75×75
midway between main posts
Cleft larch rails 100 wide
bark left on, fixed to prick
post with 100mm galv. nail

ELEVATION

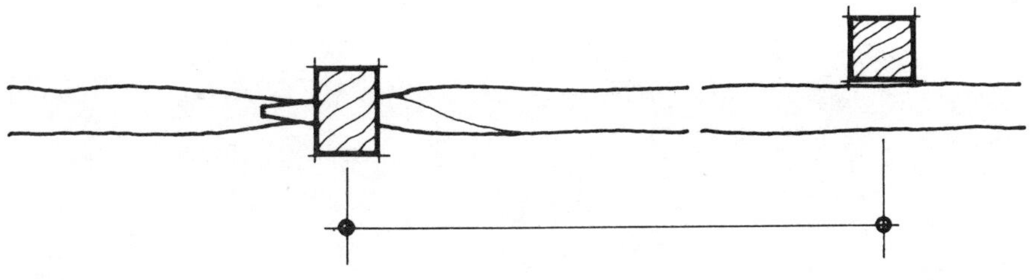

PLAN

Scale 1:10

FENCE

Lincolnshire post & rail

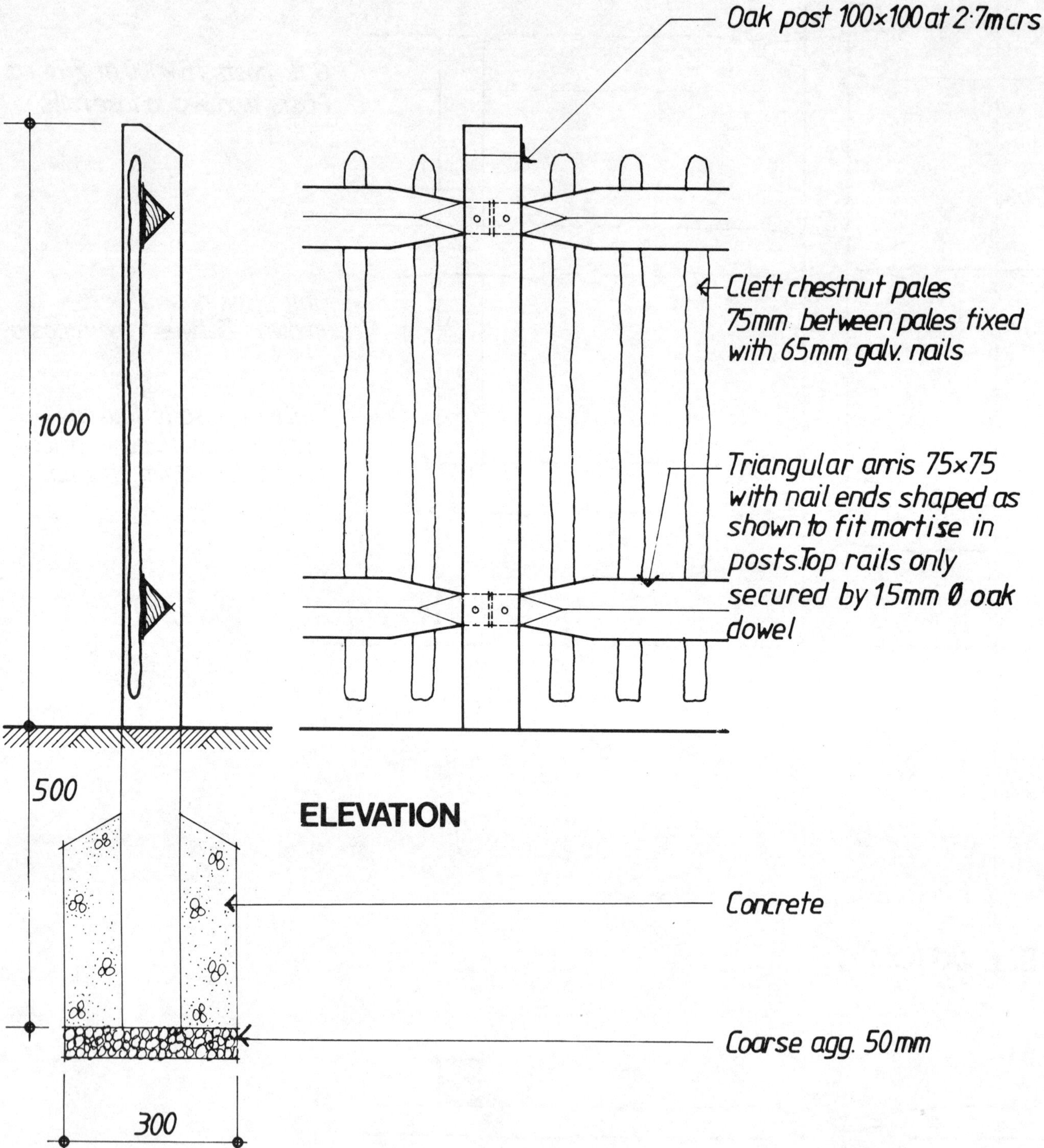

1000
500
300
Oak post 100×100 at 2·7m crs
Cleft chestnut pales
75mm between pales fixed
with 65mm galv. nails
Triangular arris 75×75
with nail ends shaped as
shown to fit mortise in
posts.Top rails only
secured by 15mm Ø oak
dowel
Concrete
Coarse agg. 50mm

ELEVATION

SECTION

Scale 1:10

FENCE

cleft chestnut

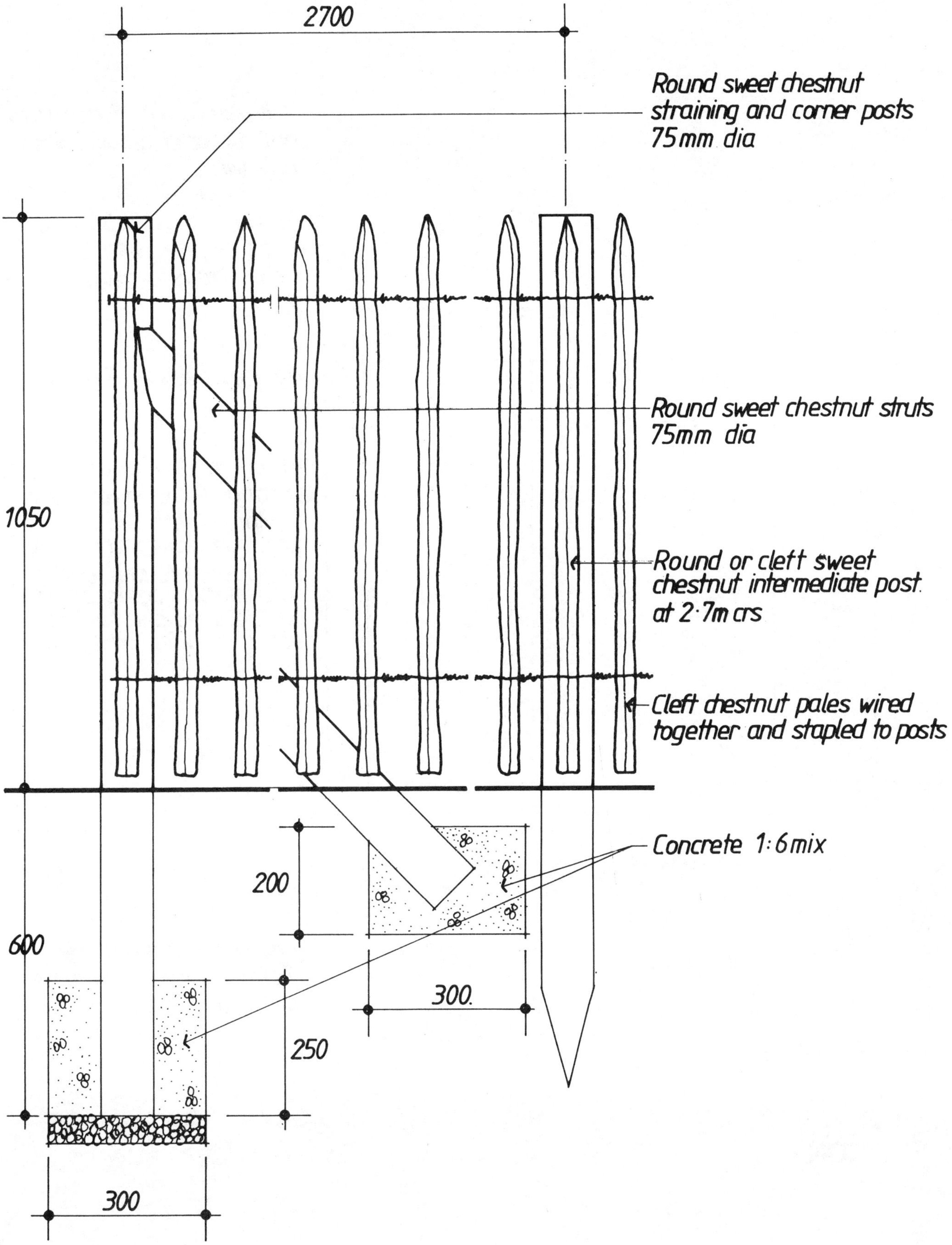
2700
Round sweet chestnut straining and corner posts 75mm dia
Round sweet chestnut struts 75mm dia
Round or cleft sweet chestnut intermediate post at 2·7m crs
Cleft chestnut pales wired together and stapled to posts
1050
Concrete 1:6 mix
200
600
300.
250
300

ELEVATION

Scale 1:10

FENCE
cleft chestnut & wire

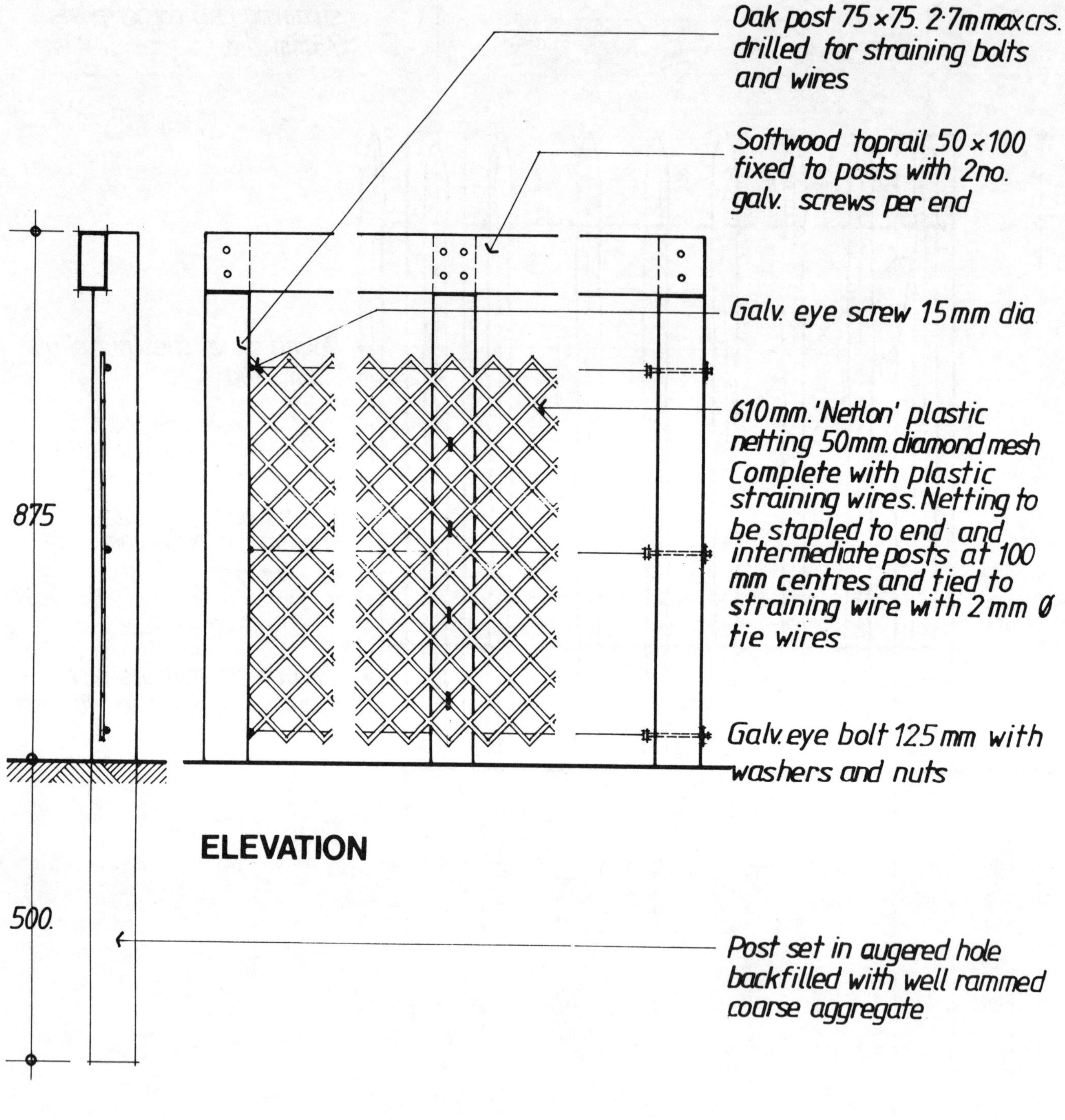

Scale 1:10

FENCE

timber & plastic mesh

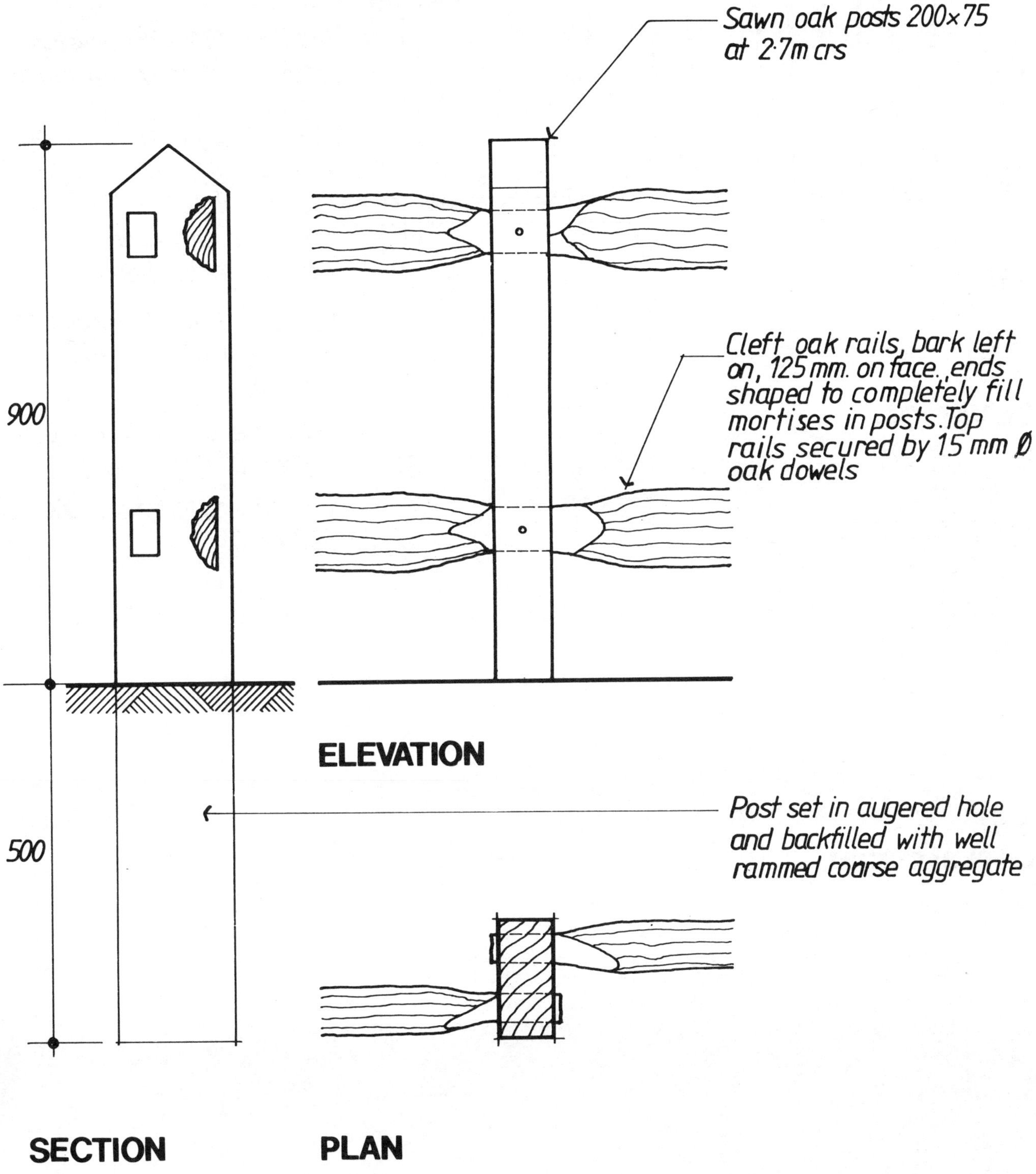
Sawn oak posts 200×75
at 2·7m crs
Cleft oak rails, bark left on, 125mm. on face., ends shaped to completely fill mortises in posts. Top rails secured by 15 mm Ø oak dowels
900
500
ELEVATION
Post set in augered hole and backfilled with well rammed coarse aggregate
SECTION
PLAN

Scale 1:10

FENCE
two rail Sussex

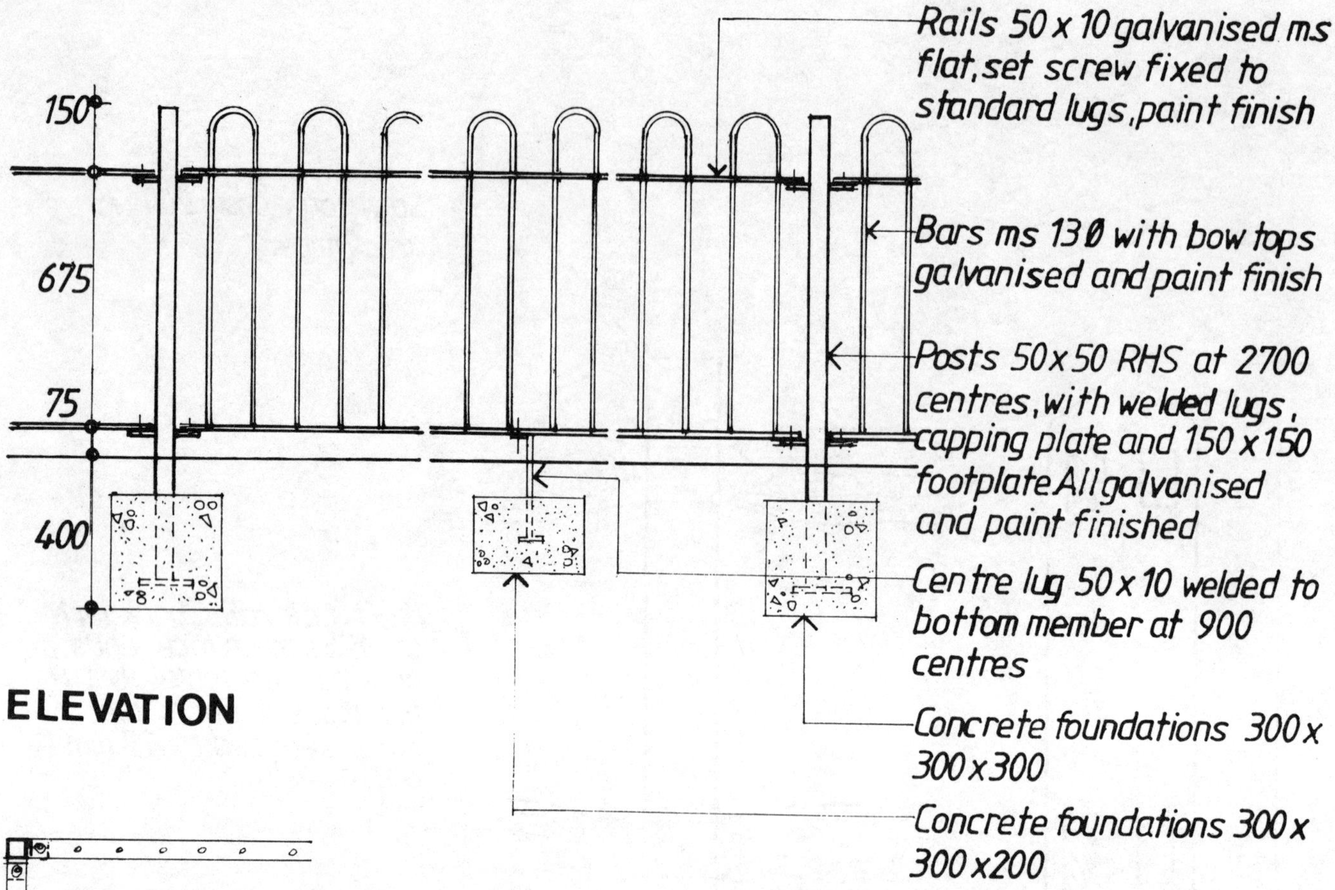

ELEVATION

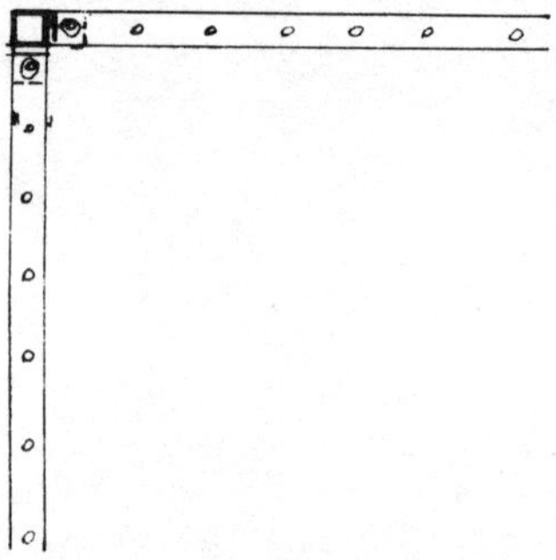

PLAN at corner

Scale 1:20

RAILINGS
metal bow topped

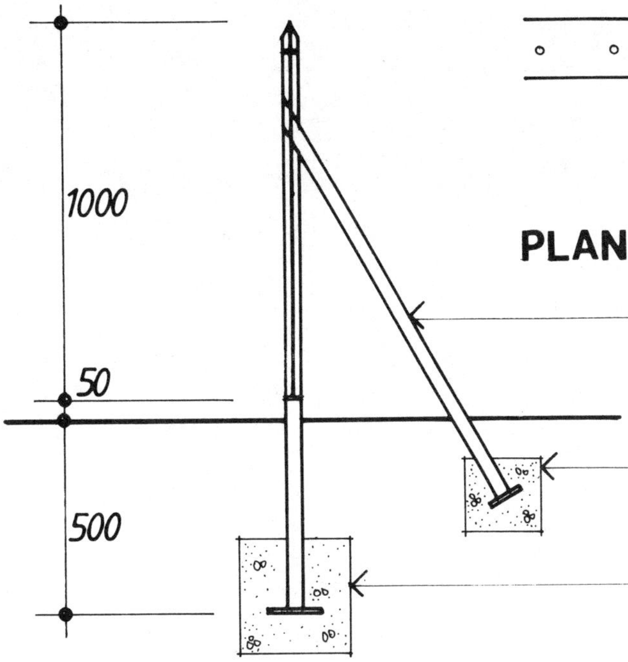

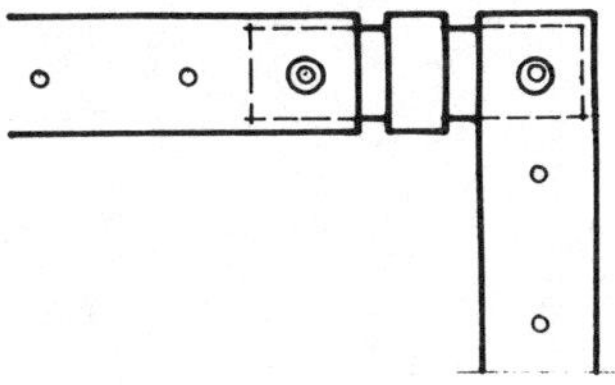

PLAN at corner

SECTION

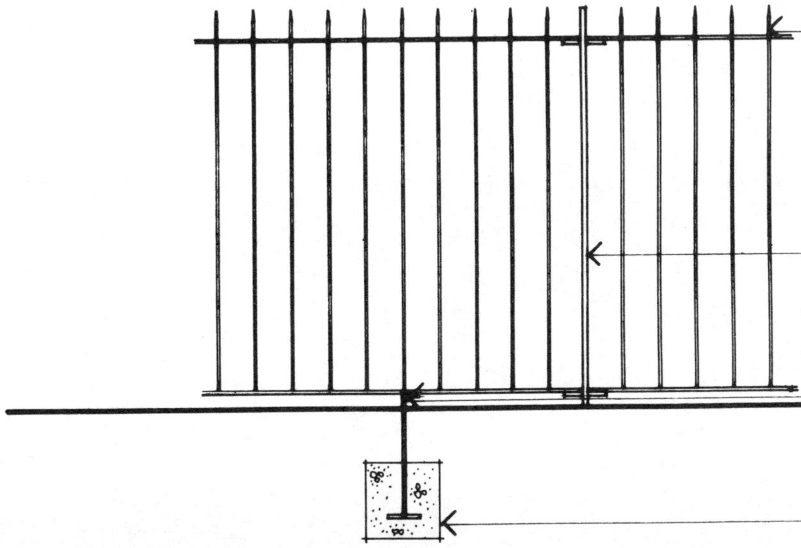

ELEVATION

Scale 1:20

RAILINGS
vertical bar

Chapter 5

Gates and barriers

BS 3470 covers the requirements for timber and steel field gates, with timber, steel and concrete gate posts. The Standard does not specify any particular design, but does set minimum units on sizes of various members. For gates in chain link and steel palisade fencing see the relevant BS fence type.

Construction

The main point about gate construction is to ensure that adequate cross bracing be provided to prevent the gate from dropping. The usual method of achieving this with timber construction is to provide a diagonal brace from the bottom corner on the hinge side so that the brace is in compression. Tall gates are provided with two separate braces. Metal gates of bolted construction are braced in the same manner. Welded metal gates are not usually cross braced.

Gate stops should be provided. The latch should not be relied on to stop the gate. Double gates should be provided with rebated meeting stiles.

Gate posts can be set in earth or concrete, and BS 3470 specifies the minimum length of post to be used in each case.

Width

For pedestrian use the structural opening width should not be less than 900 mm. Except for special designs, e.g. gallows gates, the maximum leaf size should be 1200 mm. For openings larger than this double gates should be used. For mower access to protected grass areas, a clear opening width of 2400 mm will be required. Vehicular control of estate roads or parking areas can be effected by the use of gallows gates with opening widths of up to 5200 mm.

Height

Gate height should be equal to or slightly lower than the adjacent enclosure.

Hinges, Locks and Latches

Hinges

The usual type of gate hinge is the steel band hinge. There are two basic types:

1 Hook and band

2 Reversible

Hook and band are available as light or heavy duty, straight or cranked. Reversible hinges are available as light or heavy duty. Both types are available hot-dip galvanised or sherardised. Tee hinges are also used. These are usually available in a japanned finish, but can be specially ordered with a galvanised finish. All hinge types are described in BS 1227 : Part 1A : 1967.

Locks

Locks for gates usually take the form of barrel bolts. Where these are secured with a padlock they are called padbolts. Double gates should be fitted with bolts to engage in sockets set in concrete or tarmac. A centre stop should be used in conjunction with the bolts. These can be of the fall-down type if the passage of lawn mowers is anticipated. Provision should be made for securing gates in the catches.

Latches

The type of gate latch fitted will depend on the gate height. Low gates can have an automatic latch fitted to the inside of the gate only. High gates can be fitted with a Suffolk-type thumb latch or a ring handle gate latch, both of which are operable from either side of the gate. BS 1331 describes latches suitable for gates.

References

British Standards Institute
BS 4092 Domestic front entrance gates
Part 1 : 1966 Metal gates
Part 2 : 1966 Wooden gates
BS 3470 : 1975 Field gates and posts

Timber Research and Development Association
Timber Fencing and Gates

Detail sheets

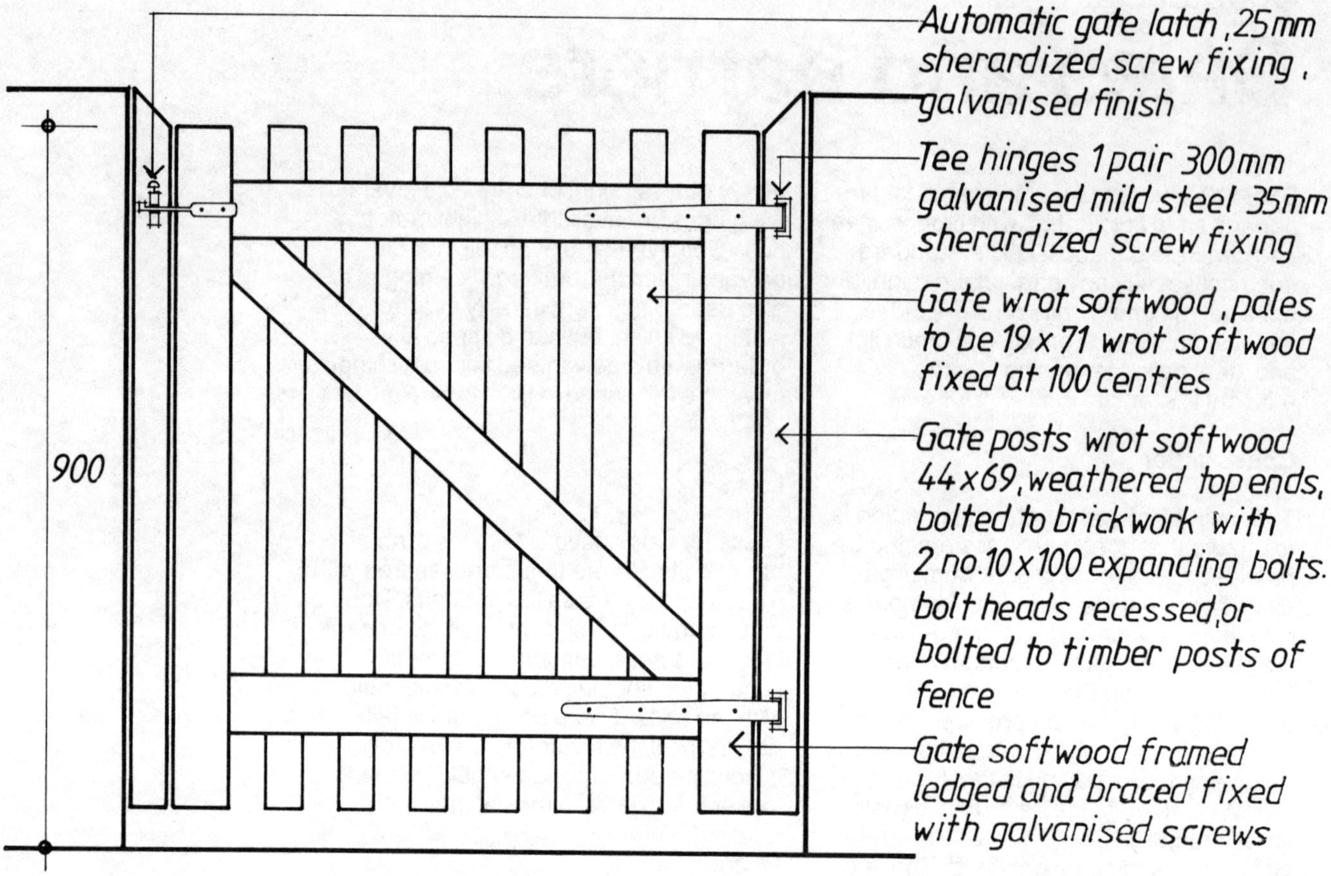

ELEVATION

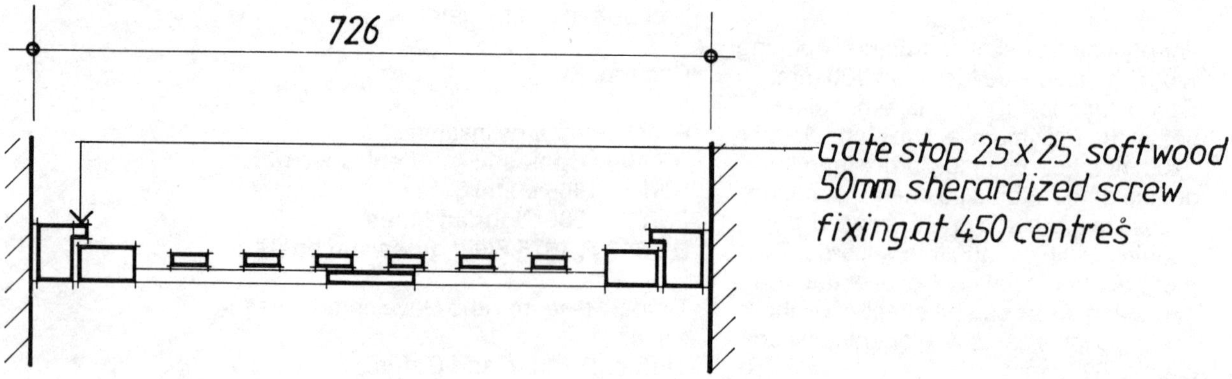

PLAN

Scale 1:10

SINGLE GATE
timber palisade

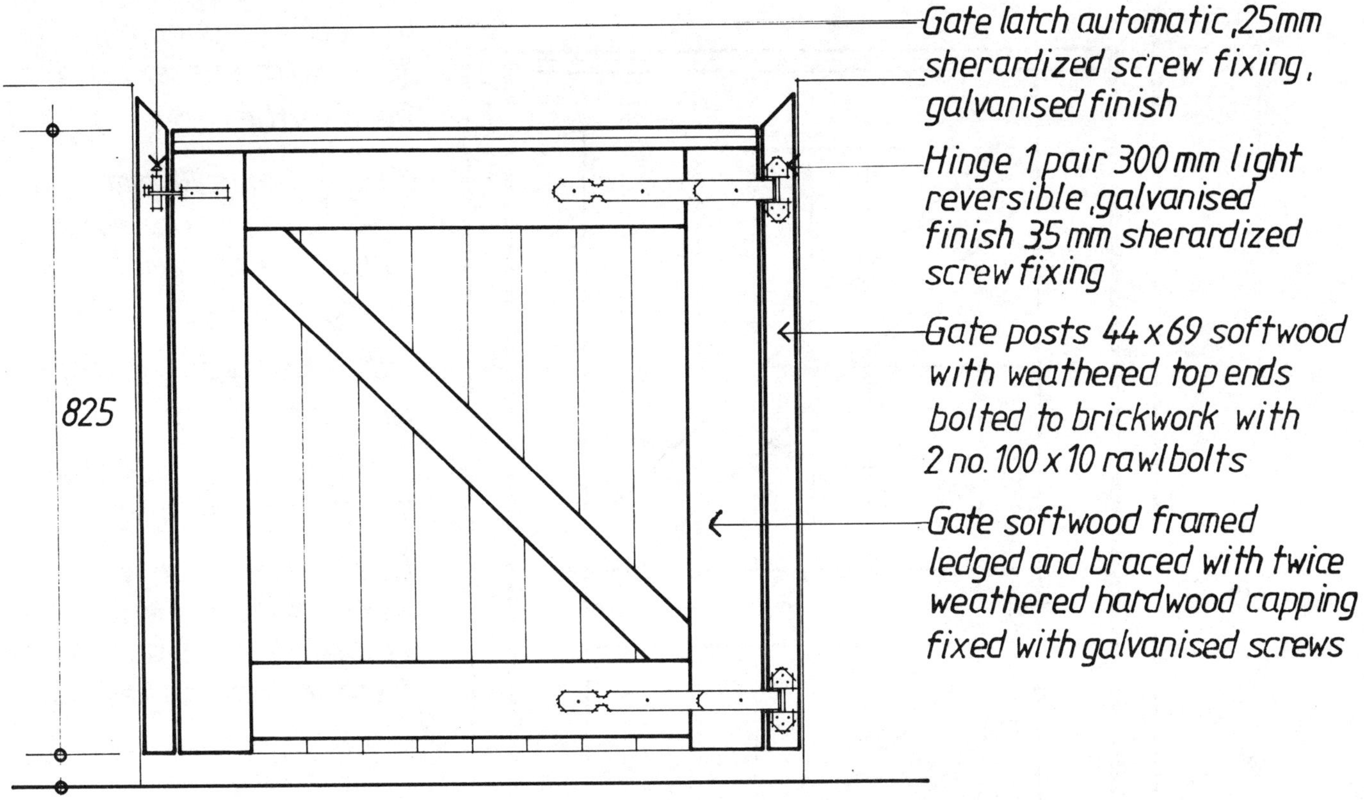

ELEVATION

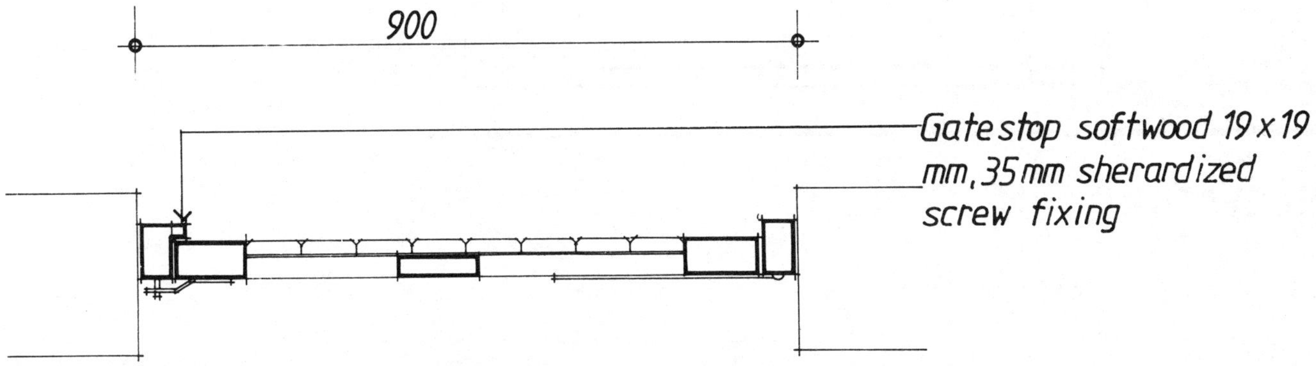

PLAN

Scale 1:10

SINGLE GATE
timber matchboard

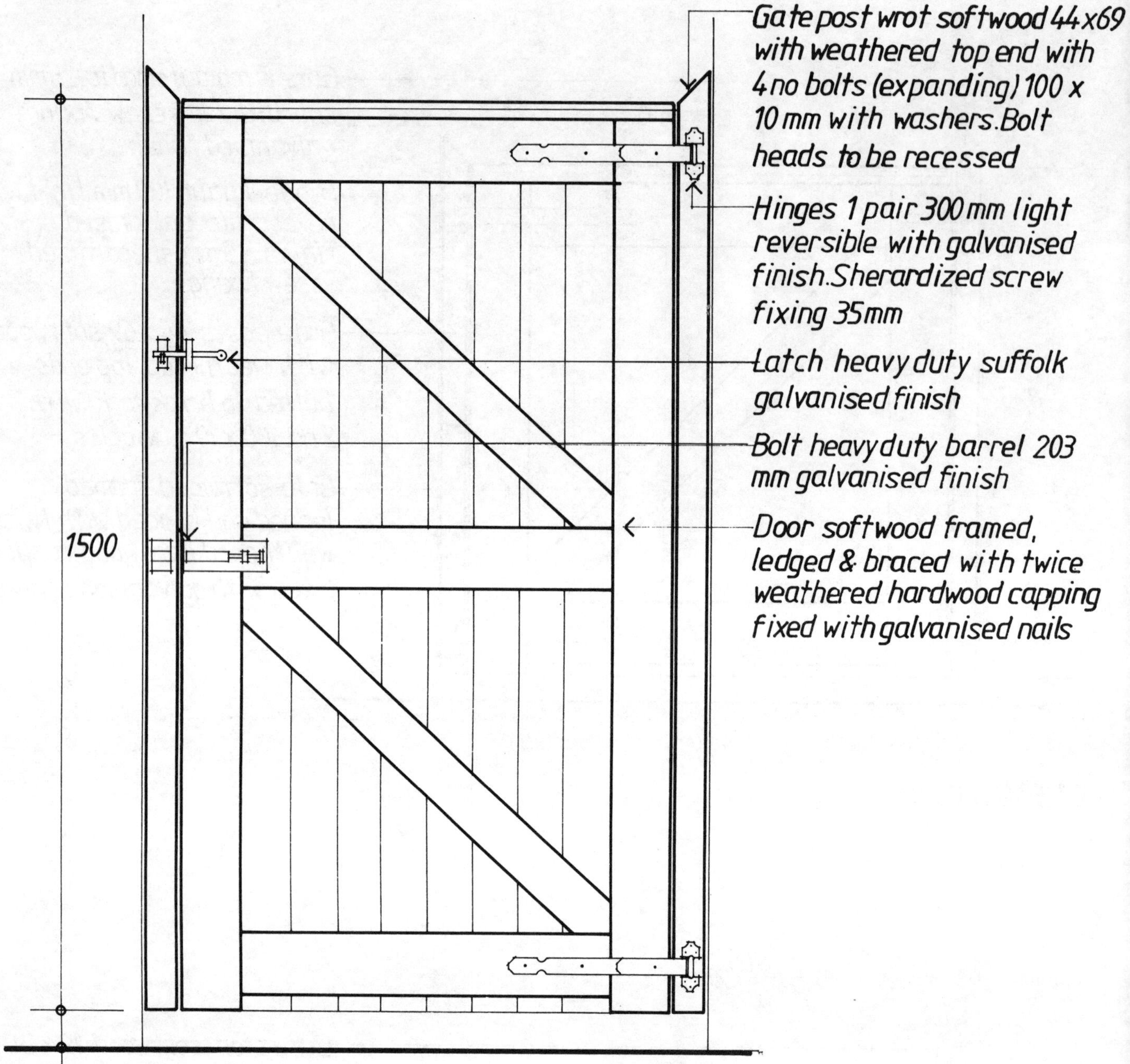

ELEVATION

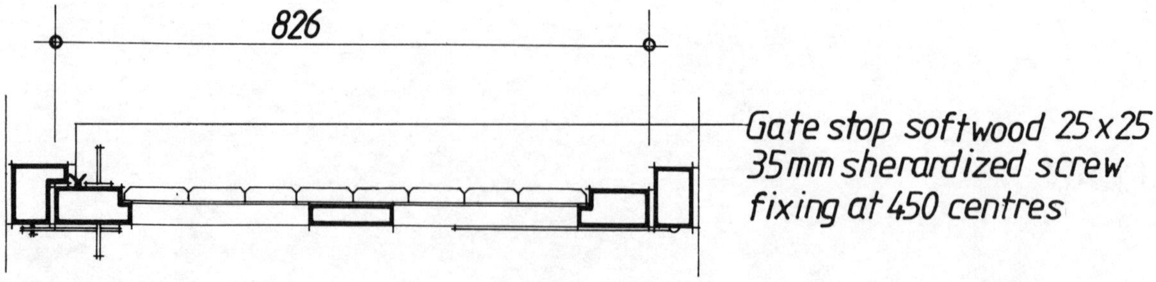

PLAN

Scale 1:10

SINGLE GATE

timber matchboard

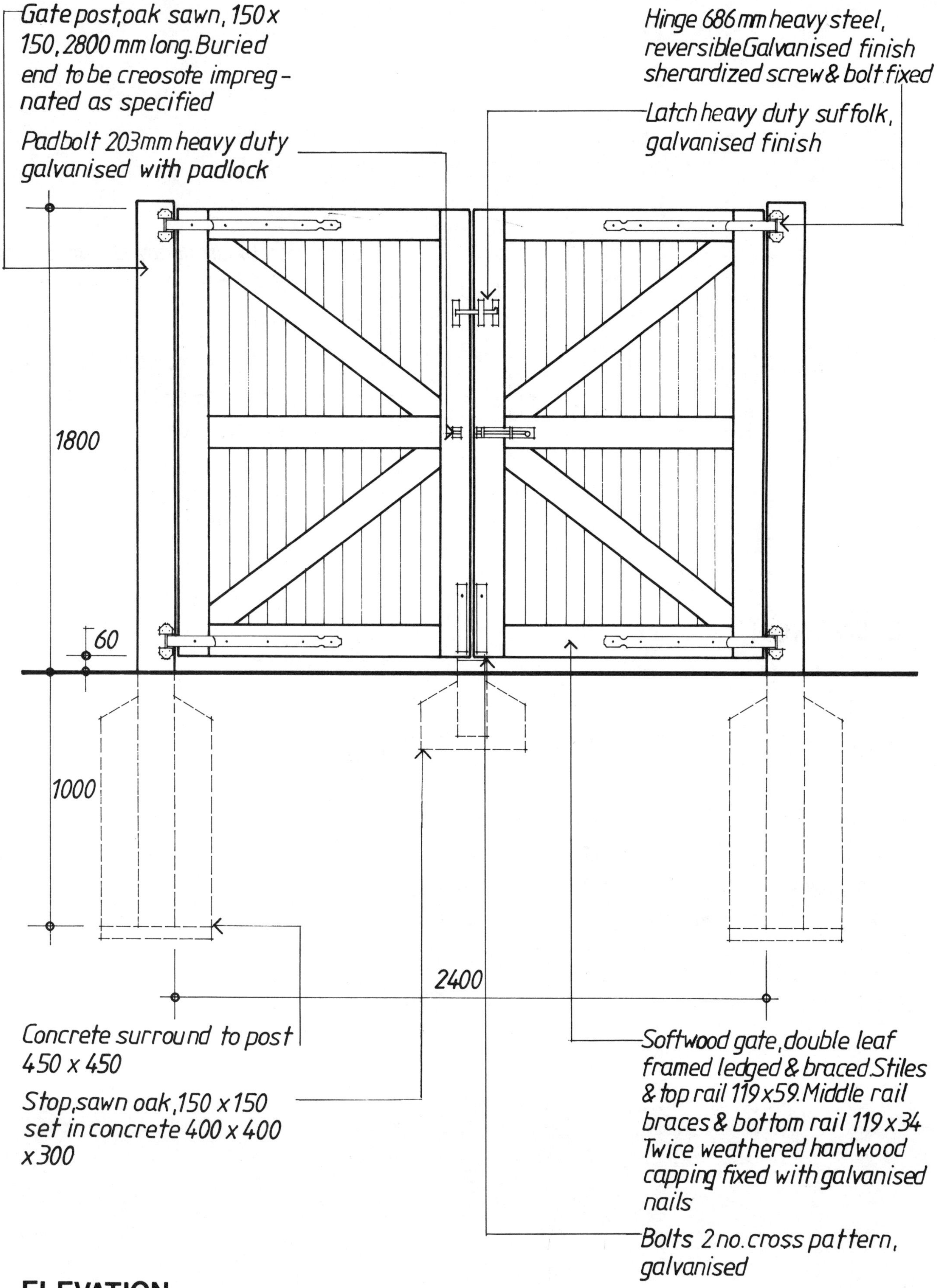

Gate post, oak sawn, 150 x 150, 2800 mm long. Buried end to be creosote impreg-nated as specified
Padbolt 203mm heavy duty galvanised with padlock
Hinge 686 mm heavy steel, reversible Galvanised finish sherardized screw & bolt fixed
Latch heavy duty suffolk, galvanised finish
1800
60
1000
2400
Concrete surround to post 450 x 450
Stop, sawn oak, 150 x 150 set in concrete 400 x 400 x 300
Softwood gate, double leaf framed ledged & braced Stiles & top rail 119 x 59. Middle rail braces & bottom rail 119 x 34 Twice weathered hardwood capping fixed with galvanised nails
Bolts 2 no. cross pattern, galvanised

ELEVATION

Scale 1:20

DOUBLE GATE

timber

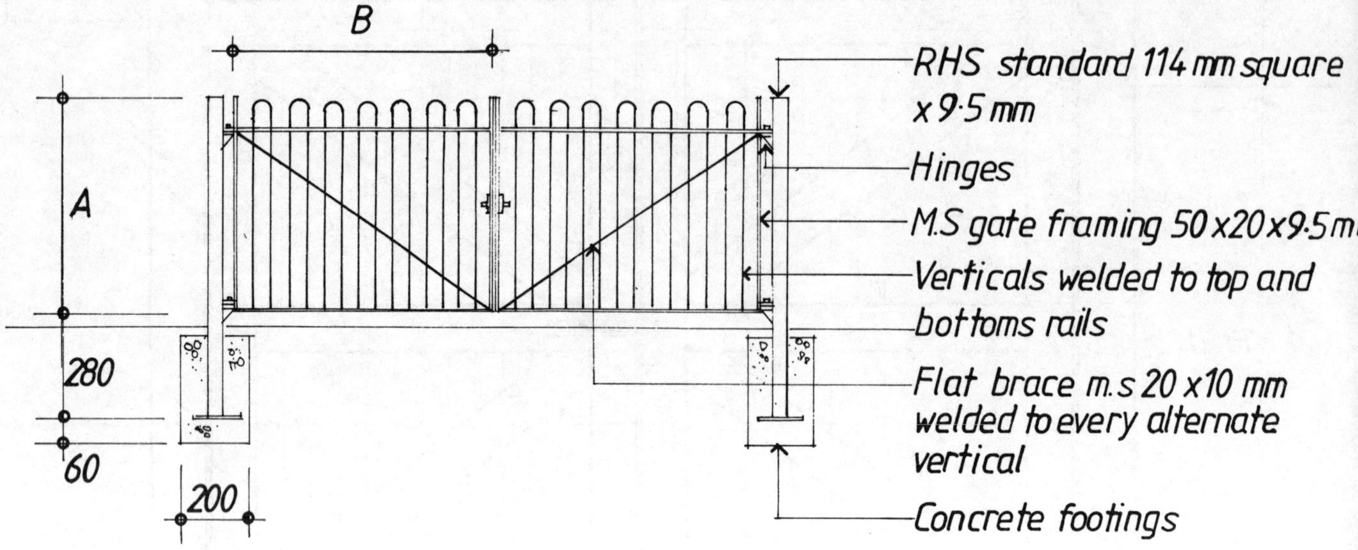

ELEVATION

Nominal Size	A	B	No of verticals/ gate & size(dia)
3800 x 1200	1125	1818	14 x 13Ø
3800 x 1400	1375	1818	14 x 13Ø
3800 x 1800	1725	1818	14 x 19Ø
4400 x 1200	1125	2118	16 x 13Ø
4400 x 1400	1325	2118	16 x 13Ø
4400 x 1800	1725	2118	16 x 19Ø

Scale 1:20

DOUBLE GATE

mild steel

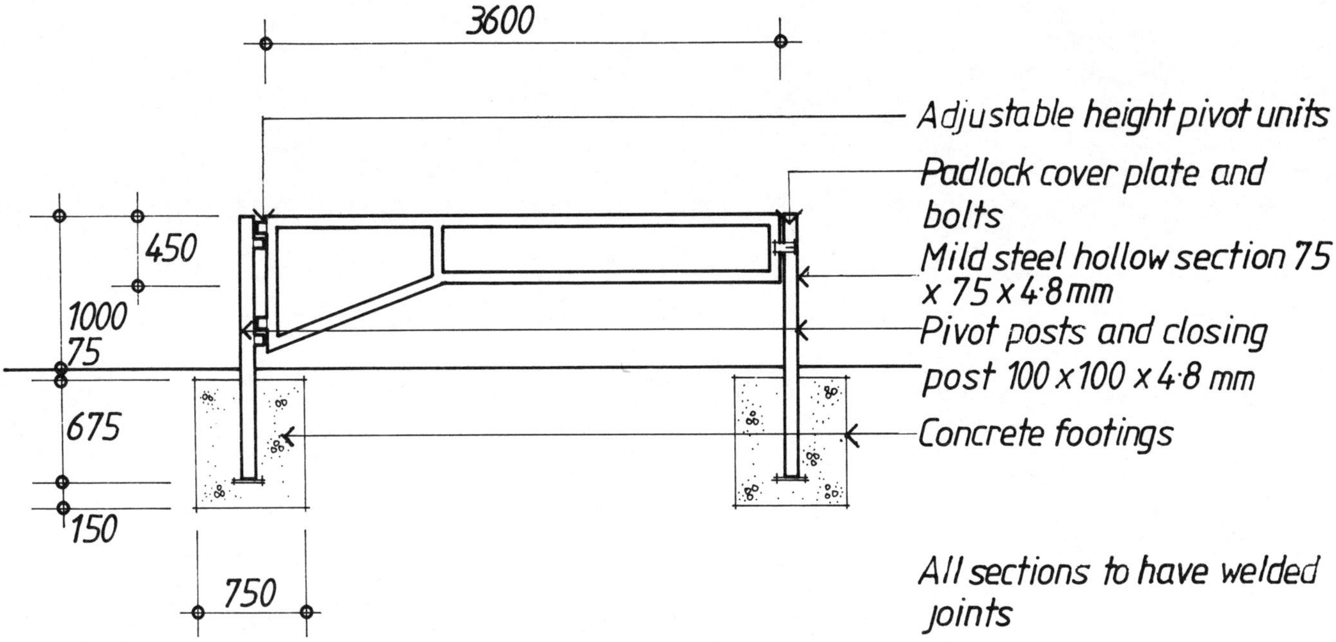

ELEVATION

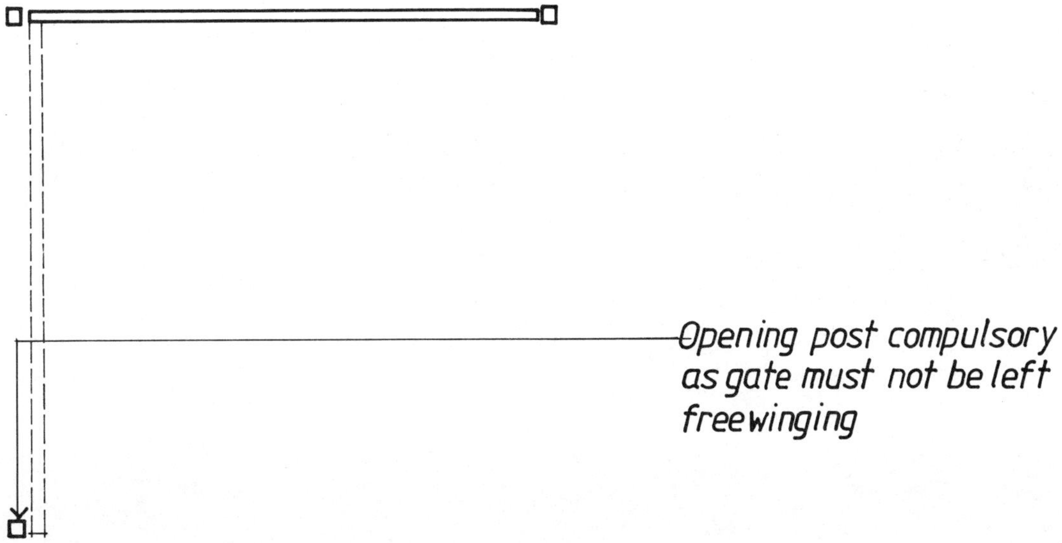

PLAN

Scale 1:20

GALLOWS GATE

metal

Chapter 6

Low rails

Low timber rails

Size

Because of their height (up to 400 mm), the designer of low rails should bear in mind their potential for being sat or balanced upon. The design should either cater for or discourage such use.

Post spacing, depth of insertion

In view of the factors mentioned above, post centres should be closer (usually 1000 mm – 1,500 mm) than in fencing intended solely as a barrier.
For pedestrian use, a post insertion depth of 300 mm is sufficient if a concrete surround is provided. For controlling vehicular traffic, an insertion depth of 750 mm is required.

Joints in top rail

The solution to the problem will vary with the design. The following general points should be observed:
1 Lapped or scarfed joints are preferable.
2 Bolts or screws should not be inserted within 25 mm of board ends.
3 Where the rail consists of two or more members, the joints in each should be staggered.

Corner detail and changes in direction

Where corners and changes in direction are infrequent, the best solution is to duplicate the post support. Where a top rail is used, adequate bearing must be arranged for a mitred joint.

Low metal rails

Size

The remarks made in regard to timber low rails apply equally in metal low rails.

Spacing of standards

The standards for low metal rails are generally spaced at 1200 mm centres. A surround of concrete must be used because of the small surface area of metal sections.

Metal protection and finish

BS 1722 : Part 8 specifies a range of ex-works finishes, the usual finish being a red-oxide primer or hot-dip galvanising after fabrication.
The finished element should be all shop welded, construction made with a loose end to the rail, which is jointed on site using a screwed sleeve or plate.
With metal rails, changes in direction are usually made in the rail; the space between standards should be closed in order to increase support at this point.

References

E and F N Spon Ltd
Spon's Landscape Handbook

NBA 'Building' Commodity File, Components (90) Section 02 : Fencing

Detail sheets

Timber
6.1 400 mm high angular
6.2 500 mm high triangular
6.3 400 mm high square
6.4 550 mm high square

Timber and steel
6.5 400 mm high
6.6 450 mm high mild steel tube

Steel
6.7 300 mm high hollow tube

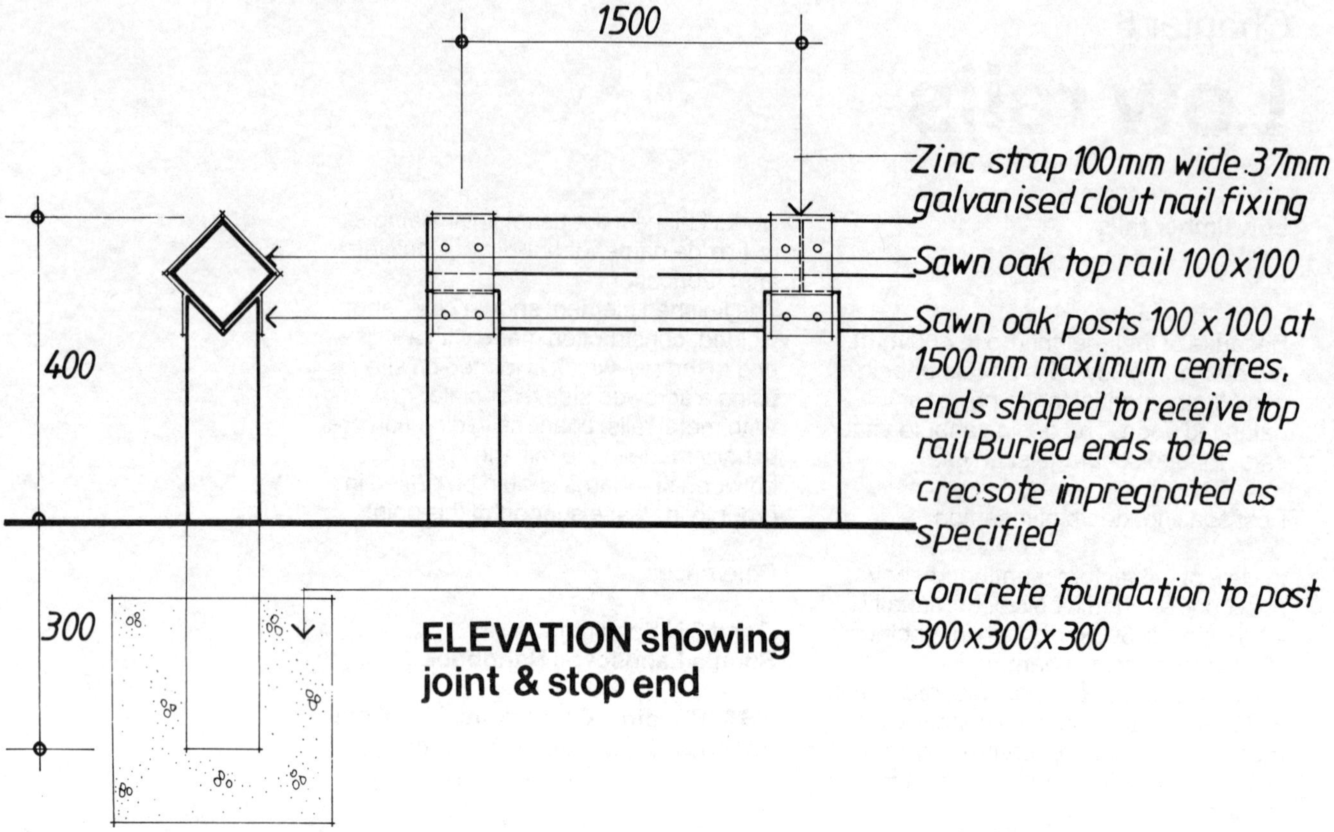
1500
400
300
Zinc strap 100mm wide.37mm galvanised clout nail fixing
Sawn oak top rail 100x100
Sawn oak posts 100 x 100 at 1500mm maximum centres, ends shaped to receive top rail Buried ends to be creosote impregnated as specified
Concrete foundation to post 300x300x300

ELEVATION showing joint & stop end

SECTION

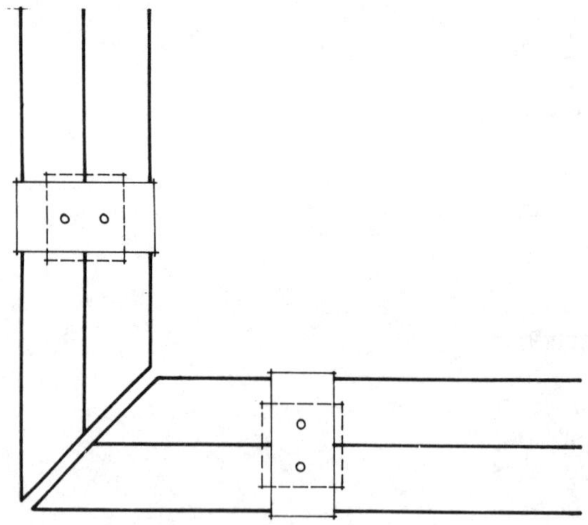

PLAN at corner

Scale 1:10

LOW RAIL

timber

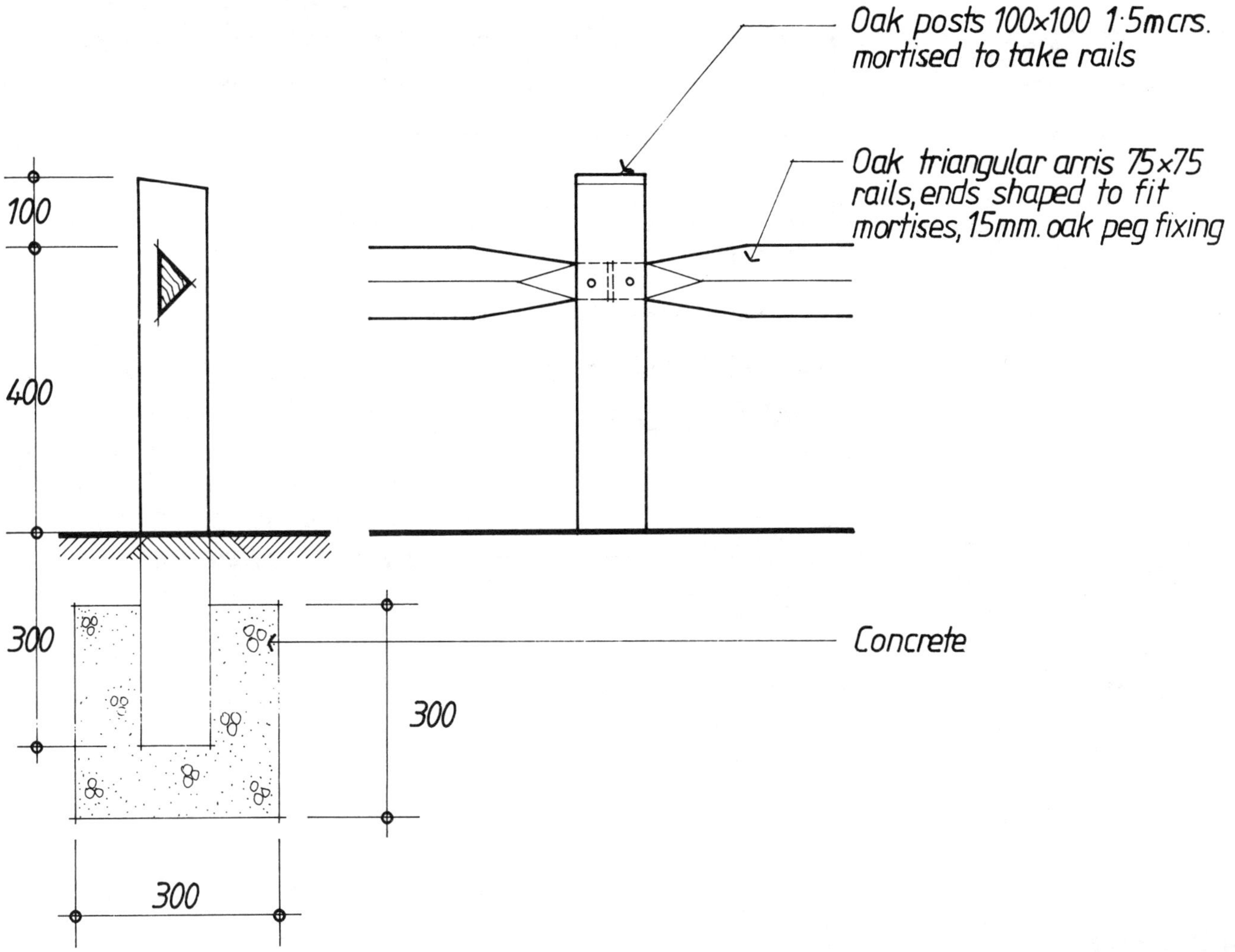

Scale 1:10

LOW RAIL
timber

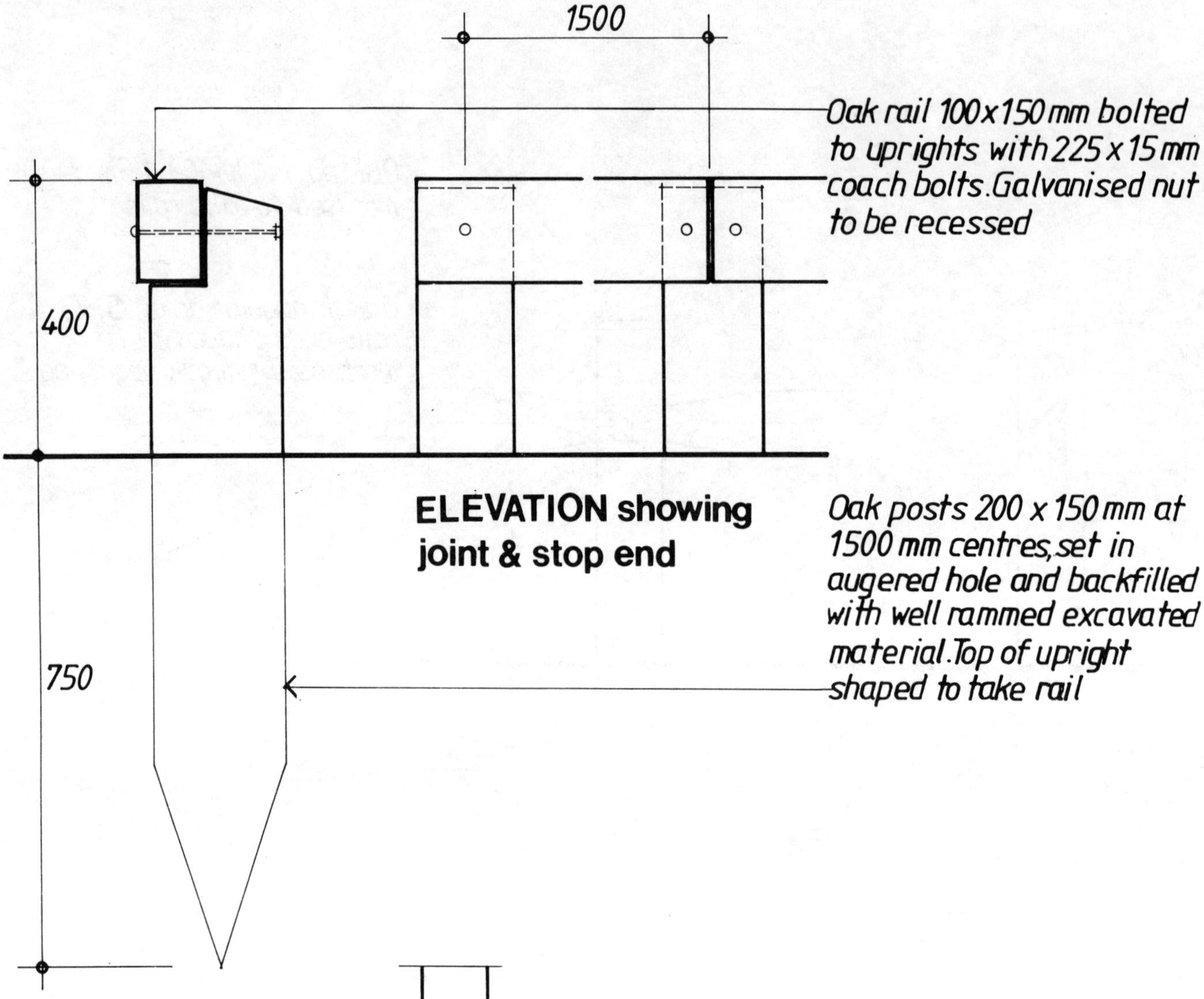
1500
400
750
Oak rail 100x150 mm bolted to uprights with 225 x 15 mm coach bolts. Galvanised nut to be recessed
Oak posts 200 x 150 mm at 1500 mm centres, set in augered hole and backfilled with well rammed excavated material. Top of upright shaped to take rail

ELEVATION showing joint & stop end

SECTION

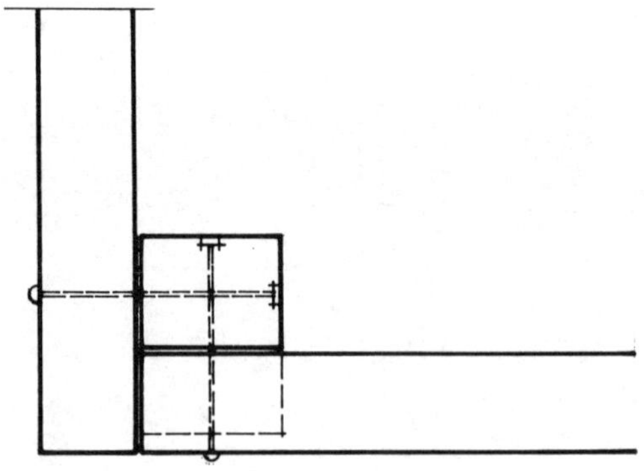

PLAN at corner

Scale 1:10

LOW RAIL
timber

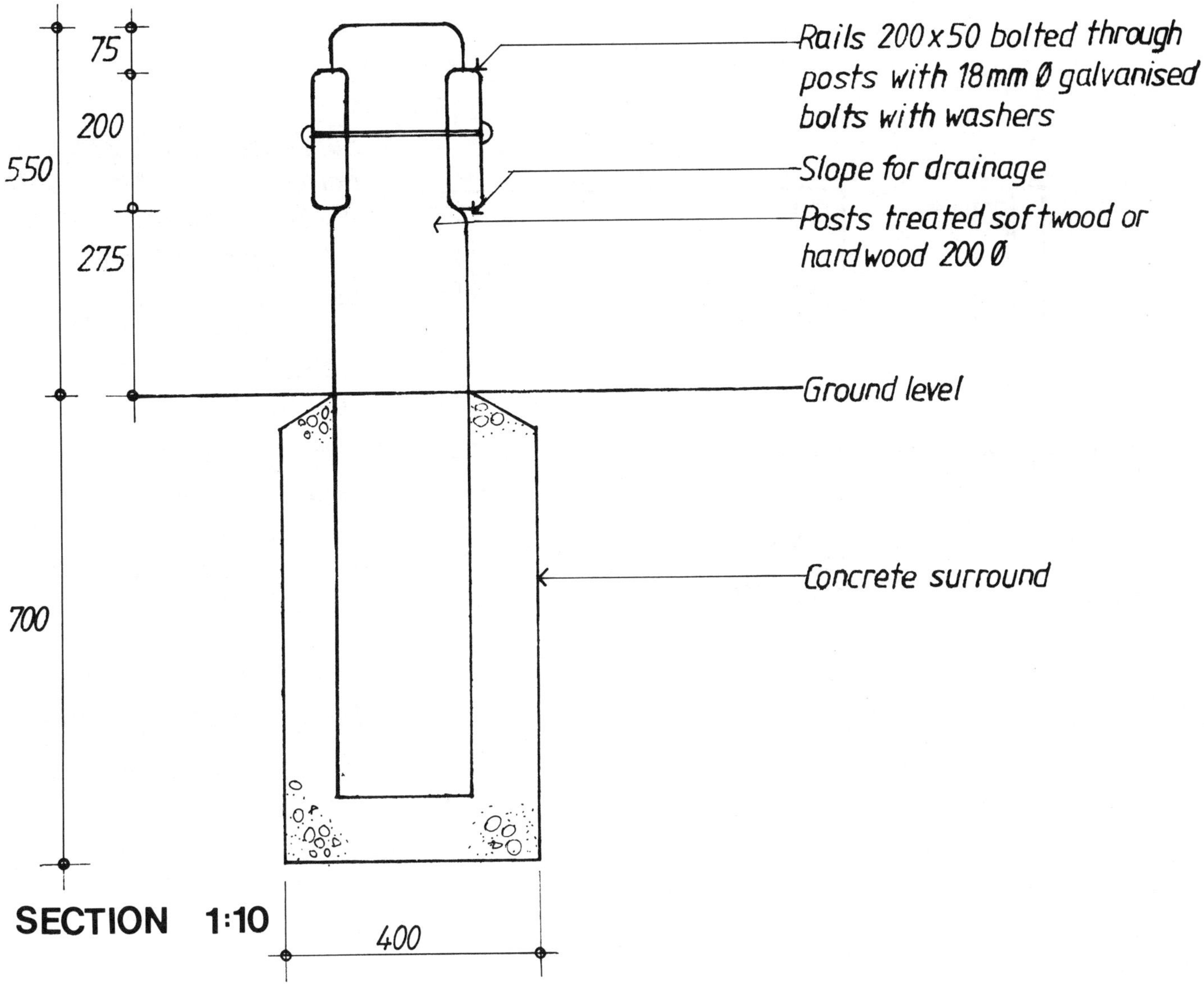
75
200
550
275
700
Rails 200x50 bolted through posts with 18mm Ø galvanised bolts with washers
Slope for drainage
Posts treated softwood or hardwood 200 Ø
Ground level
Concrete surround
400

SECTION 1:10

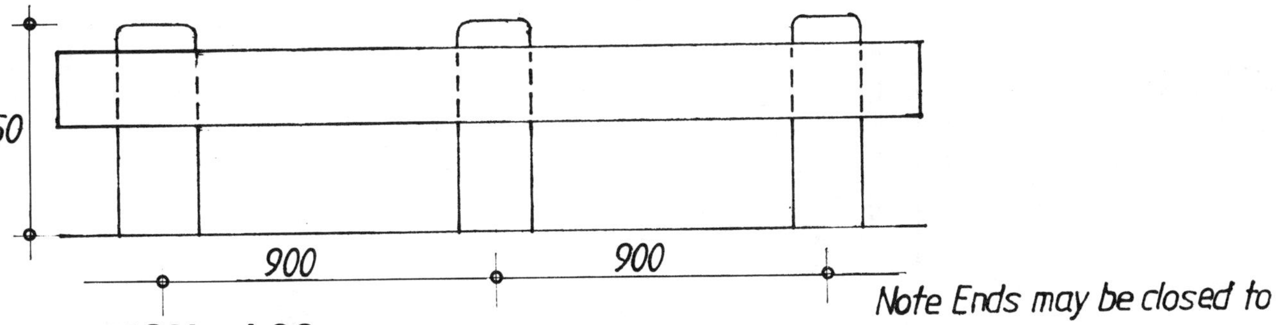
550
900
900
Note Ends may be closed to prevent bumper hooking

ELEVATION 1:20

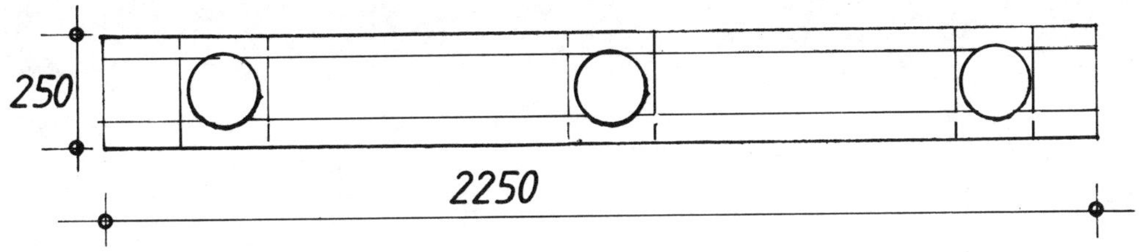
250
2250

PLAN 1:20

Scale A.S

LOW RAIL
timber

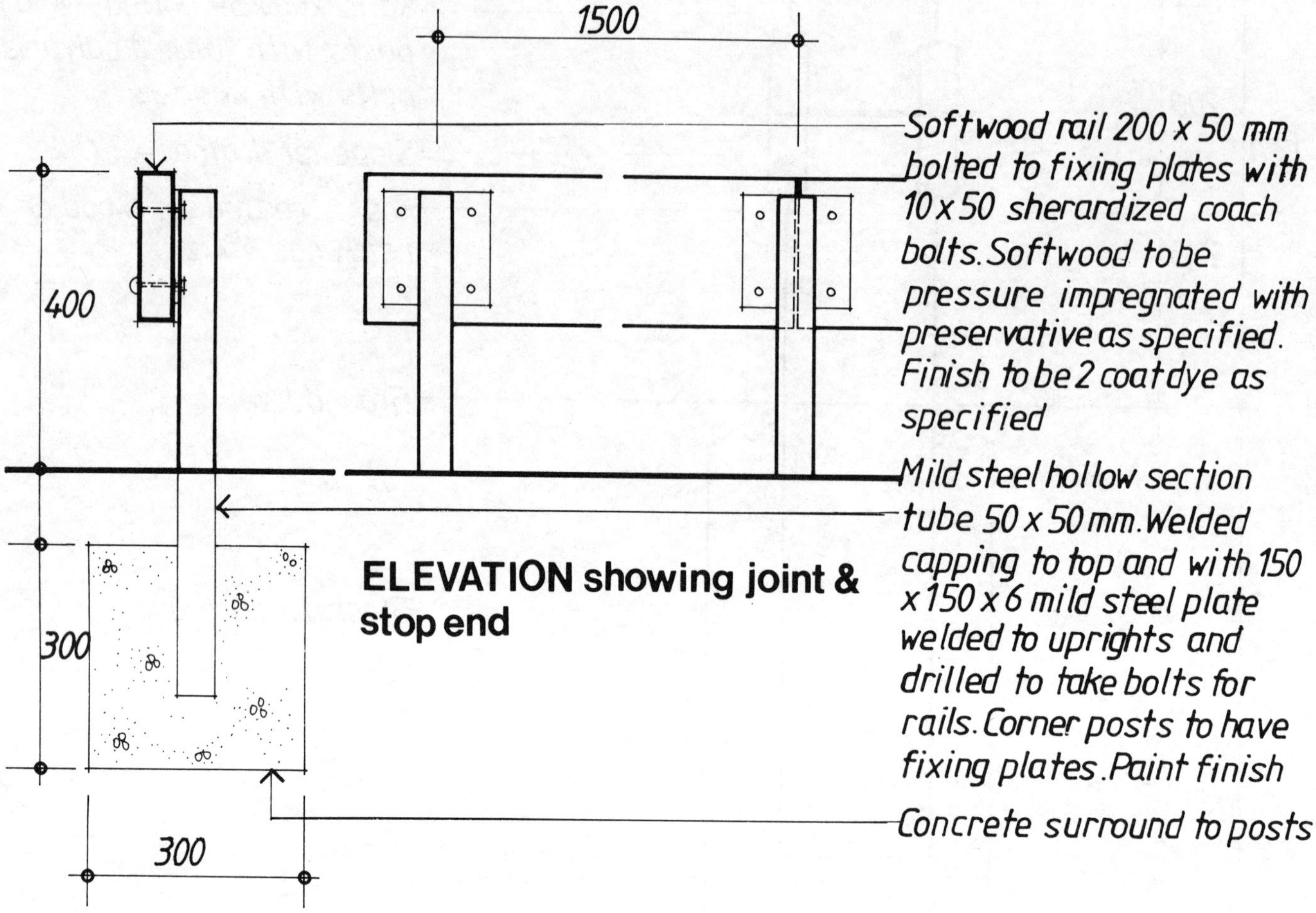

ELEVATION showing joint & stop end

SECTION

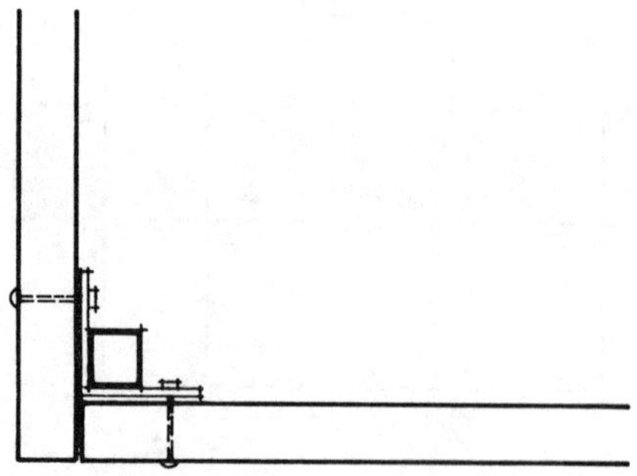

PLAN at corner

Scale 1:10

LOW RAIL
timber & steel

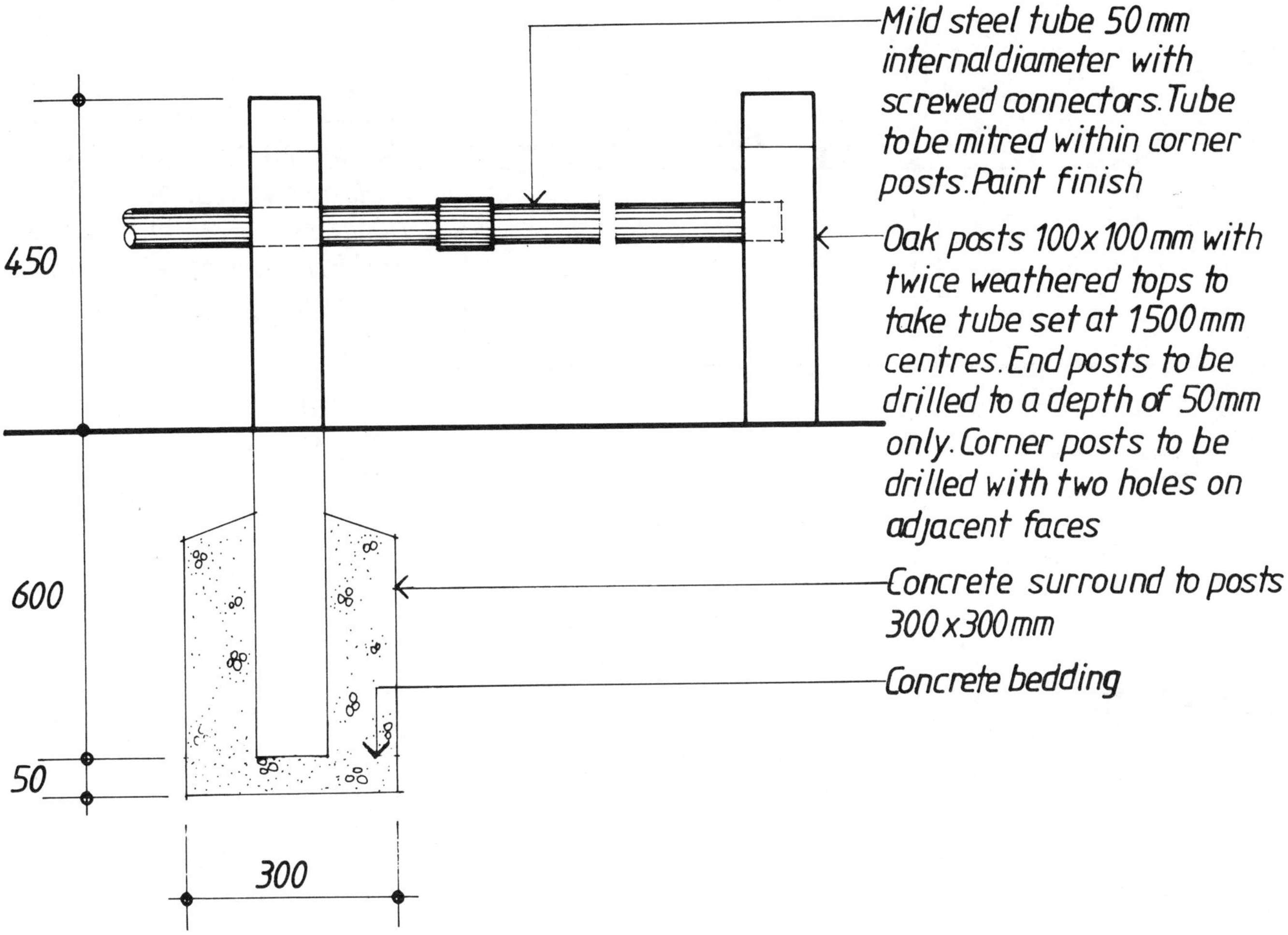

ELEVATION

Scale 1:10

LOW RAIL

timber & steel tube

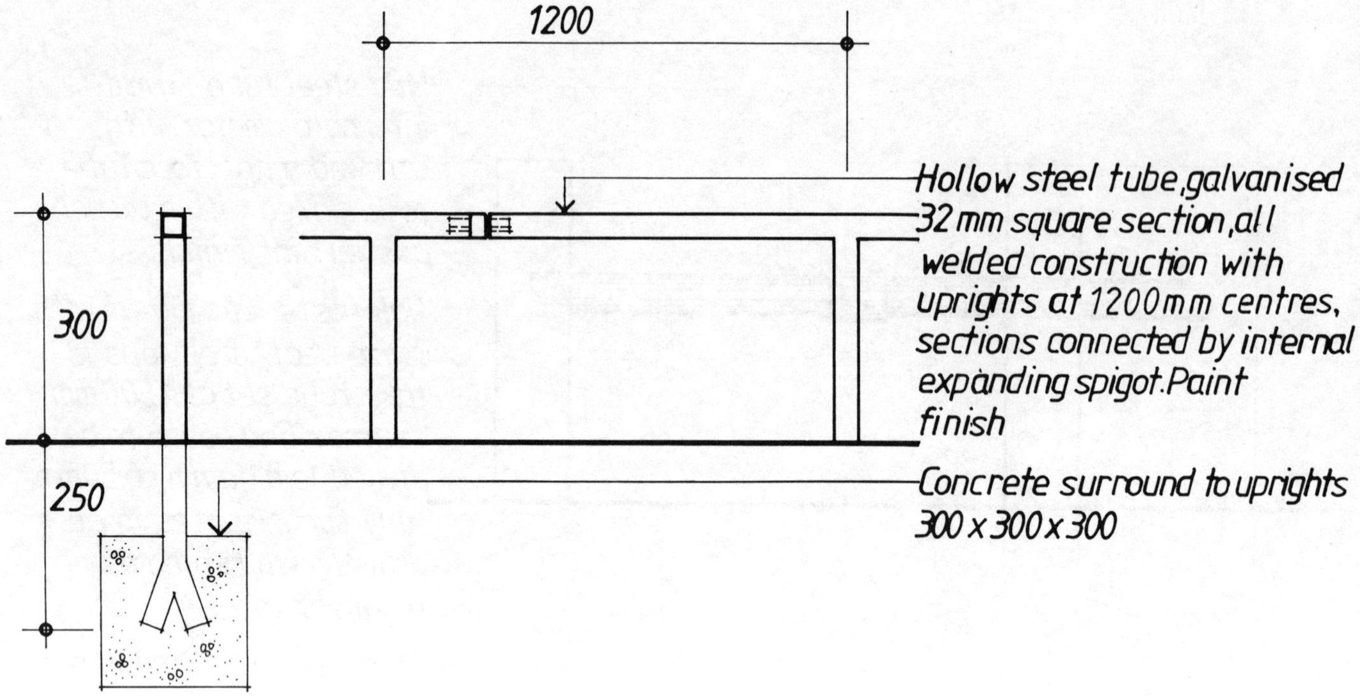

ELEVATION

Scale 1:10

LOW RAIL
steel tube

Chapter 7

Vehicular paving

The design of estate roads and their associated footpaths is subject to control by the Local Road Authority. For this reason any general design guidance will have to be modified in the light of local requirements and site conditions.

Types of road construction

Road construction can be divided into two categories:
1 Flexible pavements
2 Rigid pavements (in-situ concrete or pre-cast units)
Both types can be represented diagramatically:

WEARING COURSE →
BASE COURSE →
ROAD BASE →
SUB-BASE → grade
SUB-GRADE →

Flexible pavements

Sub-base

The material and thickness will depend entirely on the stability of the sub-grade and can be omitted altogether on very stable sub-grades.

Road base

This can be either lean-mix concrete, dense tarmacadam, dense bitumen macadam, drybound macadam or wet-mix macadam, soil-cement or a number of other materials. Each type of road base is specified in detail in the DOE's publication, Specification for Road and Bridge Works.

Base course/wearing course

A wearing course and a base course of either tarmacadam or bitumen macadam is then added to the road base. On lightly trafficked roads a single course, not less than 65 mm thick, is sometimes used.

Rigid pavements

General

The method by which the thickness of each structural layer is determined is set out in Road Note 29.
A combination construction of continuously reinforced concrete with a bituminous surface is sometimes used for city streets, but is unlikely to be used on estate roads.

In-situ concrete

Sub-base

This may be of consolidated hardcore or, if the ground is suitable, it may be eliminated provided that it can be compacted satisfactorily.

Road base

This is of either reinforced or unreinforced concrete.

Base course/wearing course

The top surface of the concrete road base is the top surface of the finished road.

Pre-cast units

Sub-base

The requirements for category of road use and type of sub-grade may be determined by consulting Road Note 29 and the DOE's Specification for Road and Bridge Works.
Alternatively, a thin concrete slab, of a minimum of 75 mm, laid direct on a suitable sub-grade will be satisfactory. The base can be laid without reinforcement or joints.

Laying course

A compacted bed of sand, approximately 50 mm thick, is spread on the sub-base. The road blocks are laid on this.

Block course

The blocks, after levelling with a vibrator, should have sand brushed over them, followed by a final vibration. All edges must be restrained to keep the blocks in compression and to prevent outward movement. The edge should be laid before the surfacing.

References

The Architectural Press Ltd, London
M Gage and M Vandenberg
Hard Landscape in Concrete, 1975: Information Sheet 2

Countryside Commission
Surfaces of Rural Car Parks

Asphalt and Coated Macadam Association
Modern Flexible Road Construction
The Types and Scope of Coated Macadam

NBA 'Building' Commodity File, Component File (90) Section 03

E and F N Spon Ltd
Spon's Landscape Handbook

Department of Transport/Department of Environment
Specification for Road and Bridge Works (5th Ed) Repr 1980
Schedule of Rates for Minor Works and Maintenance of Roads and Pavings, 1979
Roads in Urban Areas (3rd Imp 1973) Repr 1980
Metric Supplement, 1974
Design Bulletin 12 Cars in housing 2, HMSO, 1971
Design Bulletin 32 Residential roads and footpaths: layout consideration, HMSO, 1977

Transport and Road Research Laboratory
Road Note 29 A guide to the structural design of pavements for new roads (3rd Ed 1970) Repr 1980
Road Note 39 Recommendations for road surface dressing, 1973

Building Research Establishment/Transport and Road Research Laboratory/Cement and Concrete Association
D C Teychenne and others
Design of normal concrete mixes (joint publication to replace Road Note 4)

Cement And Concrete Association
Farm Construction series: Laying roads with ready-mixed concrete, 6th Ed 1979

A A Lilley and J Knapton
Concrete block paving for roads, January 1976
Concrete block paving for lightly trafficked roads and paved areas, 1980

A A Lilley and J R Collins
Laying concrete block paving
Specification for pre-cast paving blocks, September 1980

British Standards Institution
BS 12 : 1978 Specification for ordinary and rapid-hardening Portland cement
BS 63 Single-sized roadstone and chippings: Part 2 : 1971 Metric units
BS 76 : 1974 Tars for road purposes
BS 146 Portland-blast furnace cement: Part 2: 1973 Metric units
BS 434 Bitumen road emulsions : Part 1 : 1973 Requirements: Part 2: 1973 Recommendations for use
BS 594: 1973 Rolled asphalt (hot process) for roads and other paved areas
BS 598 Sampling and examination of bituminous mixtures for roads and other paved areas: Part 1: 1974 Sampling: Part 2: 1974 Testing
BS 1446: 1973 Mastic asphalt (natural rock asphalt fine aggregated) for roads and footways
BS 1447: 1973 Mastic asphalt (limestone fine aggregate) for roads and footways
BS 1521: 1972 Waterproof building papers
BS 1926: 1962 Ready-mixed concrete
BS 1984: 1967 Gravel aggregate for surface treatment (including surface dressings) on roads
BS 2499: 1973 Hot-applied joint sealants for concrete pavements
BS 3262: 1976 Hot-applied thermoplastic road marking materials
BS 3690: 1970 Bitumens for road purposes
BS 4449: 1978 Specification for hot rolled steel bars for the reinforcement of concrete
BS 4461: 1978 Specification for cold worked steel bars for the reinforcement of concrete
BS 4483: 1969 Steel fabric for the reinforcement of concrete
Bs 4987: 1973 Coated macadam for roads and other paved areas
BS 5212: 1975 Cold poured joint sealants for concrete pavements
BS 5273: 1975 Dense tar surfacing for roads and other paved areas
BS 5328: 1976 Methods for specifying concrete
BS 5931: 1980 Code of practice for machine-laid in-situ edge details for paved areas

Detail sheets

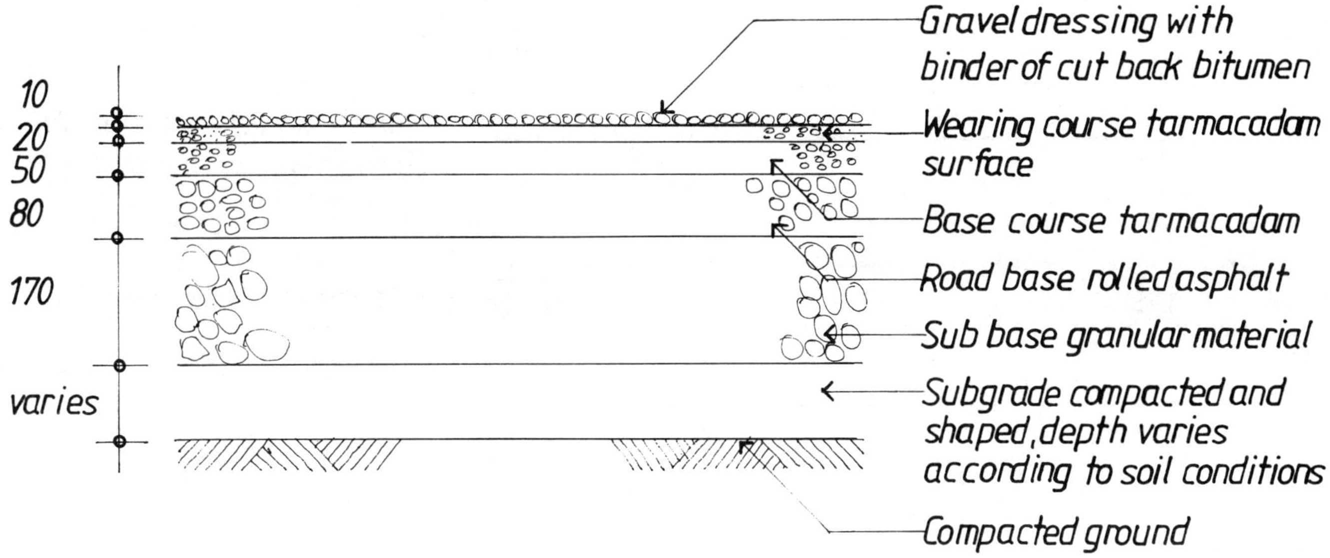

SECTION

Scale 1:10

VEHICULAR PAVING
tarmacadam

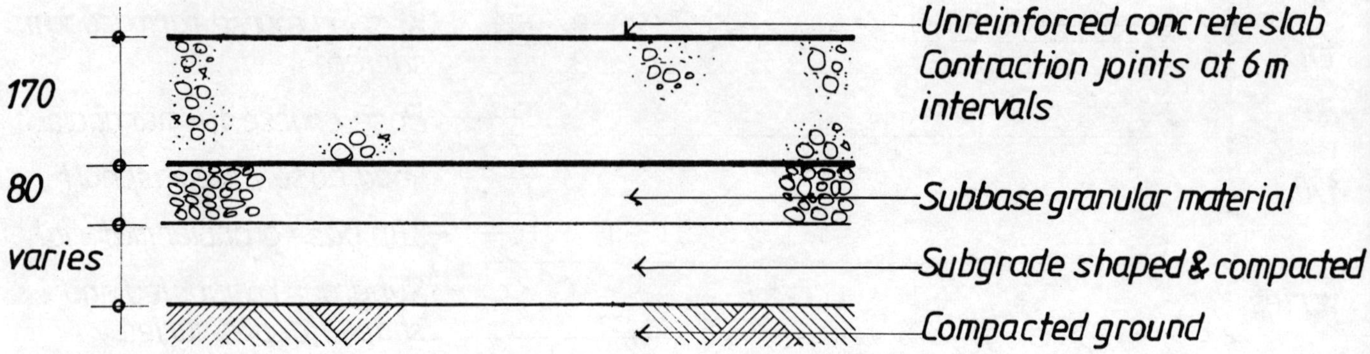

SECTION

Scale 1:10

VEHICULAR PAVING
concrete

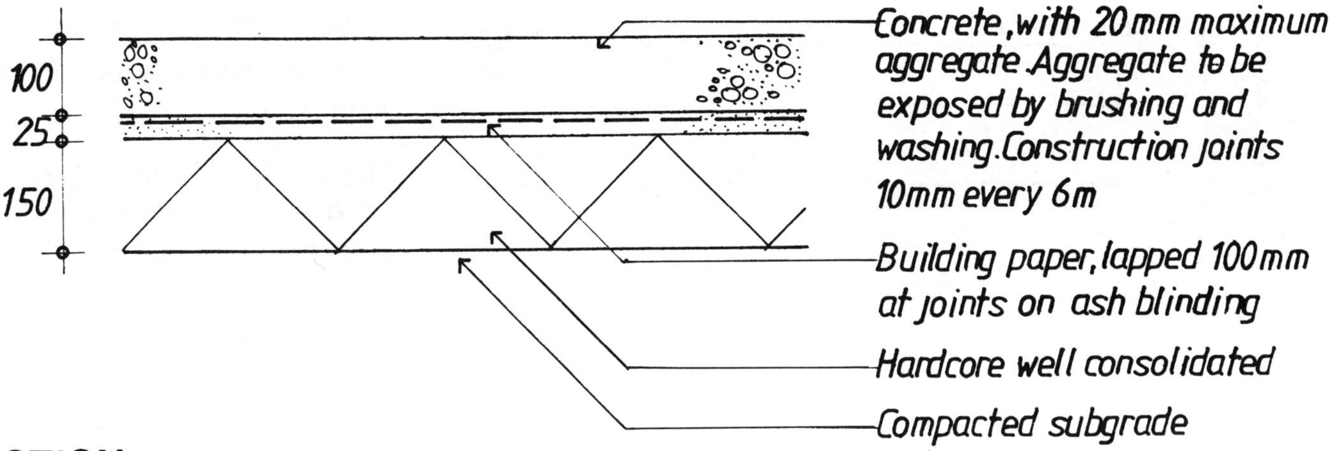

SECTION

Scale 1:10

VEHICULAR PAVING

exposed aggregate

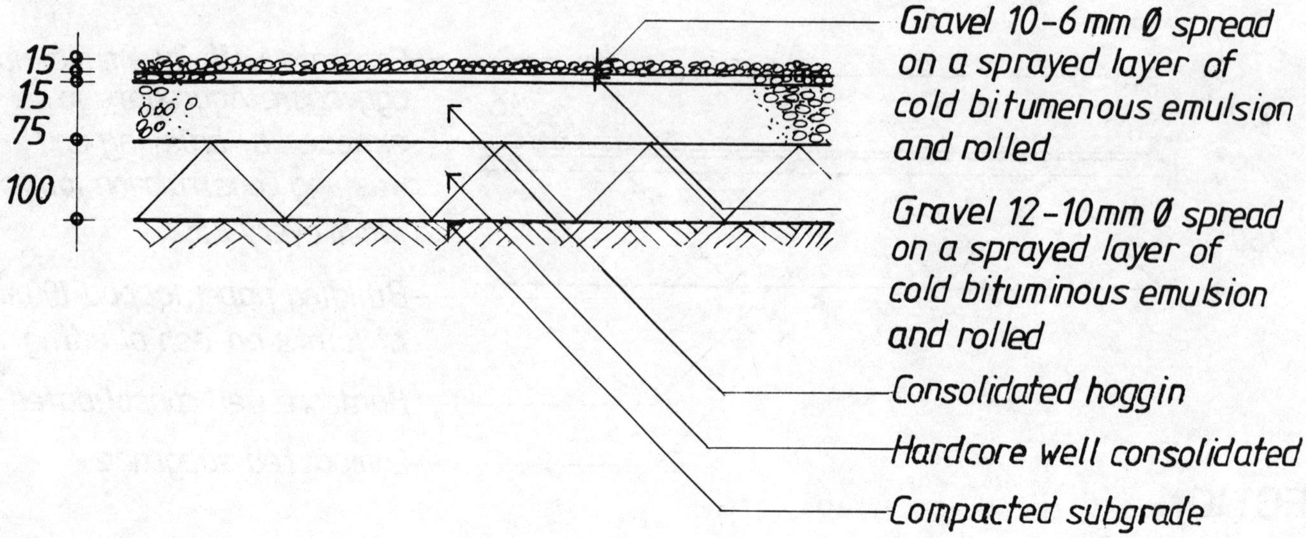

SECTION

Scale 1:10

VEHICULAR PAVING
sealed gravel

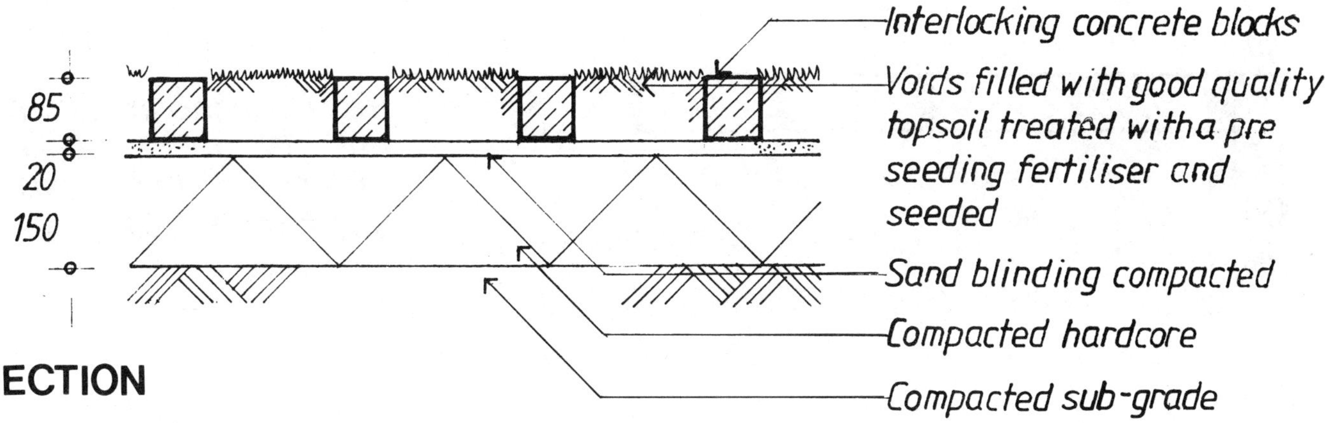

SECTION

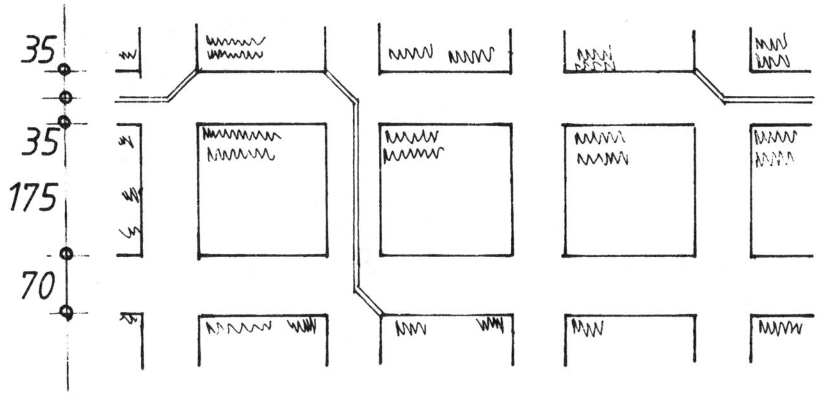

PLAN

Scale 1:10

VEHICULAR PAVING

firepath

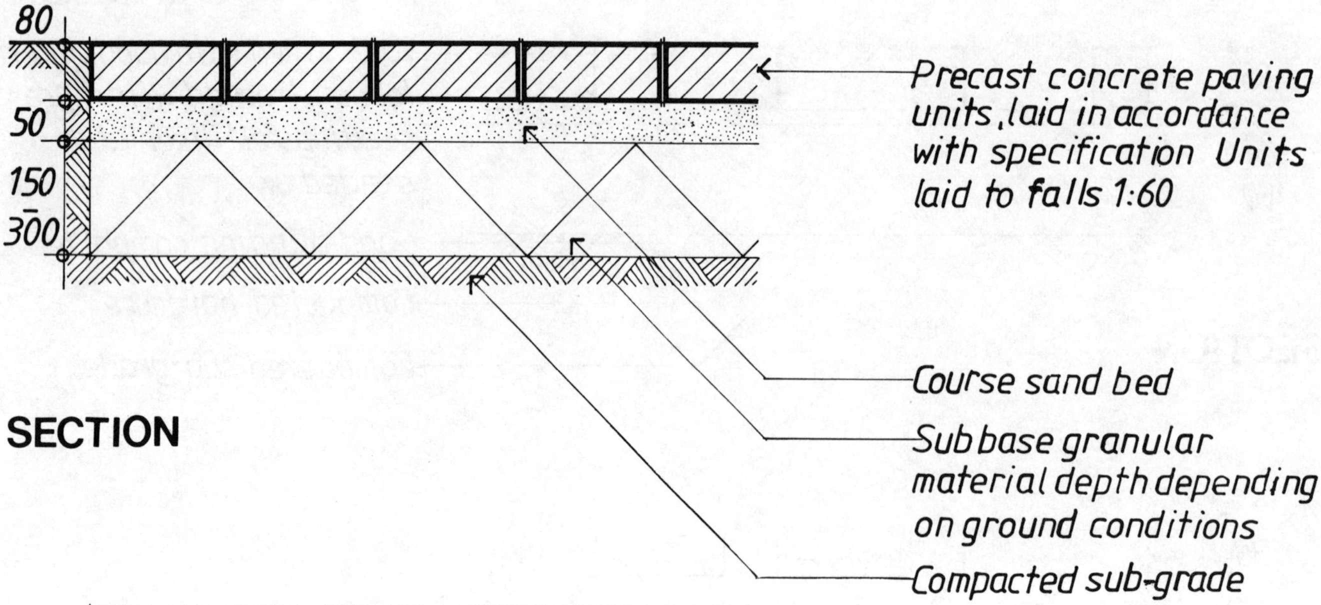
80
50
150
300
Precast concrete paving units, laid in accordance with specification Units laid to falls 1:60
Course sand bed
Sub base granular material depth depending on ground conditions
Compacted sub-grade

SECTION

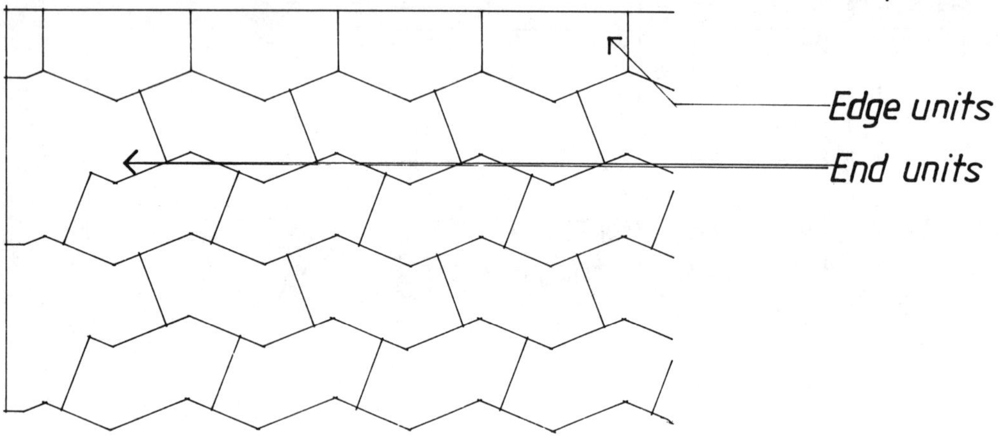
Edge units
End units

PLAN

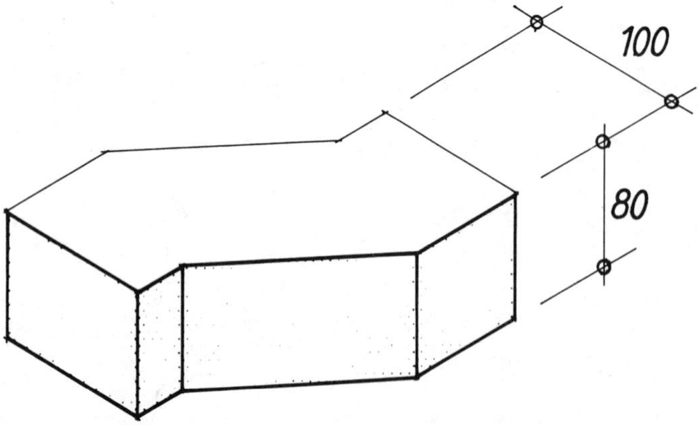
100
80

Precast concrete paving unit

Scale 1:10

VEHICULAR PAVING
interlocking conc.units

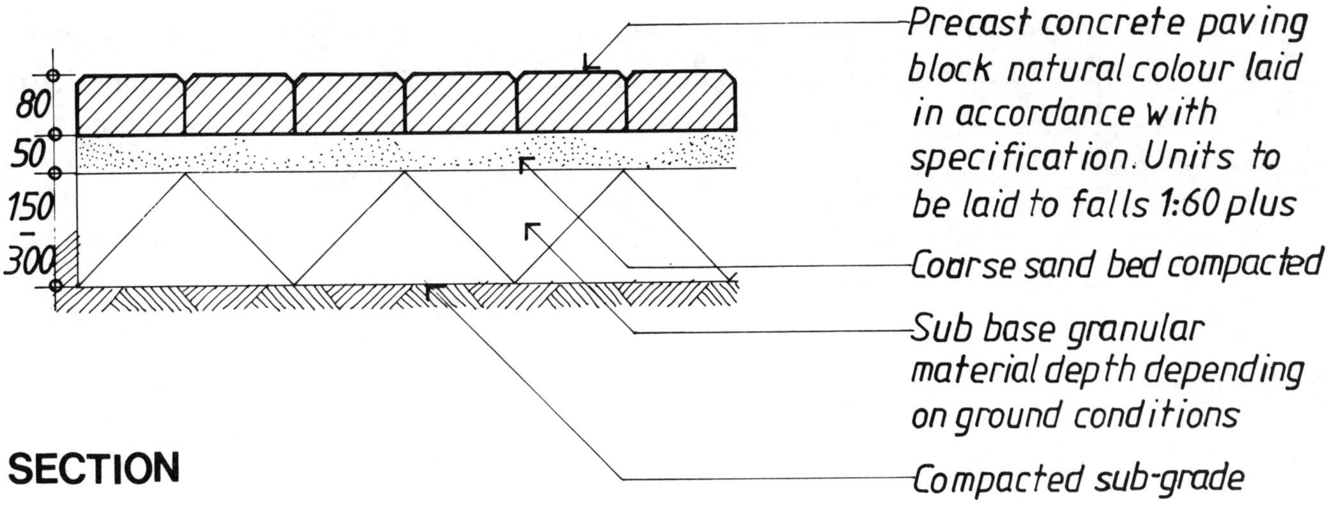

SECTION

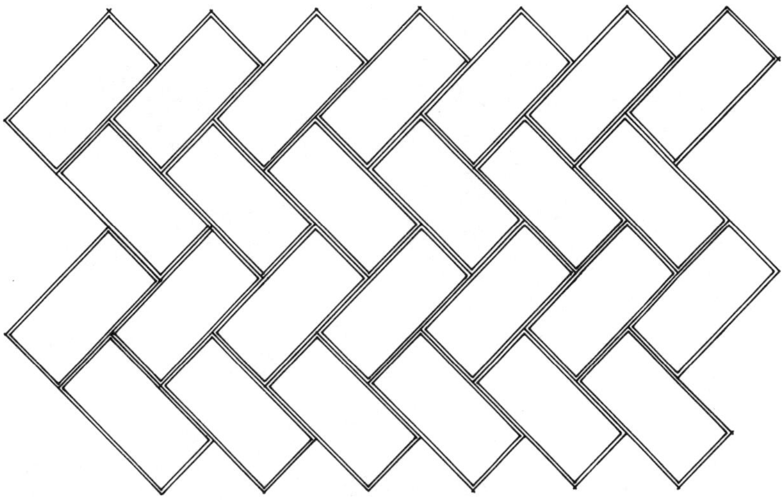

Precast concrete paving block road

PLAN

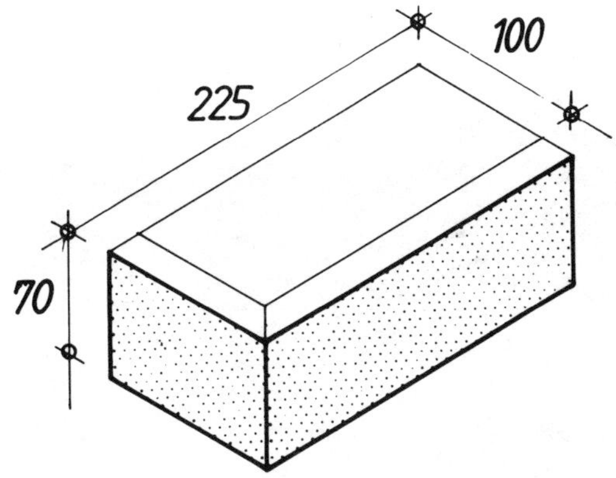

Precast concrete paving block

Scale 1:10

VEHICULAR PAVING
concrete block

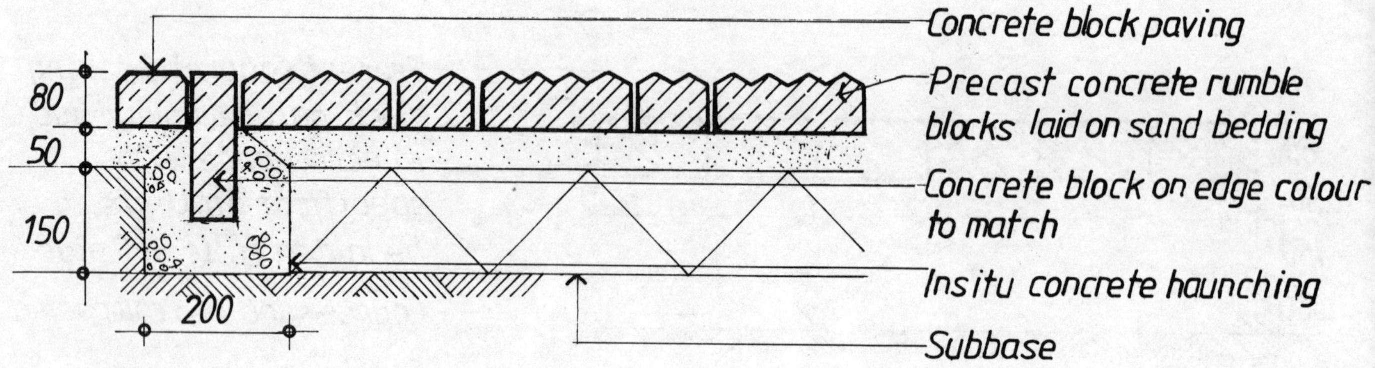

SECTION

Scale 1:10

VEHICULAR PAVING
rumble block

Chapter 8

Pedestrian paving

Choice of Material

It is preferable to reflect the local vernacular as this does create a sense of place. The separation of pedestrian from vehicular surfacing provides an opportunity to create a far more interesing design. Where it is necessary to provide for pedestrians as well as vehicles, a mixture of materials can be used, or the same material (in a different colour) can be used for vehicles, but with the appropriate increase in foundation thickness.

Sub-grade and base

To ensure that any surface paving material retain its final laid position, it is essential that both the ground and under-materials be prepared thoroughly. Paving usually has a base and sub-grade underneath, and both of these must be thoroughly compacted.

Sub-grade

This should be well compacted either by hand or by mechanical means. The required contour of the paving is obtained by shaping the sub-grade.

Base
The base is usually of hardcore, compacted by a 3-tonne roller or a 508 kg vibrating roller.

Wearing course

These can be divided into four categories:
1 Flexible (asphalt, bitumen or tarmacadam, hoggin). Flexible paving usually consists of two courses: a base course, and a wearing course of a binder with variable sizes of aggregate. Wearing course aggregate size should be 6 mm; base course aggregate size, 20 mm. The usual thickness for the wearing course is 6 mm–20 mm; base course, 50 mm.
2 Small rigid units (bricks, stone setts, concrete units). They are usually laid on a base of consolidated hardcore or clinker with a 25 mm bed of sand or 15 mm sand/lime mortar. Joints are usually sand filled, or pointed with sand/lime mortar. Small concrete interlinking units are laid in contact on a dry sand bed.
3 Large rigid units (paving slabs). These can be laid over a consolidated base of clinker on a bed of sand or sand/lime mortar dabs.
4 Rigid pavement (in-situ concrete). These are usually of unreinforced concrete laid directly on a consolidated sub-grade, or on a base of consolidated hardcore, depending on ground conditions. Expansion joints must be incorporated at 6 m centres.

Joints

Tight, unfilled joints are only possible with units of regular size and shape such as pre-cast concrete paving flags or precast concrete interlocking paving with which tight jointing is usual.
Joints between paving brick, stone setts and natural pavings are best filled with a 1 : 3 cement mortar or a 1 : 4 lime mortar. The mortar is brushed dry into the joints and then watered. This method reduces the risk of mortar staining the paving.
If plant or moss growth in the joints is to be encouraged, the joints can be filled with sifted topsoil or sand mixed with bone meal.

Edges

Flexible pavements must be contained by a rigid edge: either a pre-cast concrete edging with a concrete surround or a timber edging held by timber pegs.
Small rigid units should be contained by a row of units supported by a concrete backing.
Large rigid units need no edging when adjoined by turfed or flexible paved areas. Where adjoined by topsoil or planted areas, an in-situ concrete strip should be provided under the paving to prevent the base falling away.

Falls

The gradient of fall required to clear surface water varies according to the nature of the surface.
Recommended falls are: Concrete 1 : 60; Brick Paving 1 : 60; Bituminous Surfaces 1 : 40; Paving Slabs 1 : 70; Gravel 1 : 30; Public Pavements 1 : 50.

References

The Architectural Press Ltd, London
C C Handisyde
Hard Landscape in Brick, Chap 7, 1976

J Ashurst and F G Dimes
Stone in Building, 1977

C Tandy
A J Handbook of Urban Landscape, 1972 : Information Sheet 34

M Gage and M Vandenberg
Hard Landscape in Concrete, 1975

E Beazley
Design and Detail of the Space between Buildings, 1960

NBA 'Building' Commodity File, Component File (90) Section 01 Paving: Pre-cast Concrete

E and F N Spon Ltd
Spon's Landscape Handbook

M F Downing
Landscape Construction, 1977

Department of the Environment
Design Bulletin 5 Landscaping for Flats

Cement and Concrete Association
Specification for pre-cast paving blocks, September 1980

A A Lilley and A J Clark
Concrete block paving for lightly trafficked roads and paved areas

British Standards Institute
BS 368 : 1971 Pre-cast concrete flags
BS 4987 : 1973 Coated macadam for roads and paved areas

Detail sheets

8.1 In-situ concrete
8.2 Asphalt
8.3 Sealed gravel
8.4 Compacted hoggin
8.5 Natural York stone
8.6 Pre-cast concrete flag
8.7 Pre-cast concrete exposed aggregate
8.8 Brick stretcher bond
8.9 Brick herringbone
8.10 Brick basket weave
8.11 Cobbles laid loose
8.12 Cobbles laid flat
8.13 Granite sett (square)
8.14 Granite sett (rectangular)
8.15 Brick engineering
8.16 Re-constructed stone sett
8.17 Concrete block units (square edge)
8.18 Concrete block units (chamfered edge)

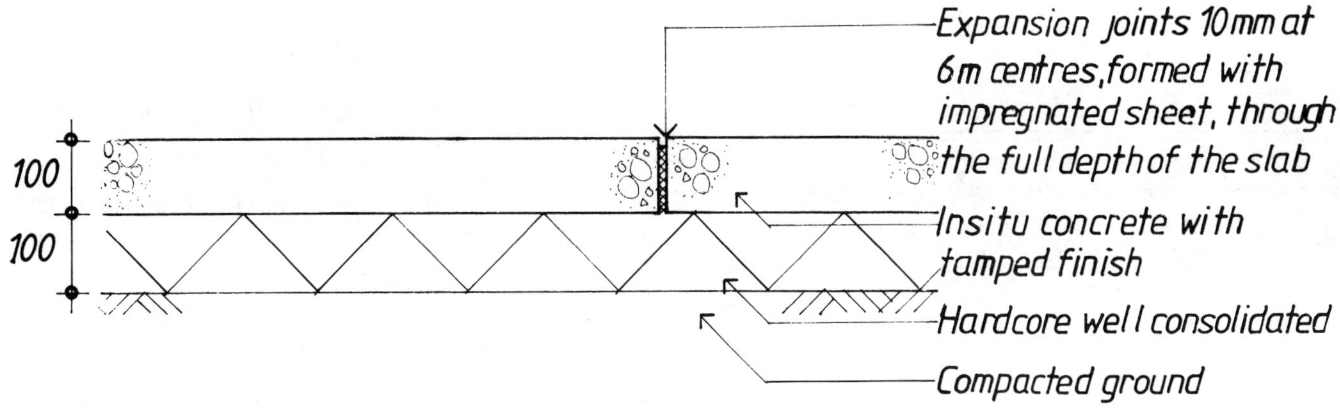

SECTION

Scale 1:10

PEDESTRIAN PAVING
concrete

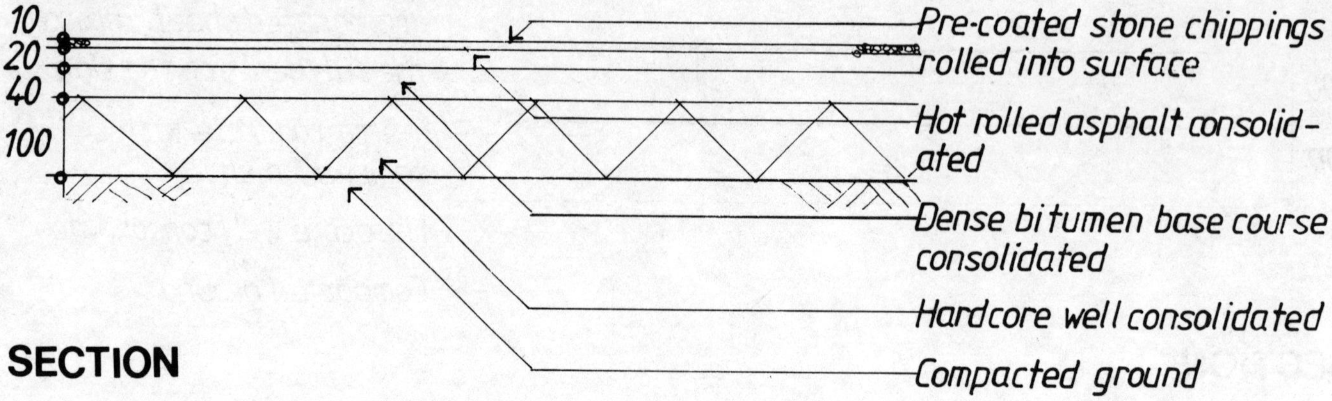

SECTION

Scale 1:10

PEDESTRIAN PAVING
asphalt

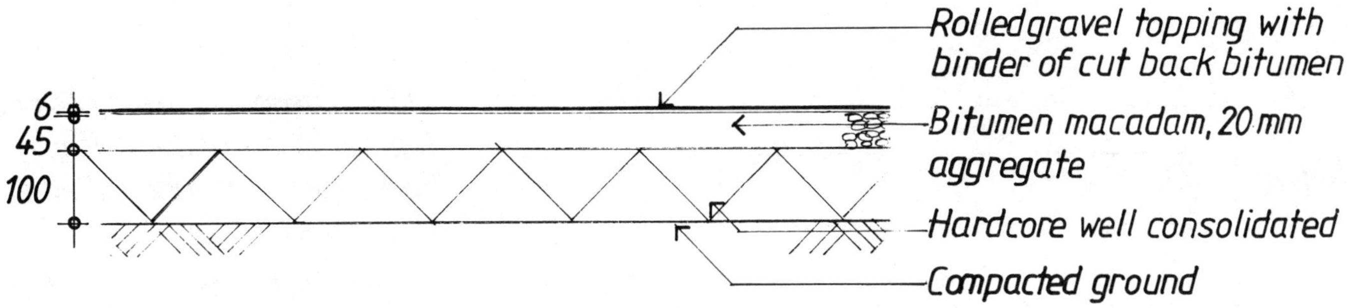

SECTION

Scale 1:10

PEDESTRIAN PAVING

sealed gravel

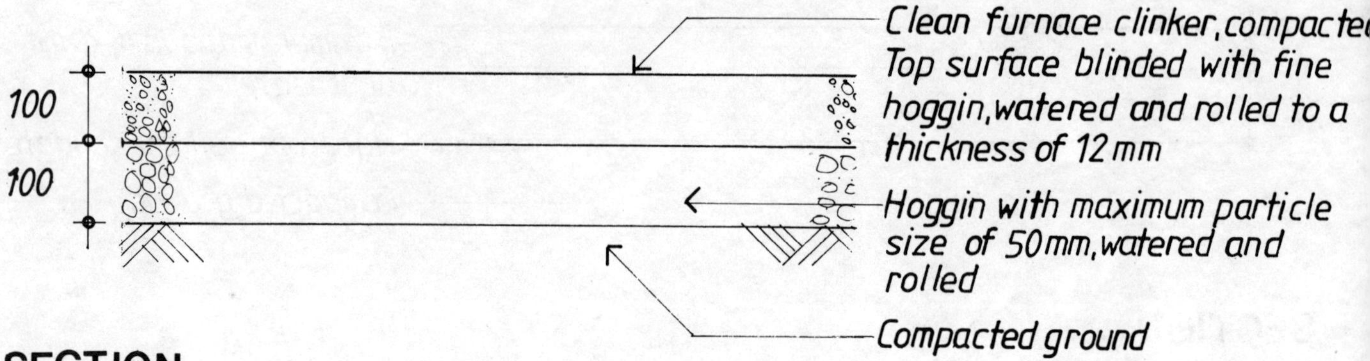

SECTION

Scale 1:10

PEDESTRIAN PAVING
compacted hoggin

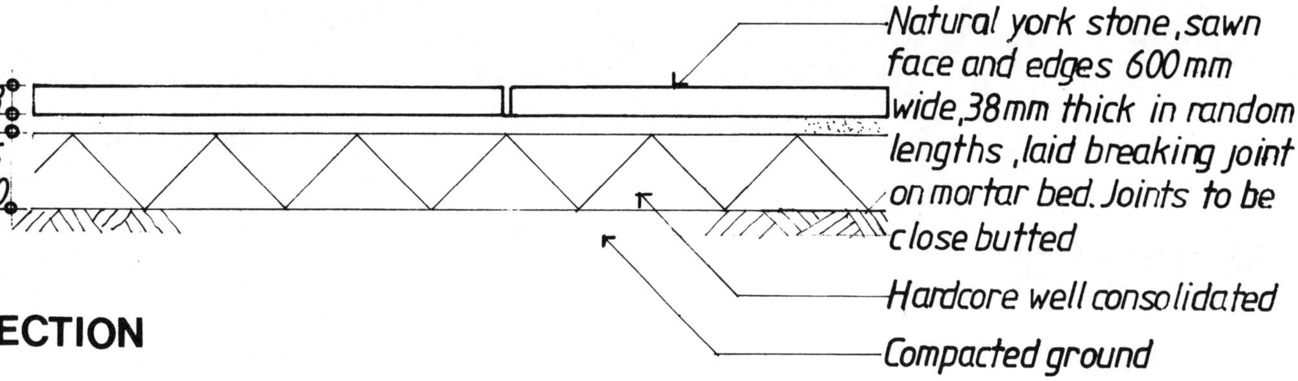
38
25
100
Natural york stone, sawn face and edges 600mm wide, 38mm thick in random lengths, laid breaking joint on mortar bed. Joints to be close butted
Hardcore well consolidated
Compacted ground

SECTION

PLAN

Scale 1:10

PEDESTRIAN PAVING
natural York stone

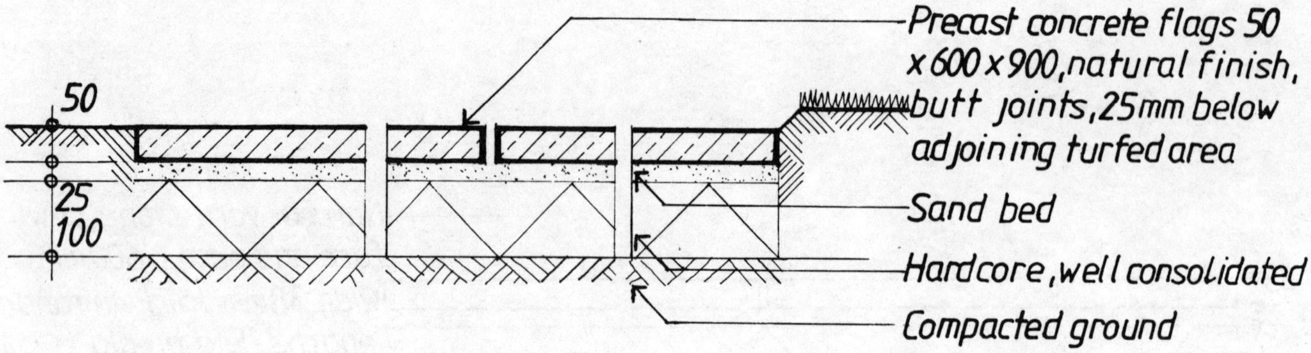

SECTION 1:10

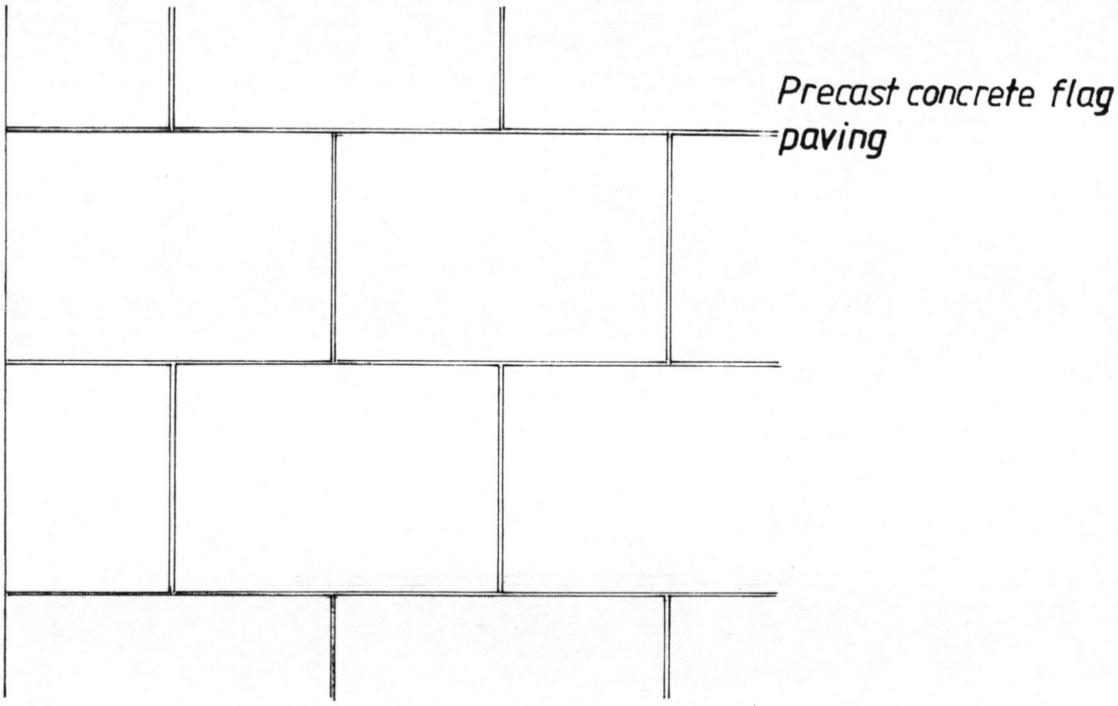

PLAN 1:20

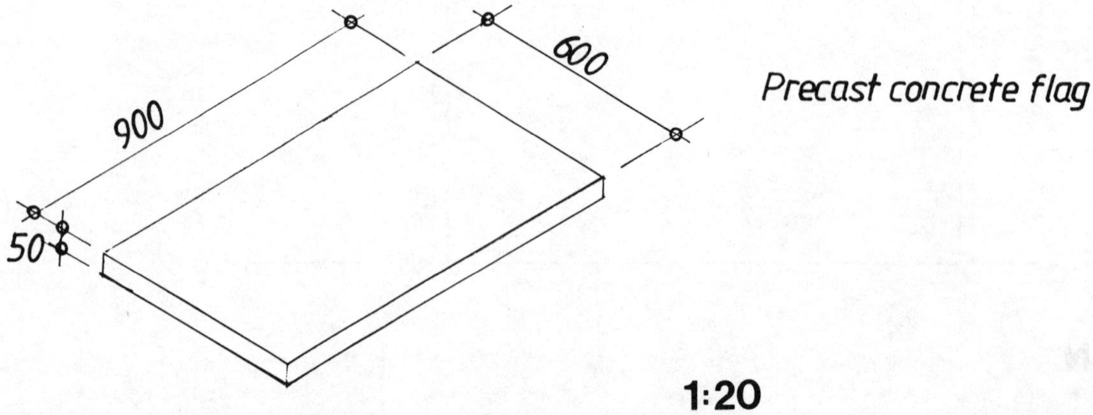

1:20

Scale A.S

PEDESTRIAN PAVING
concrete flag

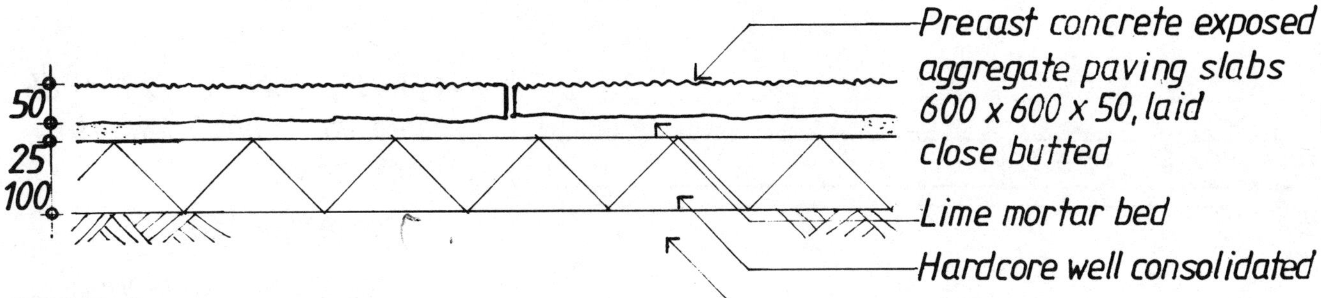
Precast concrete exposed aggregate paving slabs 600 x 600 x 50, laid close butted
Lime mortar bed
Hardcore well consolidated
Compacted ground
50
25
100

SECTION

PLAN

Scale 1:10

PEDESTRIAN PAVING
exposed aggregate concrete

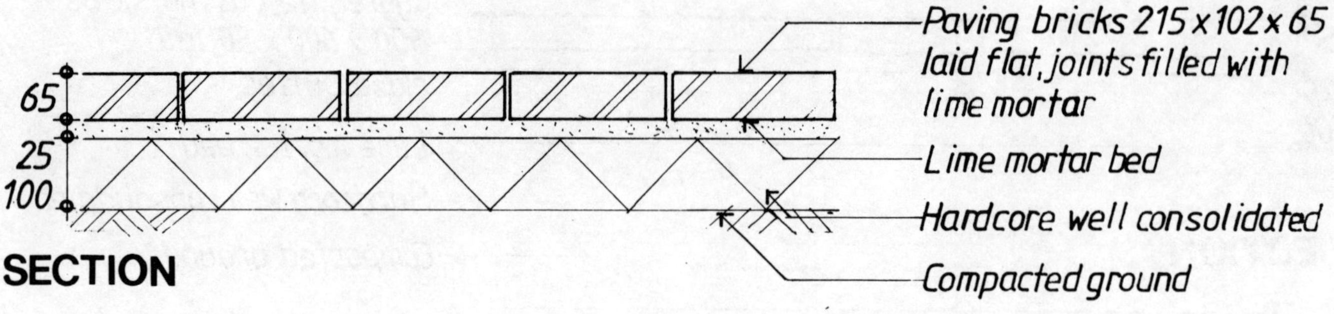
65
25
100
Paving bricks 215 x 102 x 65 laid flat, joints filled with lime mortar
Lime mortar bed
Hardcore well consolidated
Compacted ground

SECTION

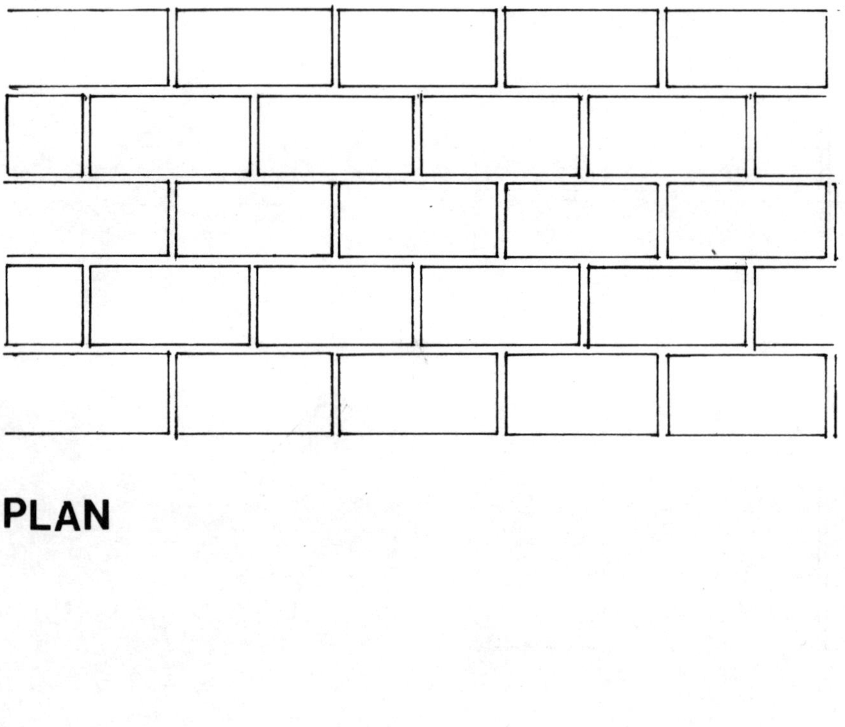

PLAN

Scale 1:10

PEDESTRIAN PAVING
brick (stretcher bond)

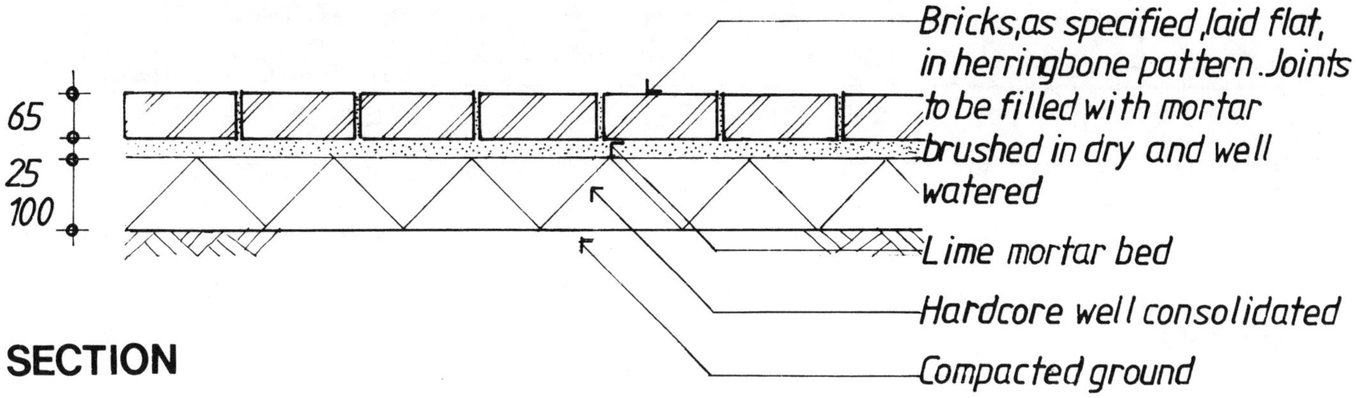

SECTION

PLAN

Scale1:10

PEDESTRIAN PAVING
brick (herringbone)

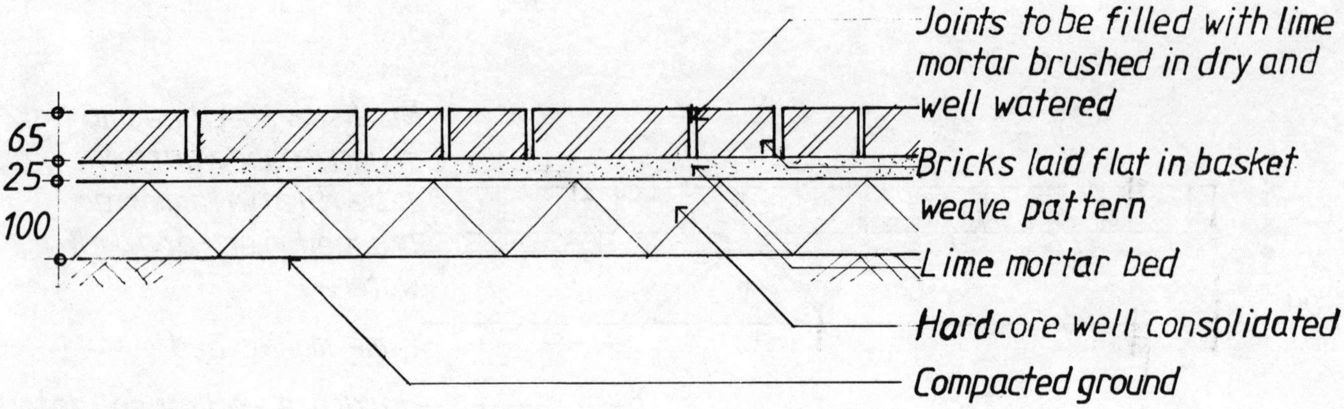

SECTION

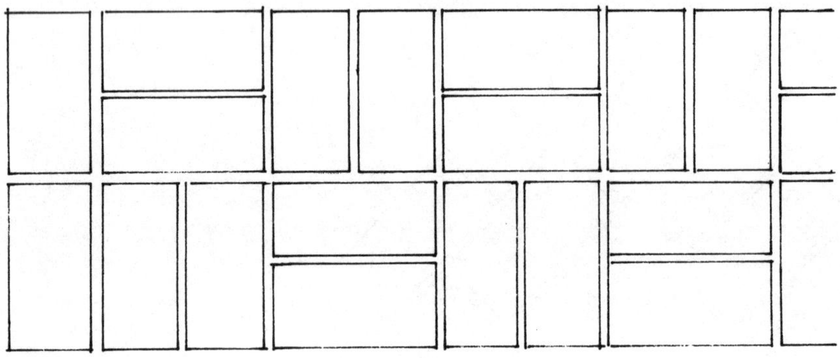

PLAN

Scale 1:10

PEDESTRIAN PAVING
brick (basket weave)

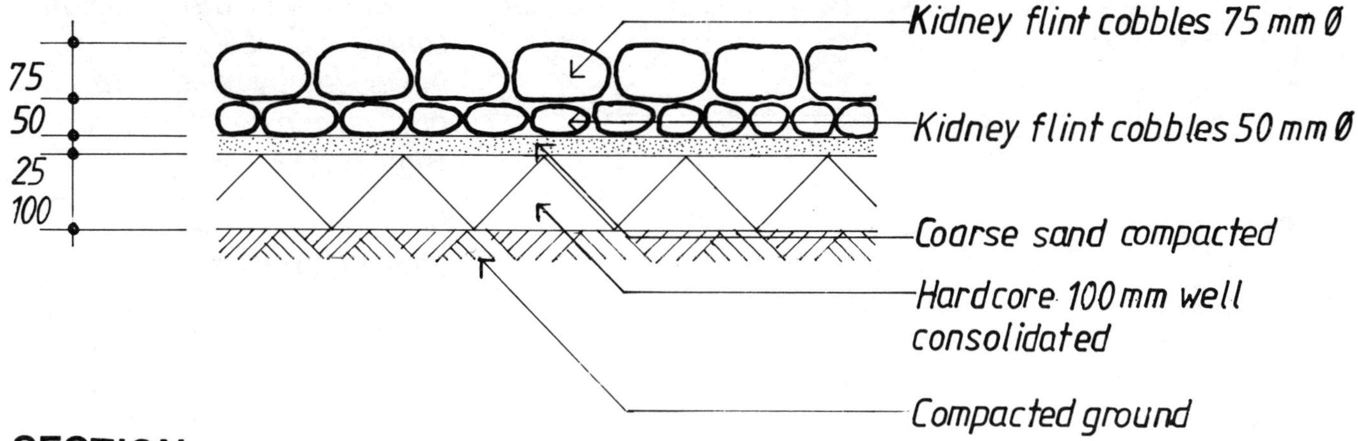

SECTION

Scale 1:10

PEDESTRIAN PAVING
cobbles loose laid

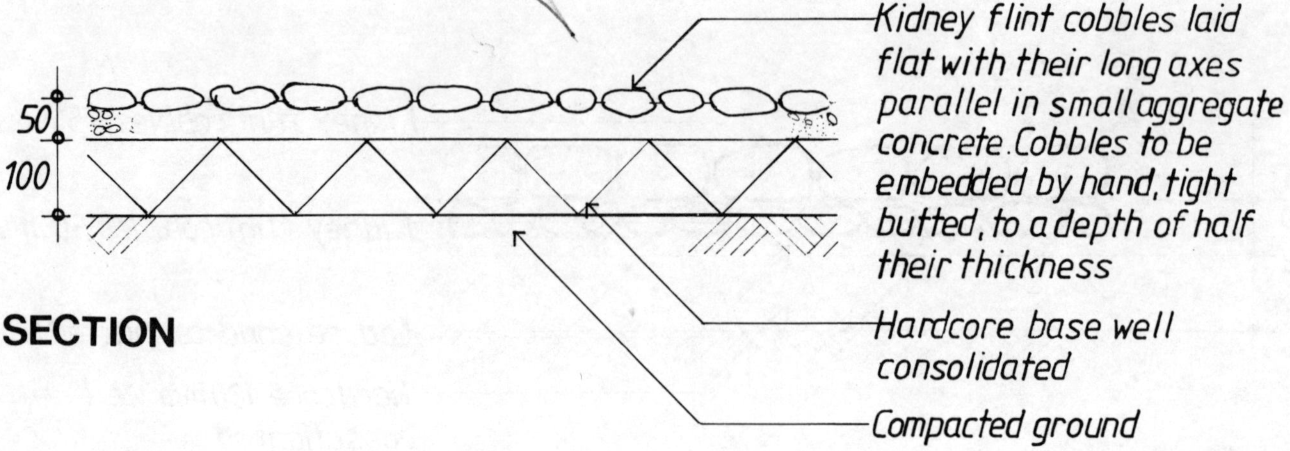

SECTION

PLAN

Scale 1:10

PEDESTRIAN PAVING
cobbles laid flat

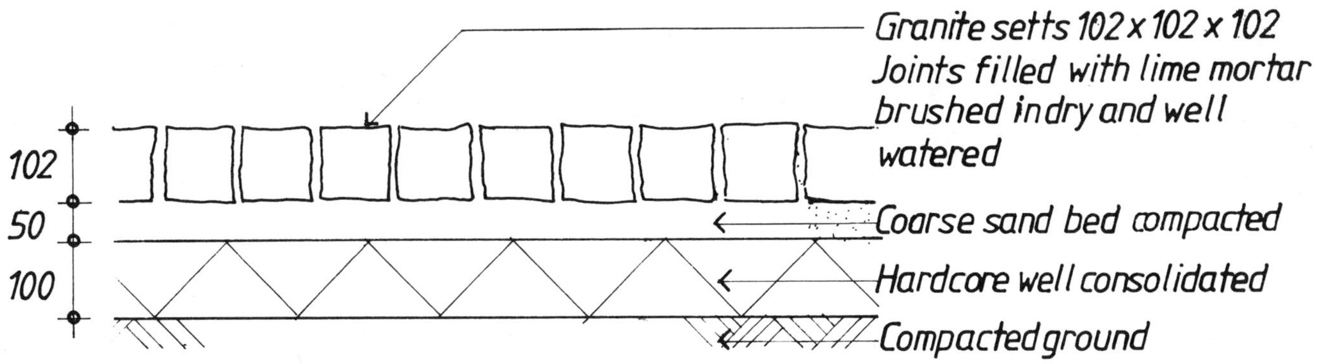

SECTION

PLAN

Scale 1:10

PEDESTRIAN PAVING
granite sett (square)

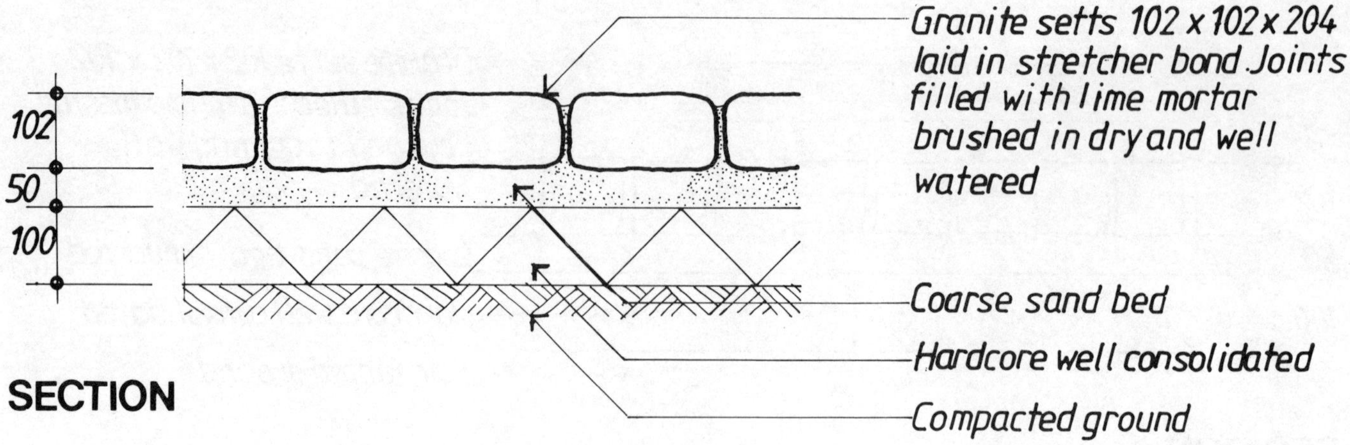

SECTION

PLAN

Scale 1:10

PEDESTRIAN PAVING

granite sett

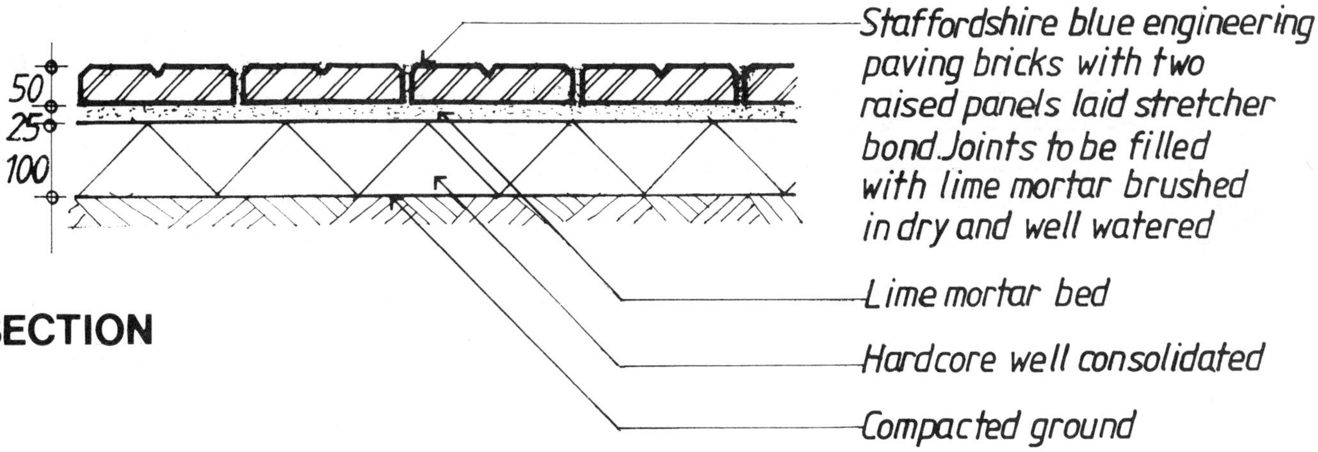

SECTION

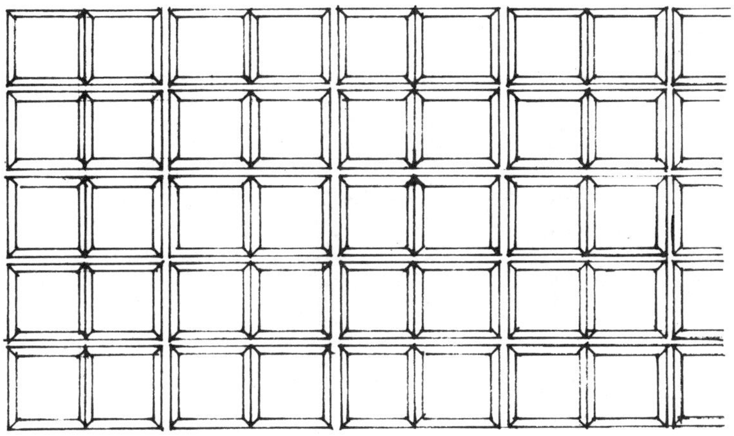

PLAN

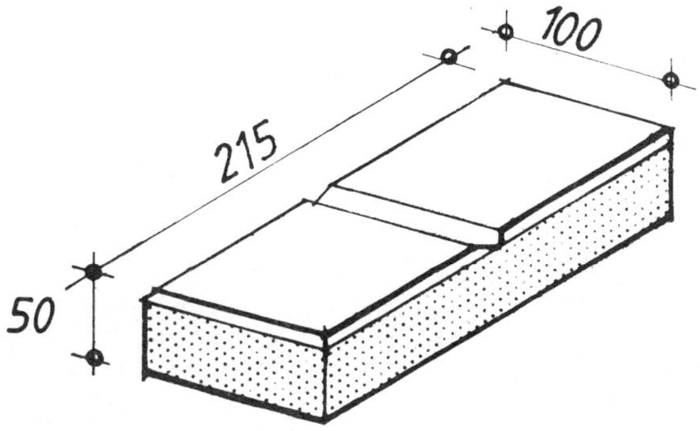

UNIT

Scale 1:10

PEDESTRIAN PAVING
brick (engineering)

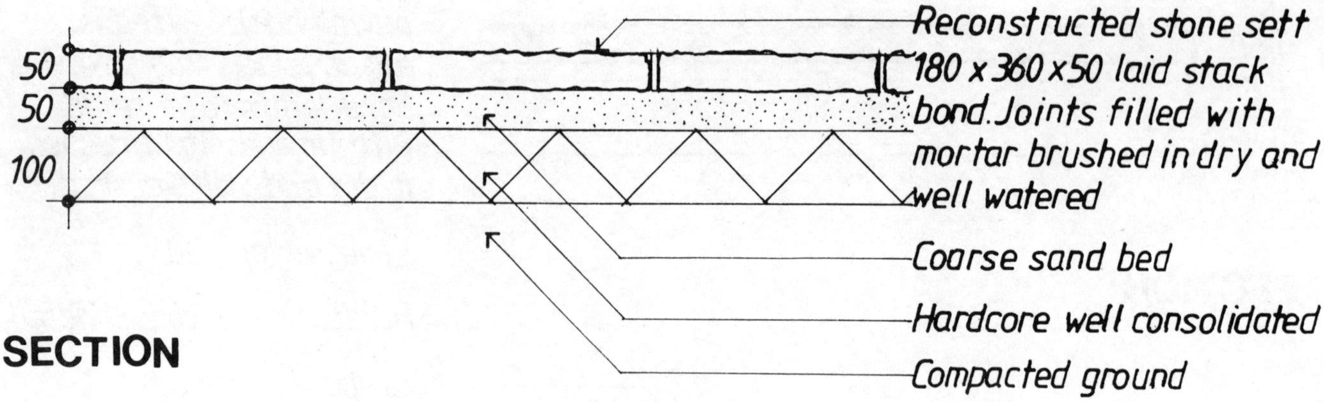

SECTION

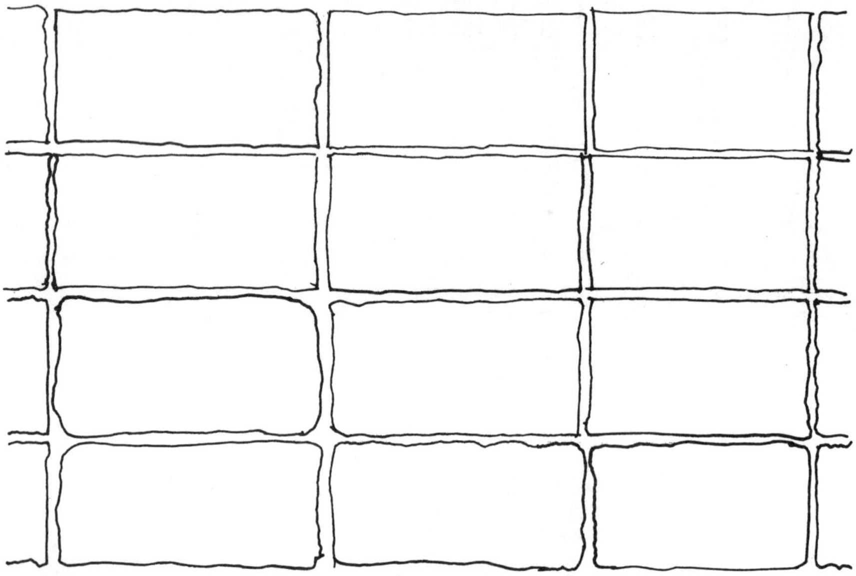

PLAN

Scale 1:10

PEDESTRIAN PAVING
reconstructed stone

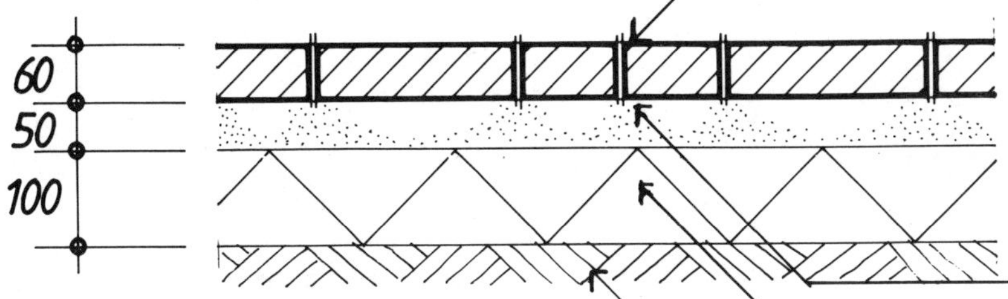

SECTION 1:10

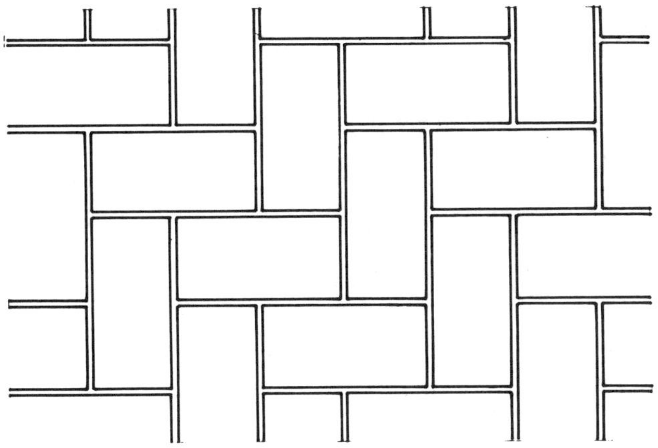

Rectangular concrete paving laid in herringbone pattern with 1:40 cross fall

PLAN 1:20

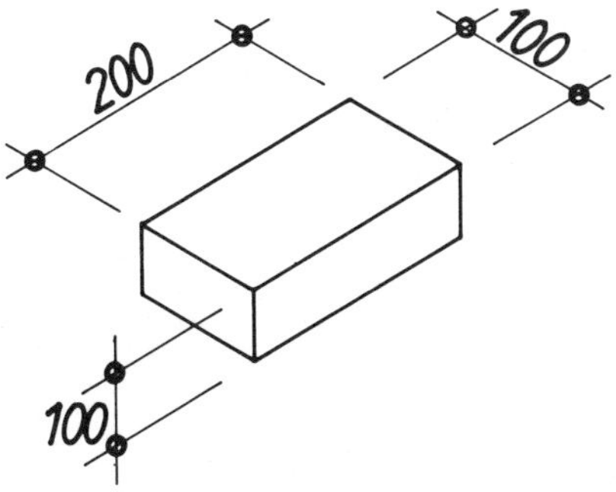

Rectangular concrete paving block

UNIT 1:20

Scale A.S

PEDESTRIAN PAVING
concrete block

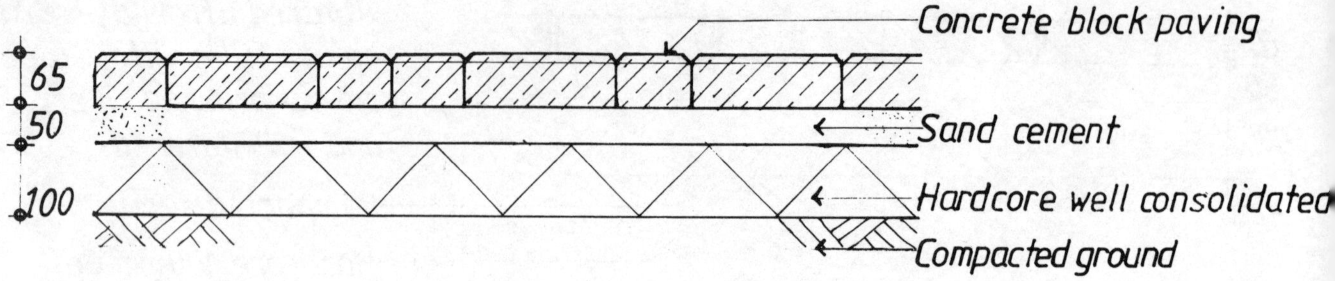

SECTION

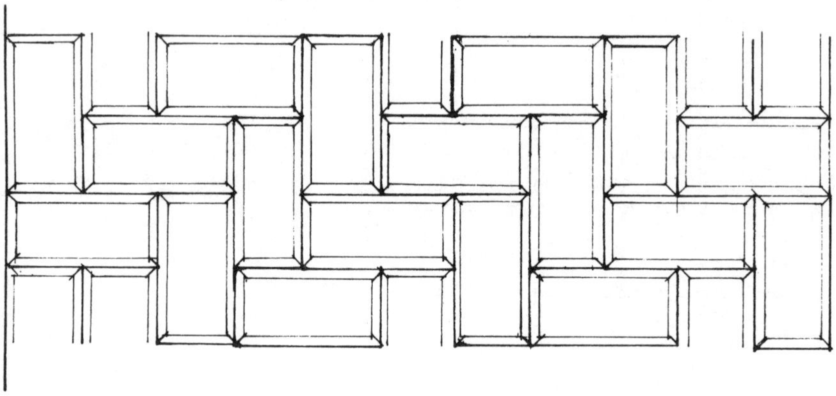

PLAN

Scale 1:10

PEDESTRIAN PAVING
concrete block

Chapter 9

Steps and ramps

Steps

The two main components of steps are the risers and treads and their size plays a significant part in their overall appearance. External steps can be far more generous in their size then internal ones, but they should have a rise of between 80 mm and 160 mm. The outdoor scale makes the use of any formula for calculating the size of risers and treads extremely difficult.

Treads

These should be not less than 300 mm; the width should not be less than the going. Each tread should have a fall of 5 mm to ensure that no water is retained which might make the steps dangerous, especially in very cold weather. Non-slip materials are preferable. Where slab treads are used they should overhang the risers by 15 mm. Falls will affect the total rise of long flights.

Risers

These should be well marked, especially where the material used is different from the treads.

Landings

Long flights of steps should be broken up by generous landings of between one and two metres wide, with the maximum number of steps between landings limited to twelve. Flights should not exceed nineteen steps.

Handrails

If extensive use by old people is anticipated, or if the vertical drop at the side of the steps exceeds 600 mm, a handrail should be included.

Stepped ramps

These are generally used on ground slopes of between 1 in 12 (8.3%) and 1 in 4 (25%). The ramp going should have a constant slope of 1 in 12 (8.3%) and the step riser height should be varied to suit the slope of the land.
Stepped ramps can be used to reduce the apparent steepness of a long ramp. To allow easy negotiation by prams and wheelchairs, riser dimension should not exceed 100 mm and tread dimension should be not less than 900 mm and preferably 1500 mm. Allow for three paces to each tread. Nosings of treads should be clearly defined by a change of colour or texture.

Ramps

These should have a maximum gradient of 1:10. For wheelchairs the maximum should be 1:12. The surface should be non-slip and surface water should be shed across the ramp, preferably into a drainage channel. Ramp lengths should not exceed 10 m. Level landings should be provided at intervals. Ramps that are parallel to a street are safer than those at right angles to it.

References

The Architectural Press Ltd, London
C Tandy
A J Handbook of Urban Landscape, 1972: Information Sheet 35

C C Handisyde
Hard Landscape in Brick, 1976

E Beazley
Design and Detail of the Space between Buildings, 1960

M Gage and M Vandenberg
Hard Landscape in Concrete, 1976

E and F N Spon
Spon's Landscape Handbook

M F Downing
Landscape Construction, 1977

William Heinemann Ltd, London
A E Weddle
Landscape Techniques, 1979

Detail sheets

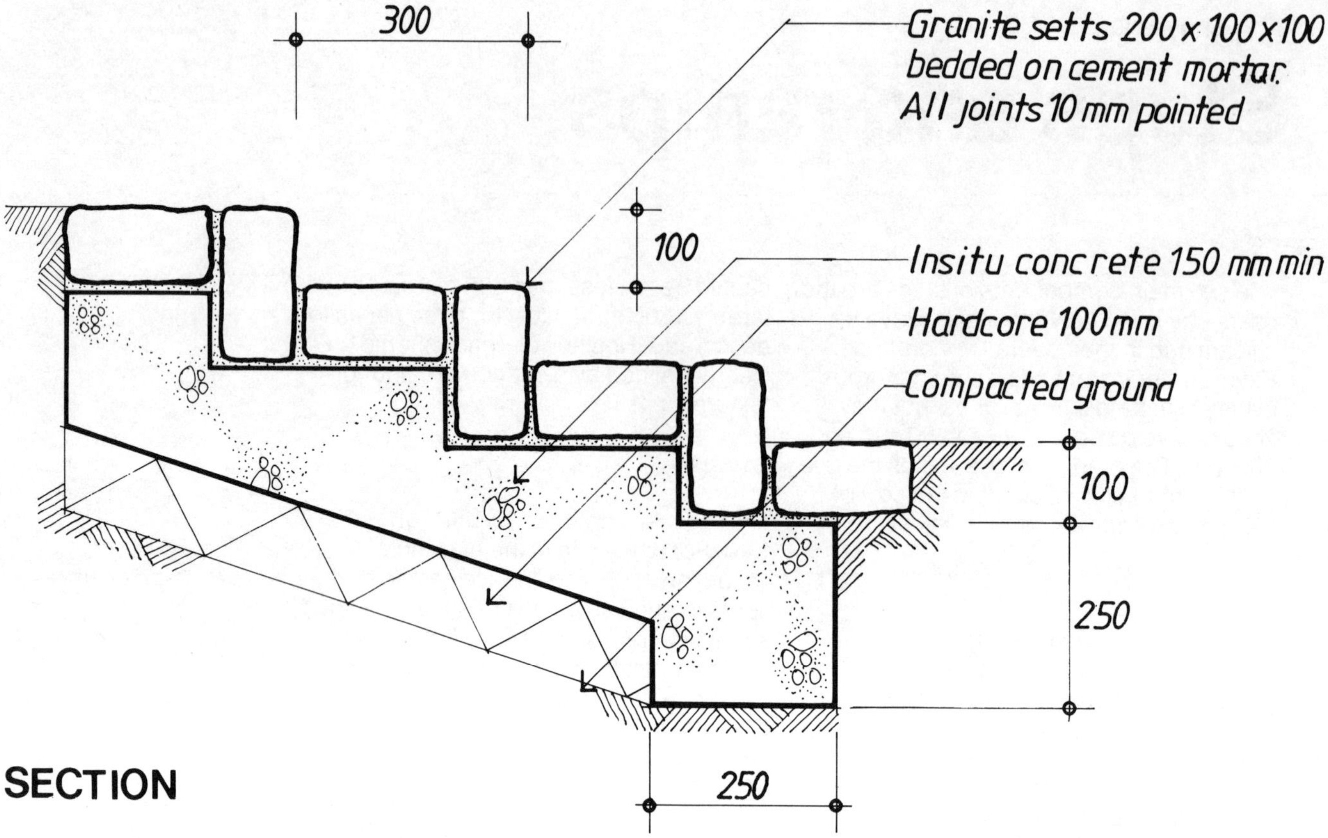

SECTION

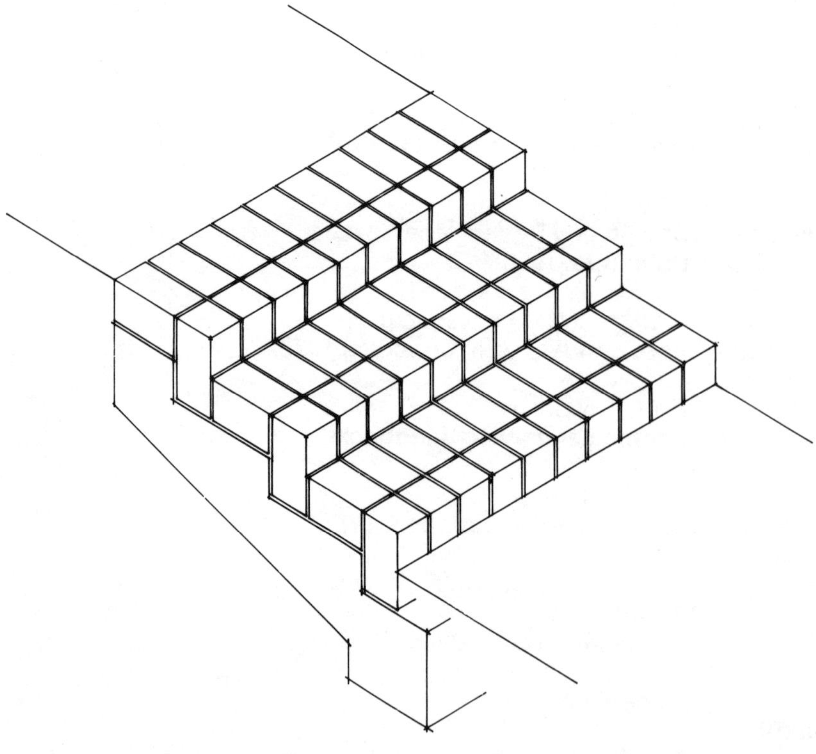

Scale 1:10

STEPS

granite sett

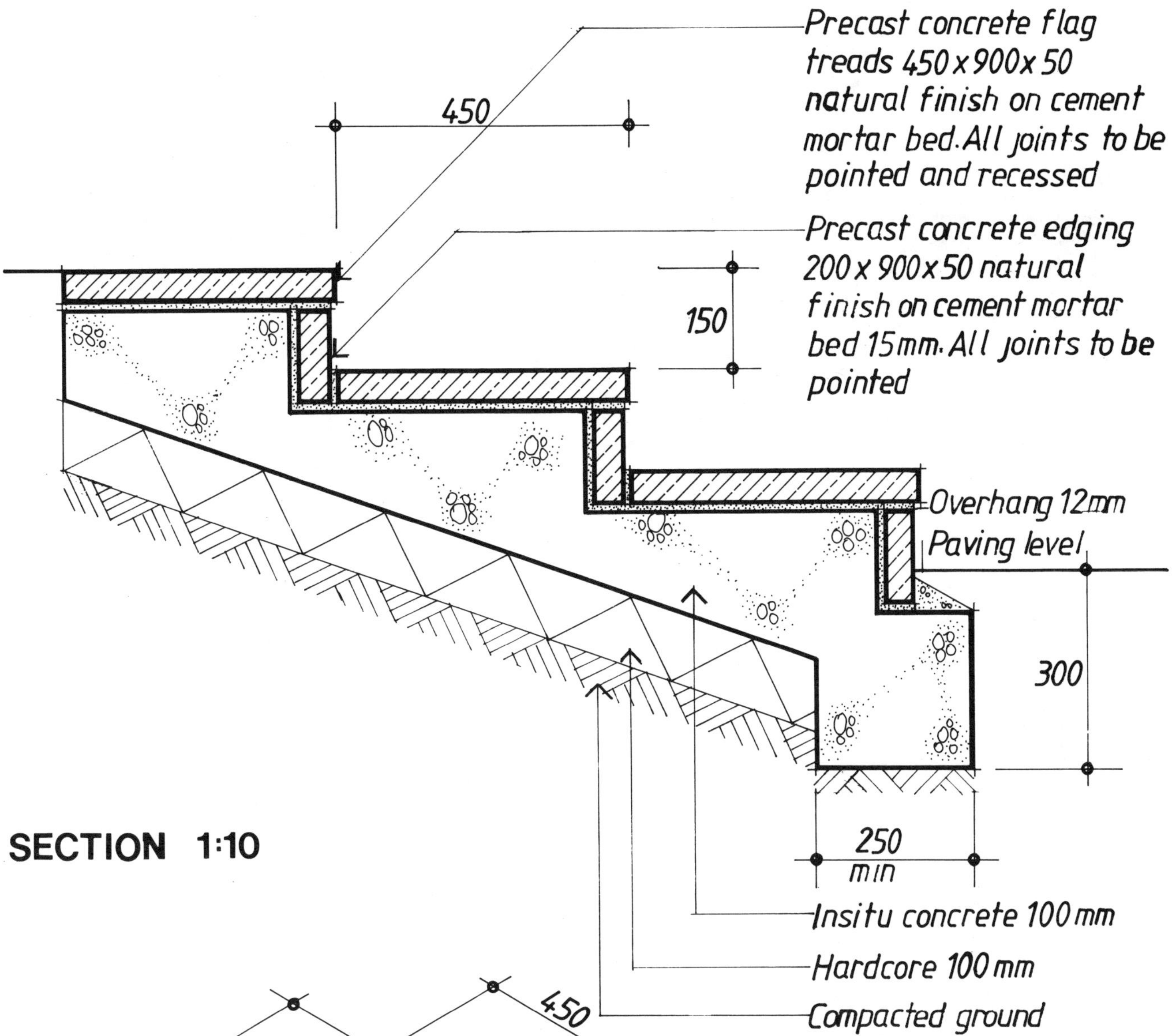
Precast concrete flag treads 450 x 900 x 50 natural finish on cement mortar bed. All joints to be pointed and recessed
Precast concrete edging 200 x 900 x 50 natural finish on cement mortar bed 15mm. All joints to be pointed
450
150
Overhang 12mm
Paving level
300
250 min
Insitu concrete 100 mm
Hardcore 100 mm
Compacted ground

SECTION 1:10

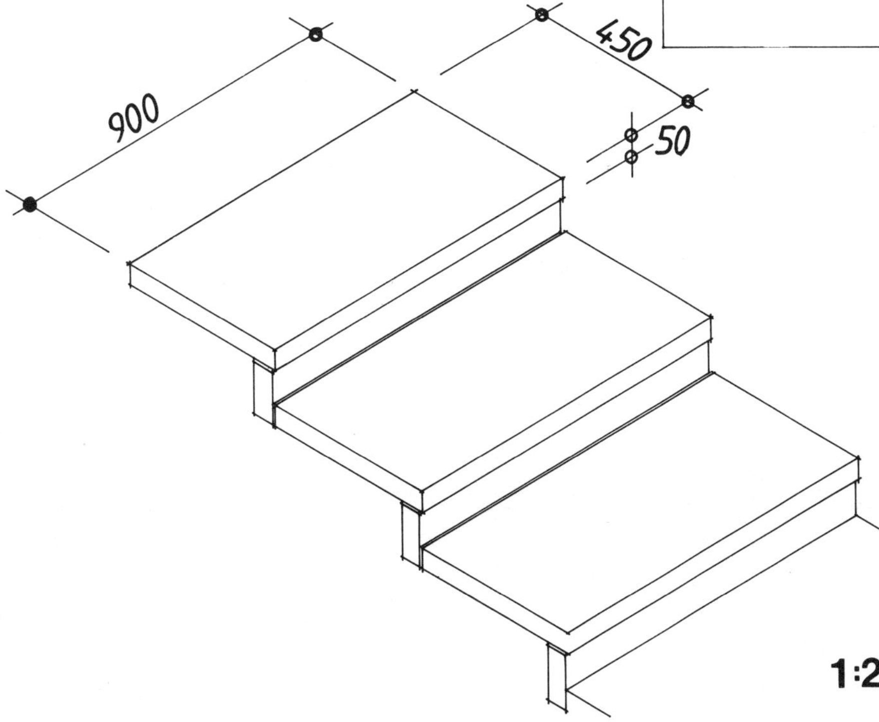
900
450
50

1:20

Scale A S

STEPS

concrete slab

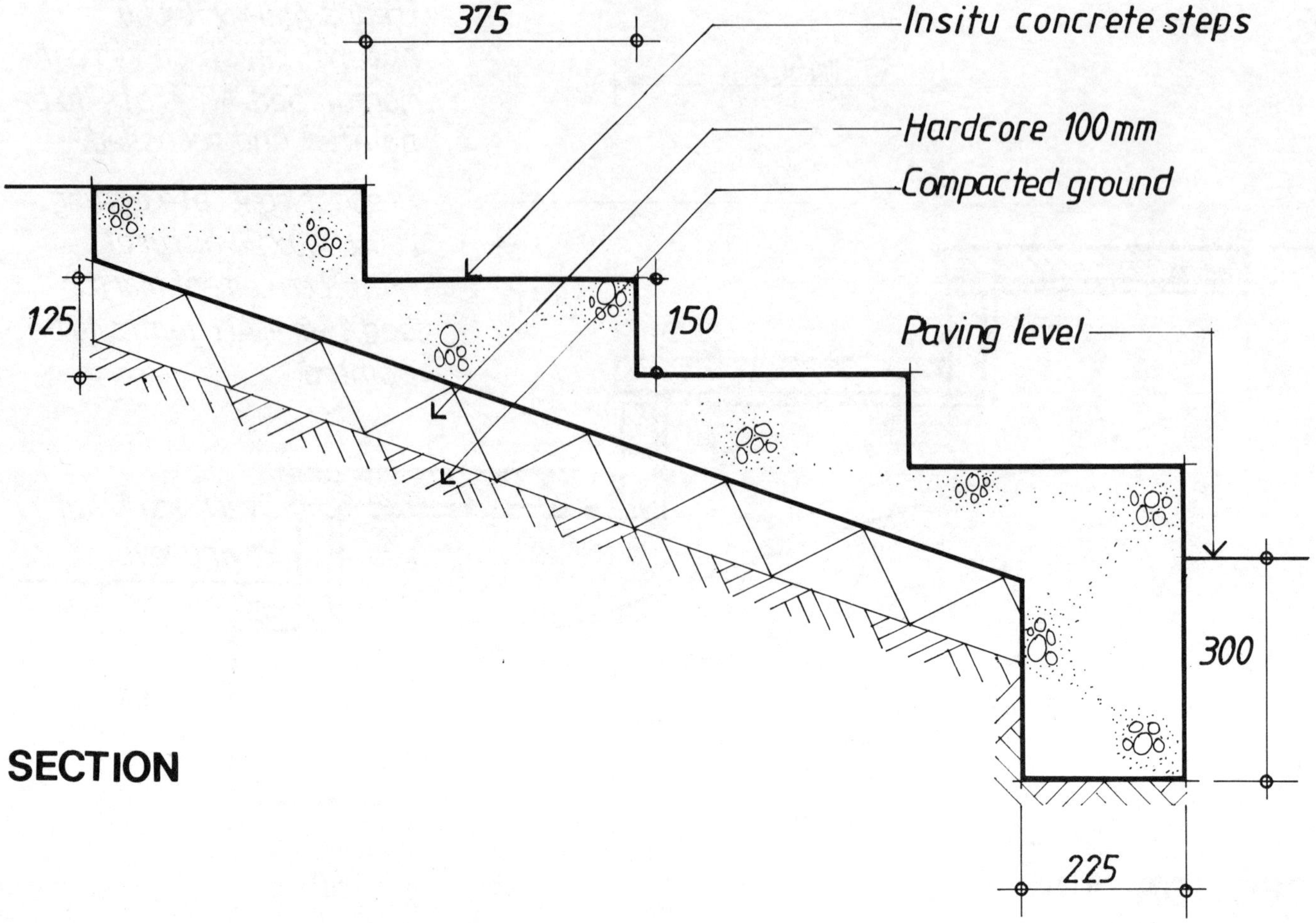
375
Insitu concrete steps
Hardcore 100mm
Compacted ground
125
150
Paving level
300
225

SECTION

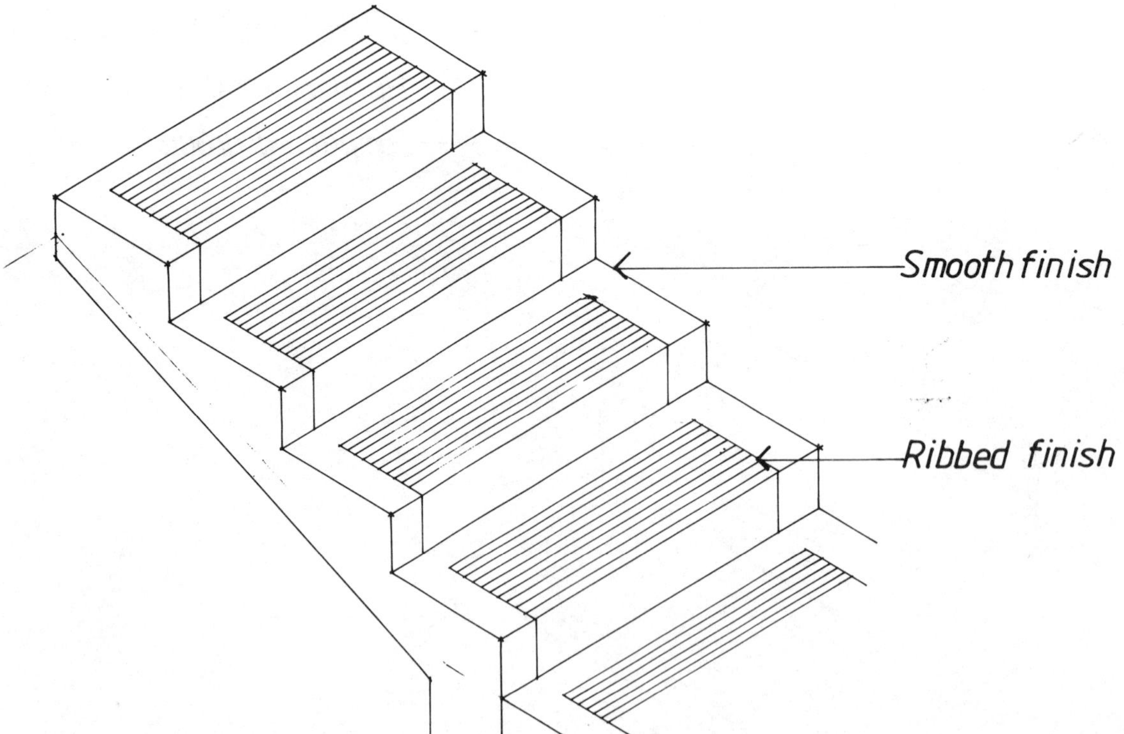
Smooth finish
Ribbed finish

Scale 1:10

STEPS
concrete

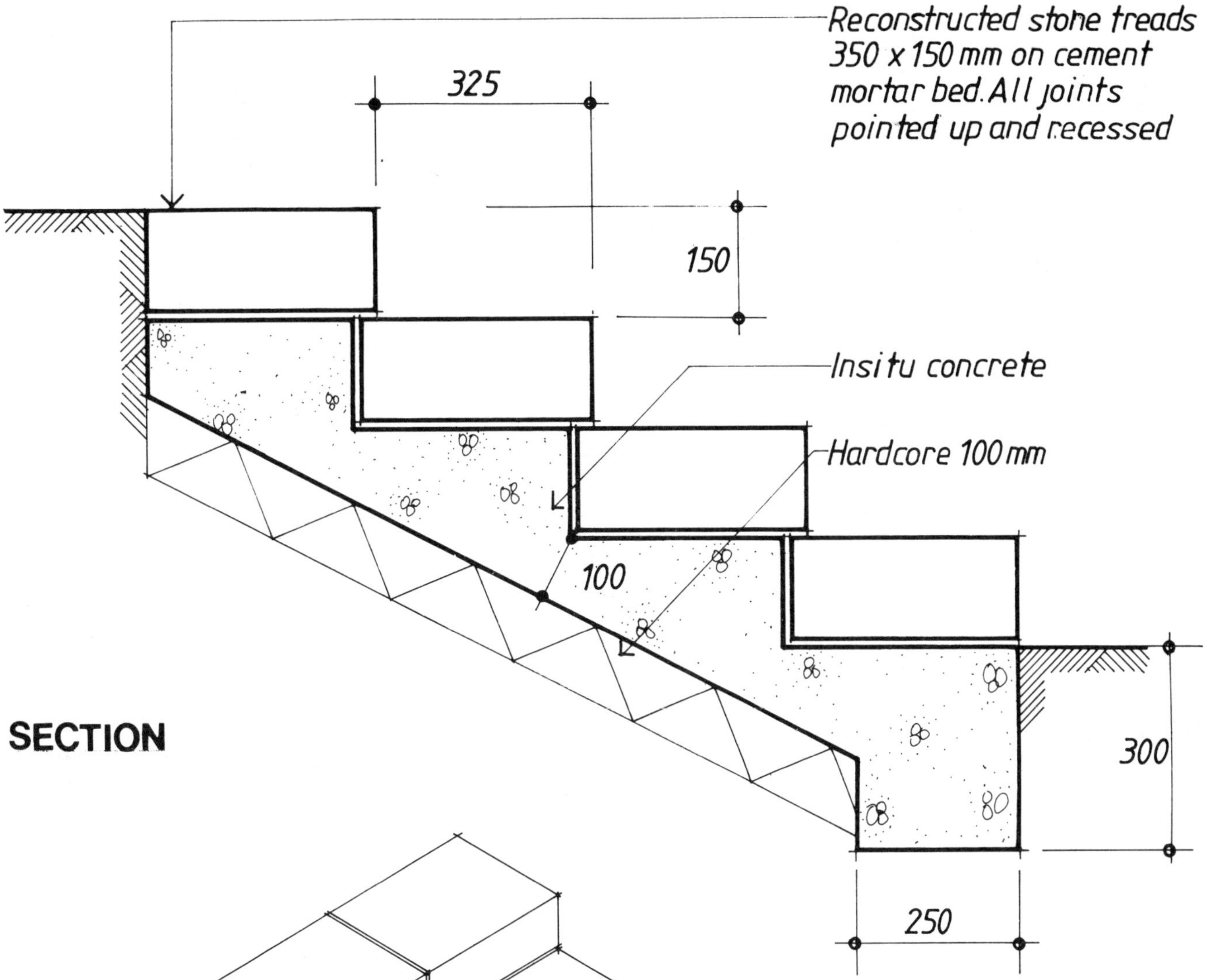
Reconstructed stone treads
350 x 150 mm on cement
mortar bed. All joints
pointed up and recessed
325
150
Insitu concrete
Hardcore 100 mm
100
300
250

SECTION

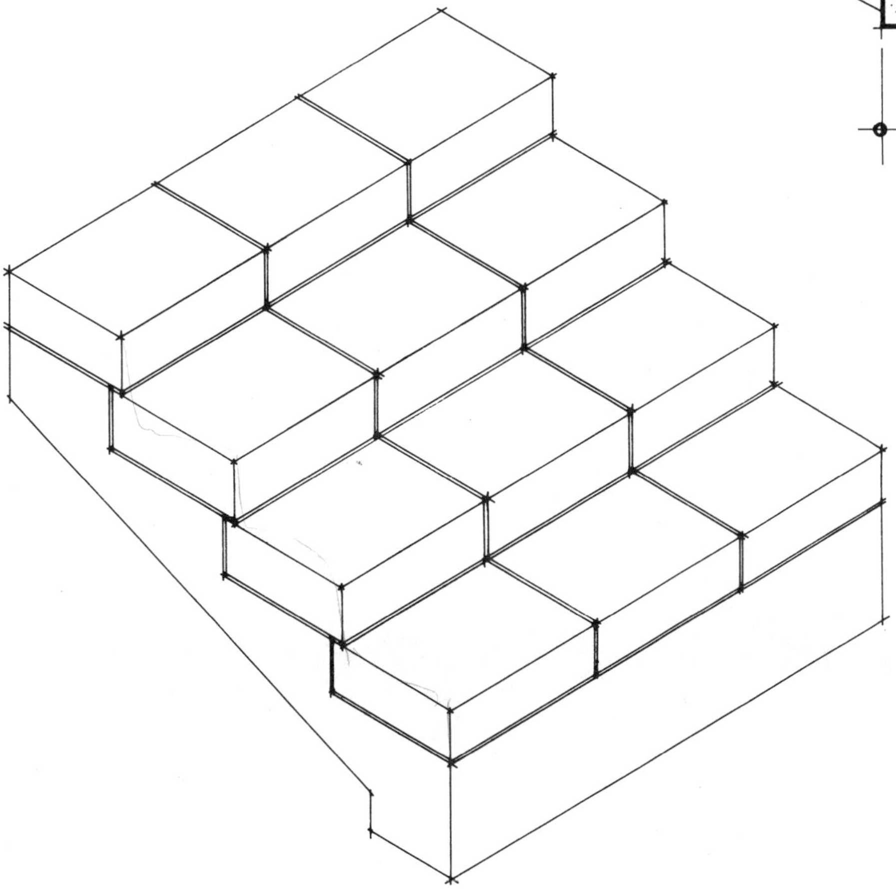

Scale 1:10

STEPS

reconstructed stone

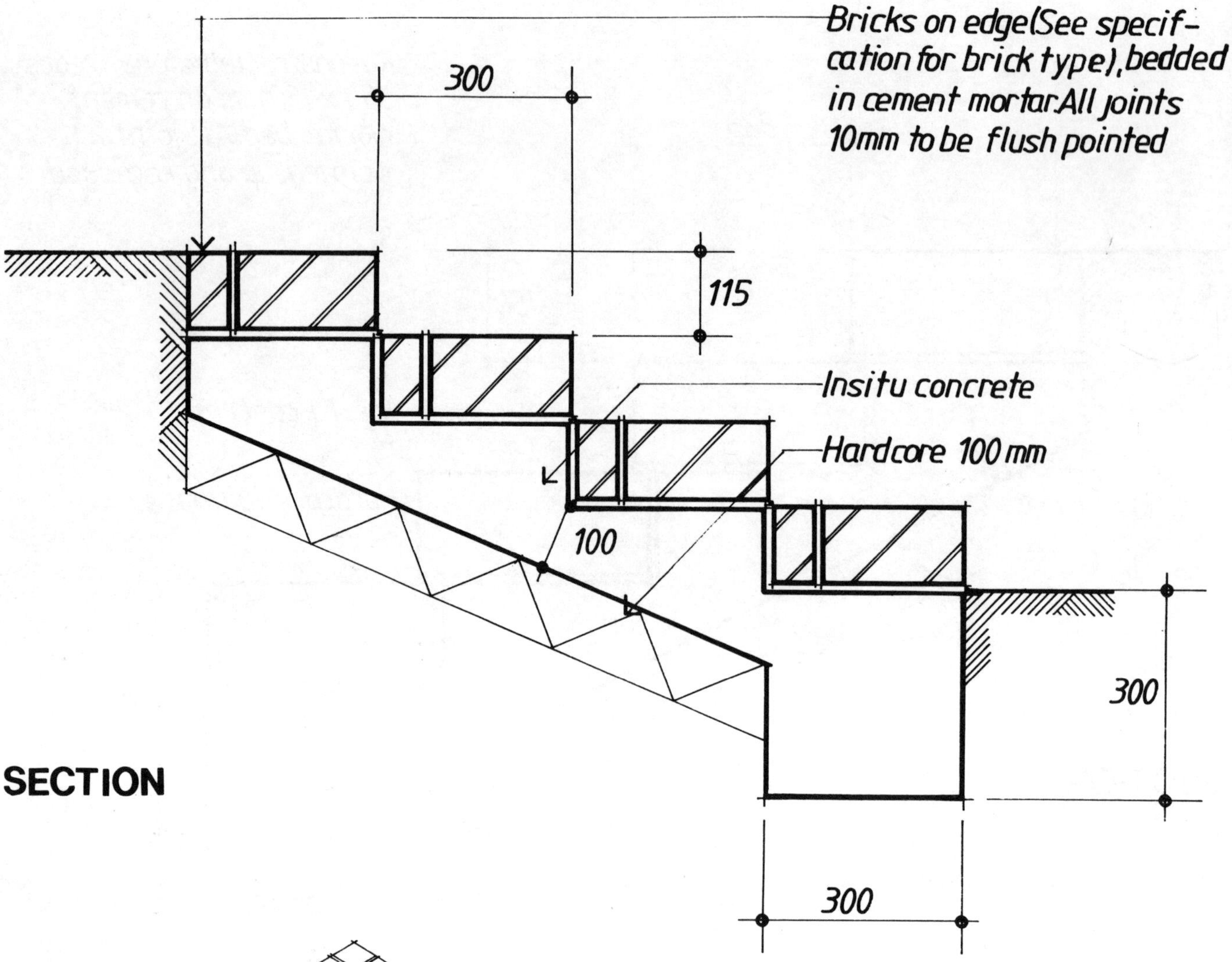
Bricks on edge(See specif-
cation for brick type), bedded
in cement mortar. All joints
10mm to be flush pointed
300
115
Insitu concrete
Hardcore 100mm
100
300
300

SECTION

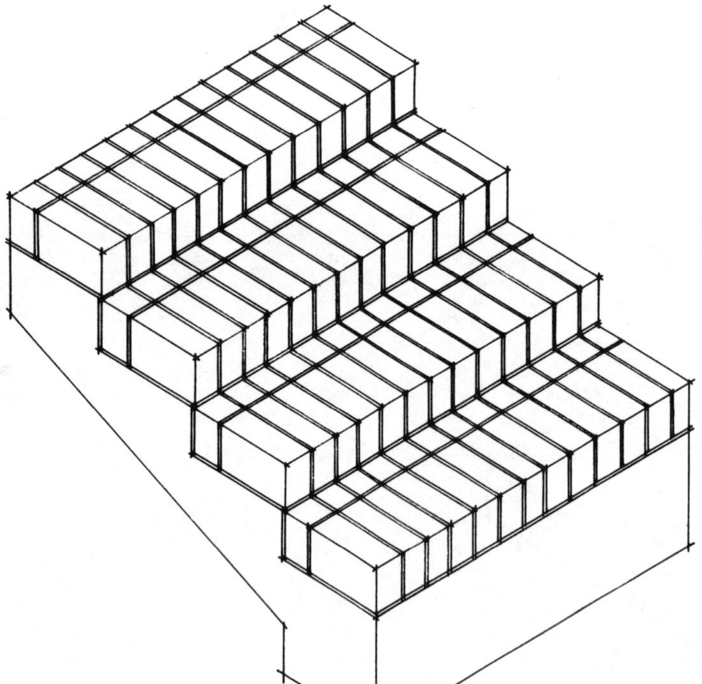

Scale1:10

STEPS
brick paving

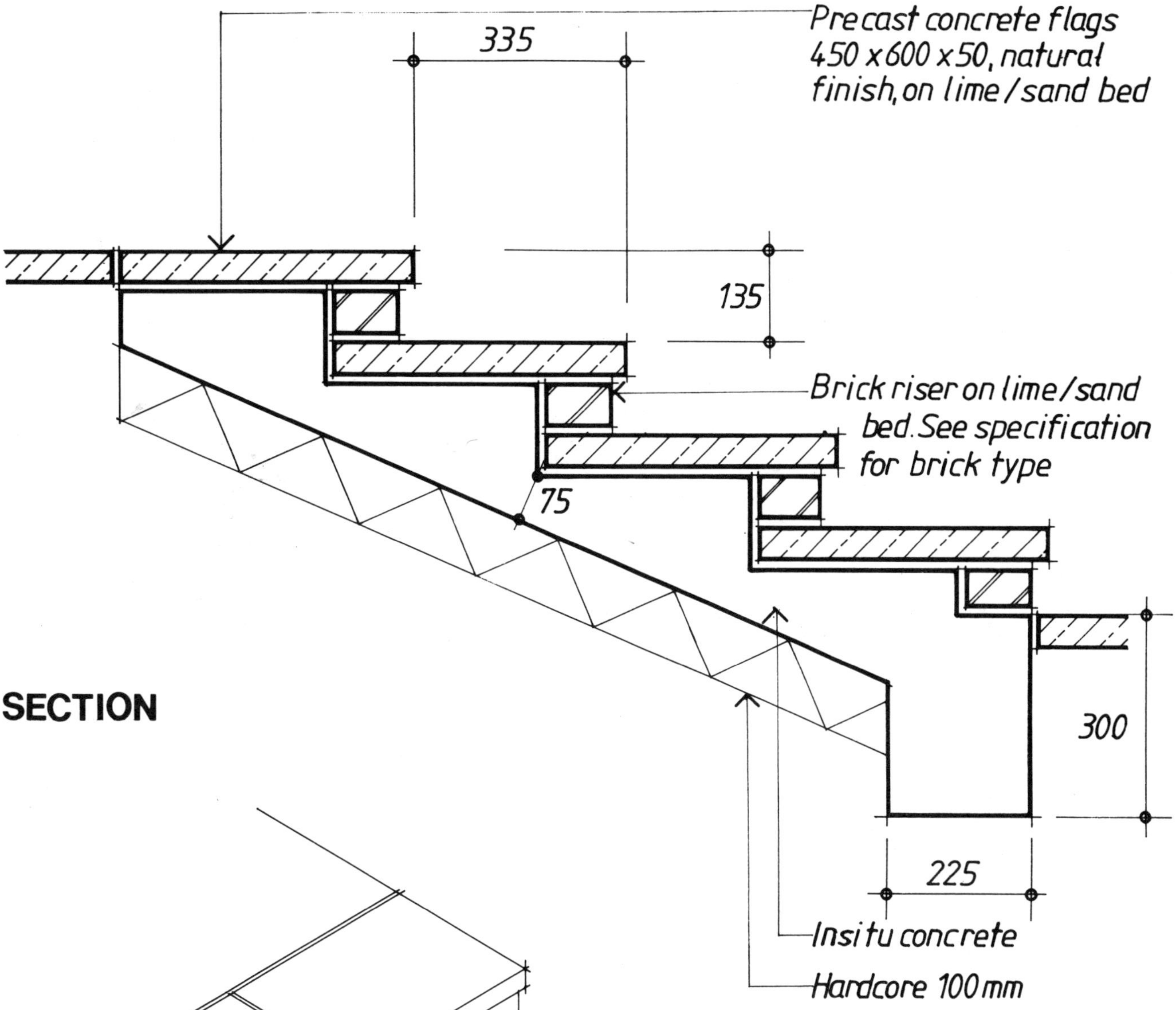
Precast concrete flags
450 x 600 x 50, natural
finish, on lime / sand bed
335
135
Brick riser on lime / sand
bed. See specification
for brick type
75
300
225
Insitu concrete
Hardcore 100 mm

SECTION

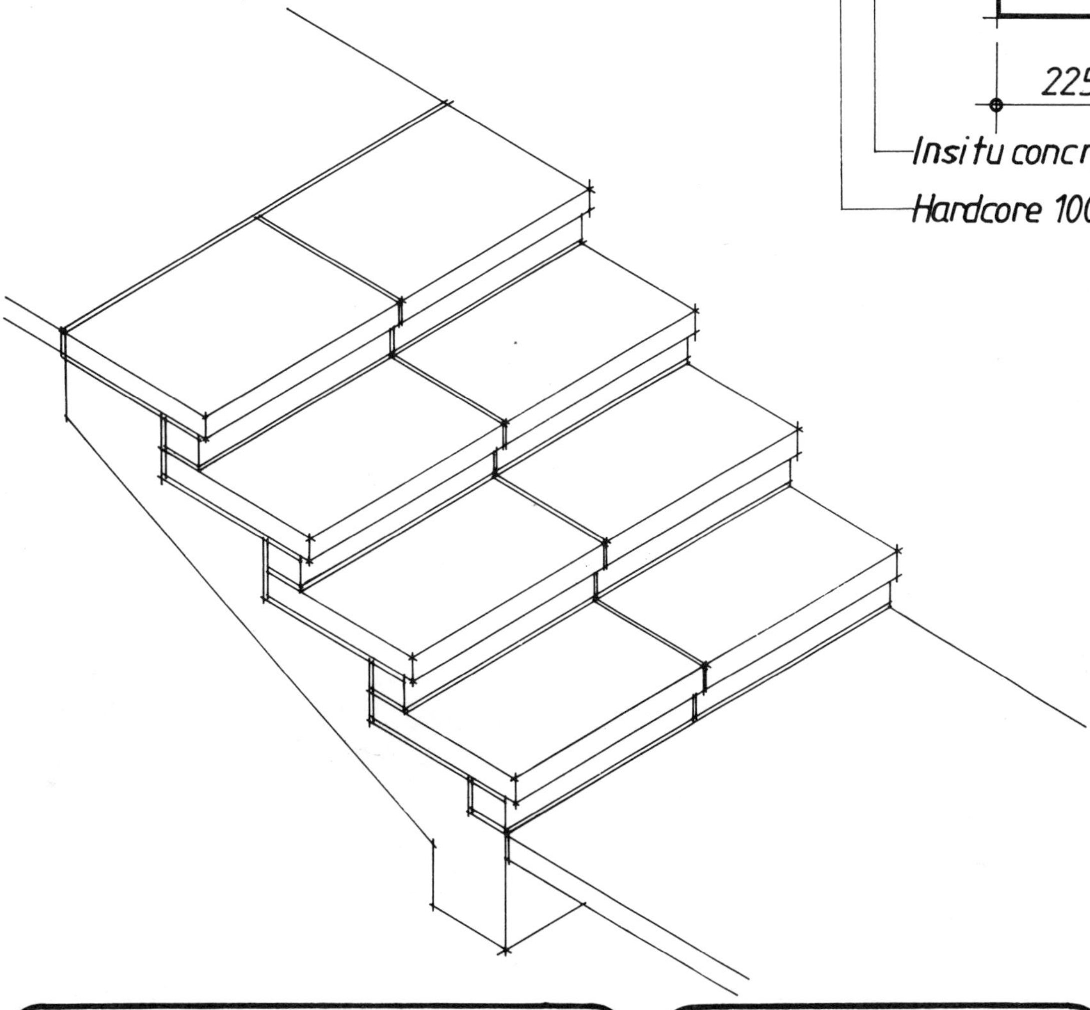

Scale 1:10

STEPS

brick & concrete flag

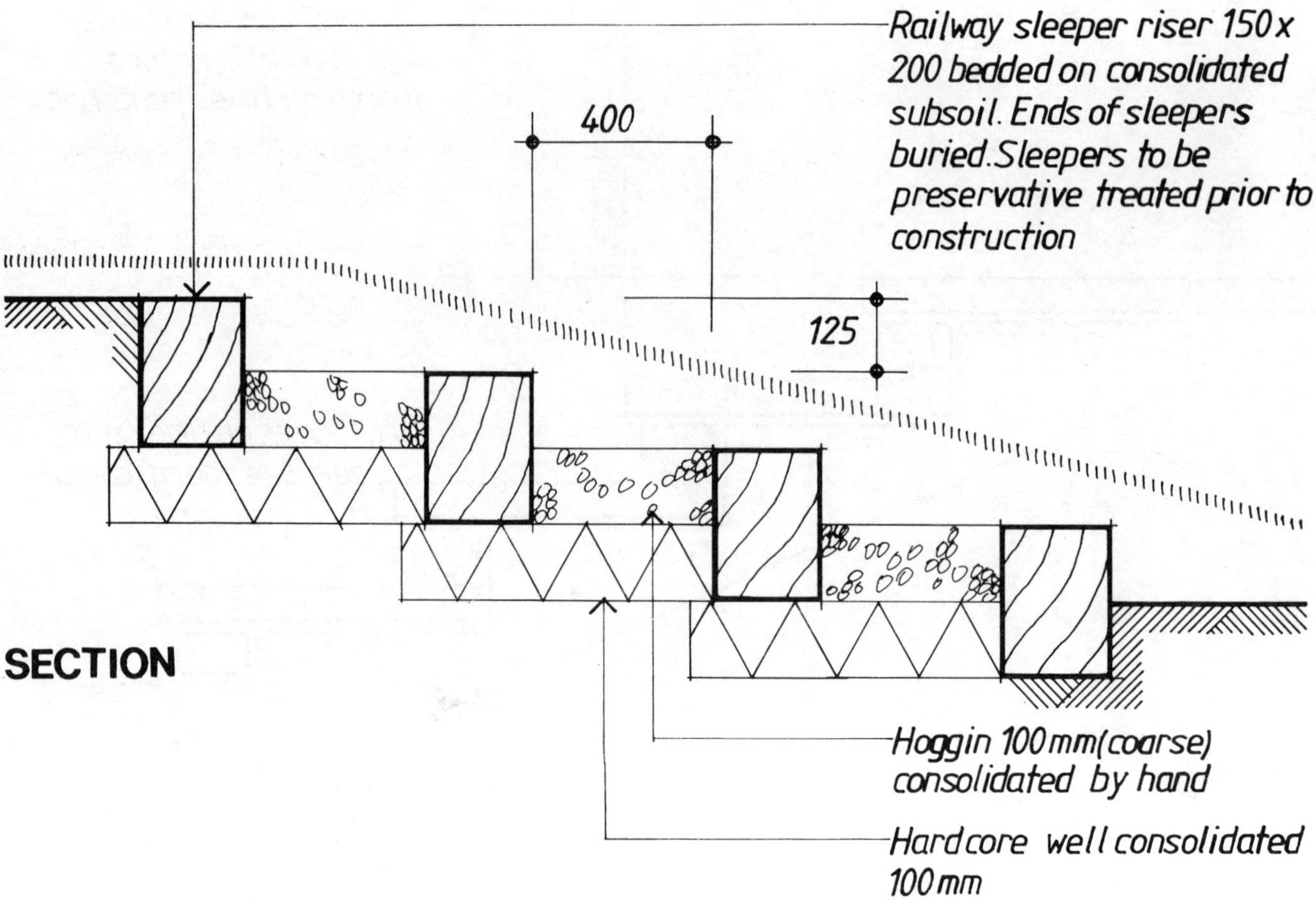
Railway sleeper riser 150x 200 bedded on consolidated subsoil. Ends of sleepers buried. Sleepers to be preservative treated prior to construction
400
125
Hoggin 100mm (coarse) consolidated by hand
Hardcore well consolidated 100mm

SECTION

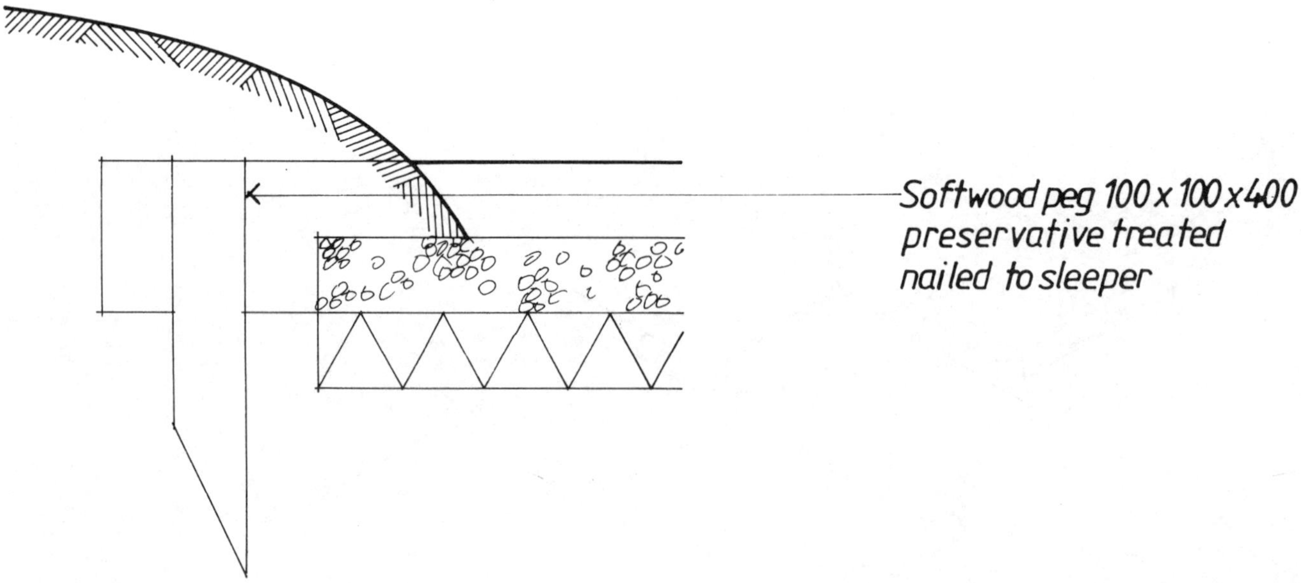
Softwood peg 100x100x400 preservative treated nailed to sleeper

SECTION

Scale 1:10

STEPS
timber & hoggin

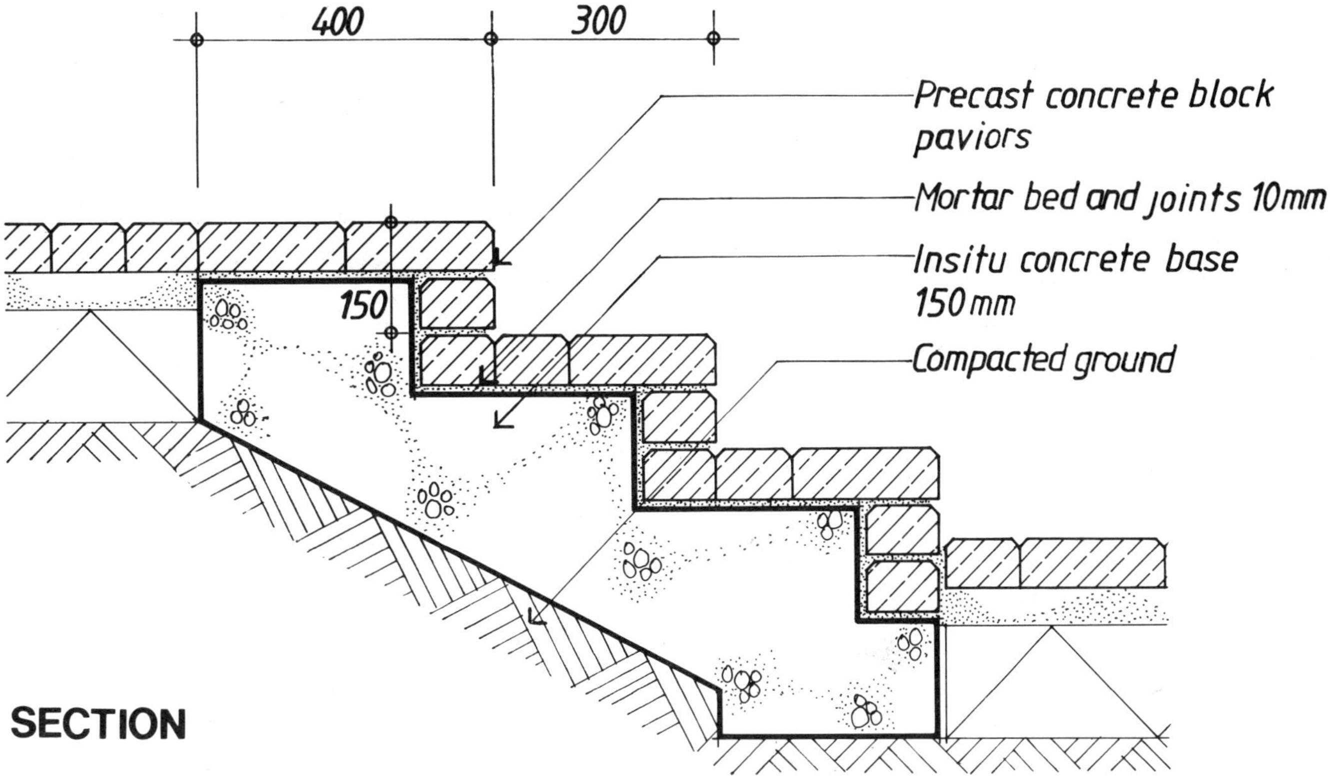

SECTION

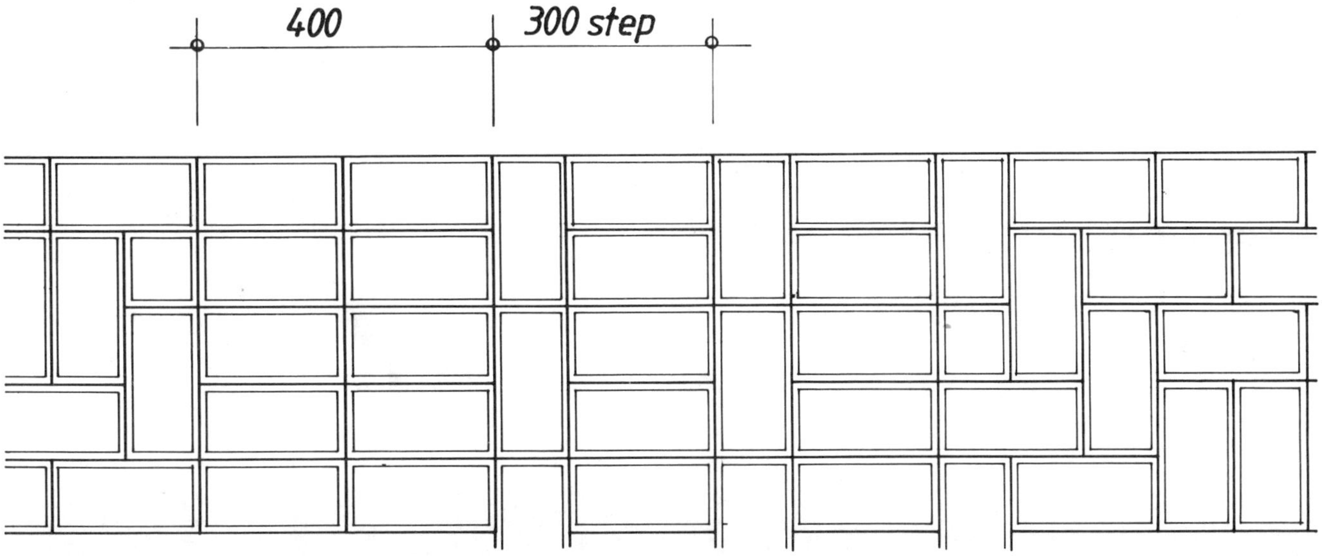

PLAN

Scale 1:10

STEPS

conc. block paviors

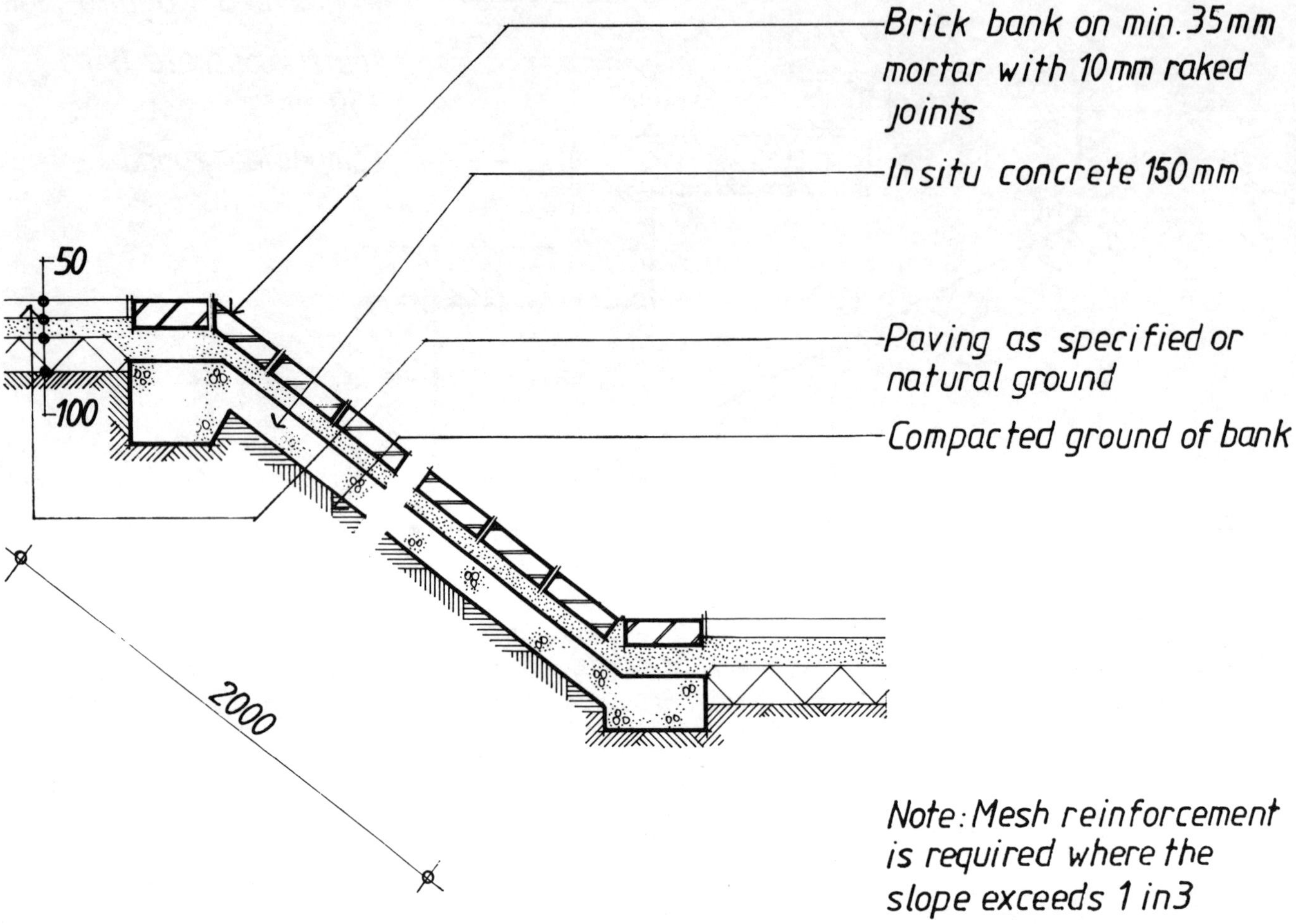

SECTION

Scale1:10

EMBANKMENT

brick

Chapter 10

Margins and trims

Mowing margins

An important aim in the detailing of grass areas is the elimination of edge trimming. Grass edges should be kept at least 225 mm away from walls and other obstructions, and should abut a hard edge. The infill can be of any material that will not support plant growth. Loose gravel and hoggin should be approached with discretion because they require a high standard of maintenance. Mowing strips can also be used around planted areas.

Trims and edges

These are necessary to retain the substrata of paving and to prevent the edges breaking away. They should be retained by a concrete foundation and haunching, except where timber has been used. Trims are also used to mark limits of ownership or to subdivide areas of concrete paving.

References

The Architectural Press Ltd, London
C Tandy
A J Handbook of Urban Landscape, 1972: Information Sheet 35

C C Handisyde
Hard Landscape in Brick, 1976

E Beazley
Design and Detail of the Space between Buildings, 1960

M Gage and M Vandenberg
Hard Landscape in Concrete, 1976

E & F N Spon
M F Downing
Landscape Construction, 1977

E and F N Spon
Spon's Landscape Handbook

Department of The Environment: Housing Development Notes
4 Grass and Small Plants
11 Landscape of New Housing

NBA 'Building' Commodity File, Components File (90) Section 02

British Standards Institute
BS 340 : 1963 Pre-cast concrete kerbs, channels, edgings and quadrants
BS 435 : 1931 Granite and whinstone kerbs, channels and quadrants

Detail sheets

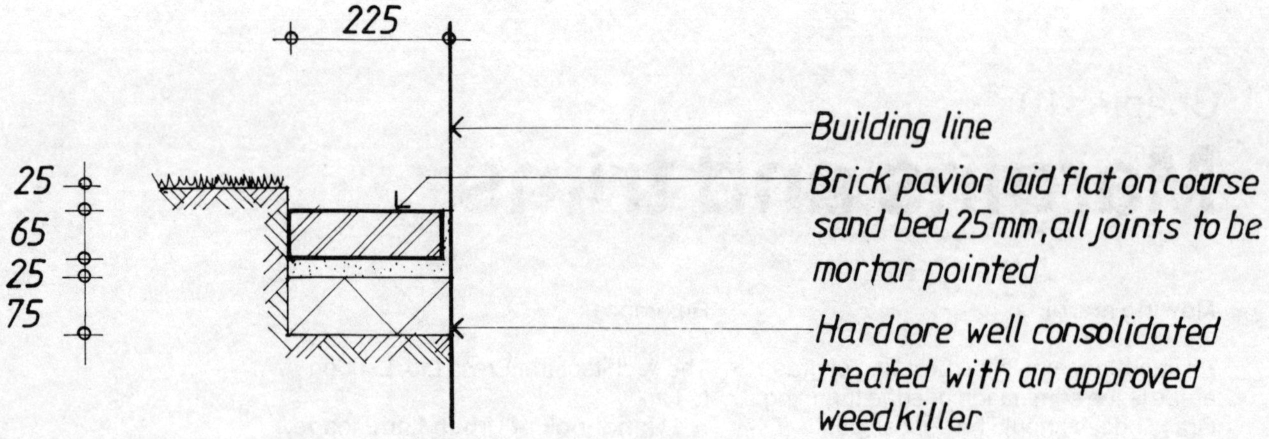

SECTION

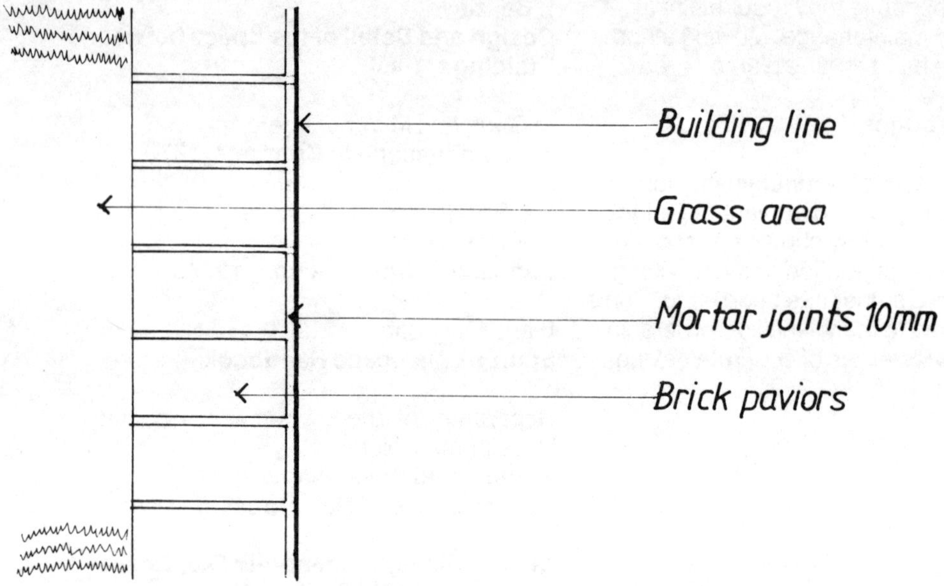

PLAN

Scale 1:10

MARGIN
brick

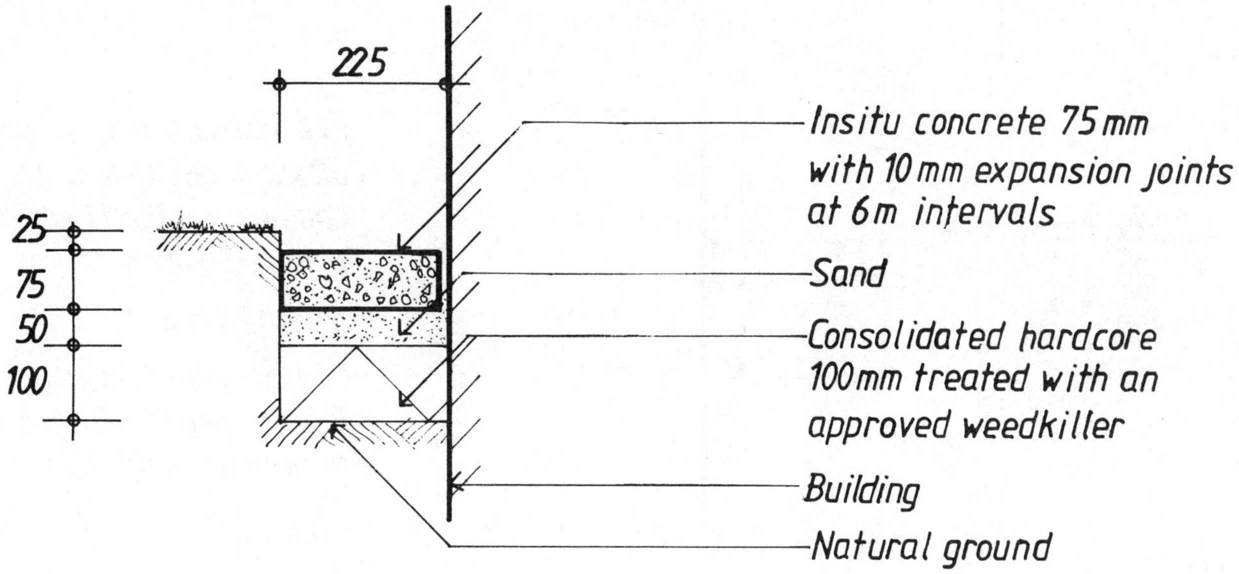

SECTION

Scale 1:10

MARGIN
concrete

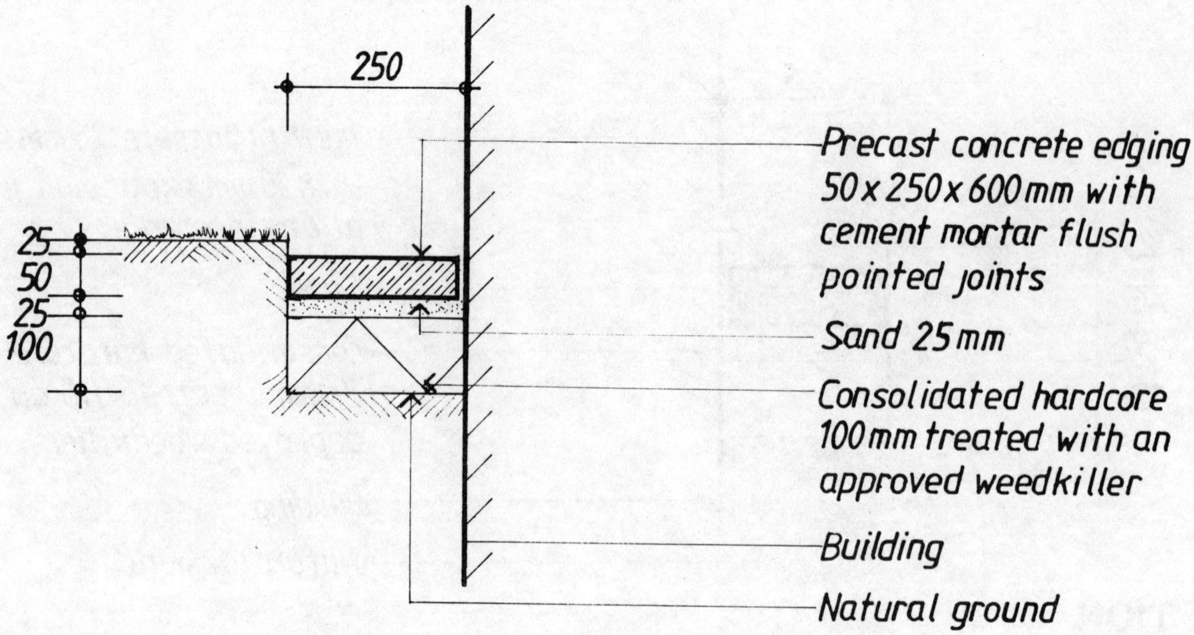

SECTION

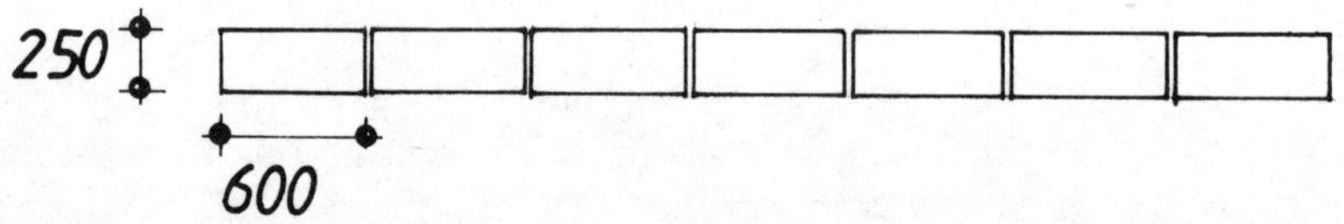

PLAN

Scale 1:10

MARGIN
paving slab

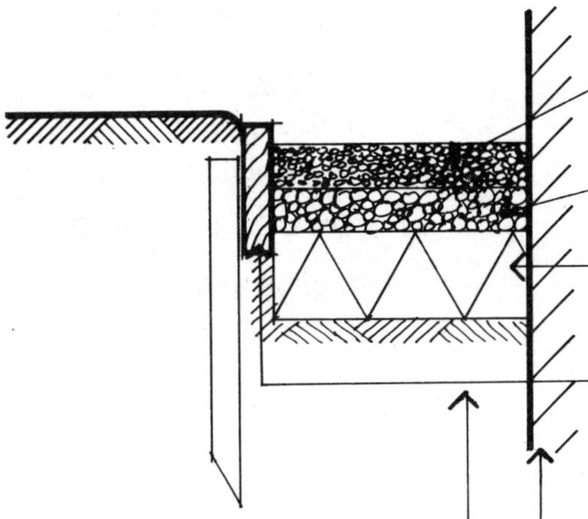

SECTION

Scale 1:10

MARGIN
hoggin

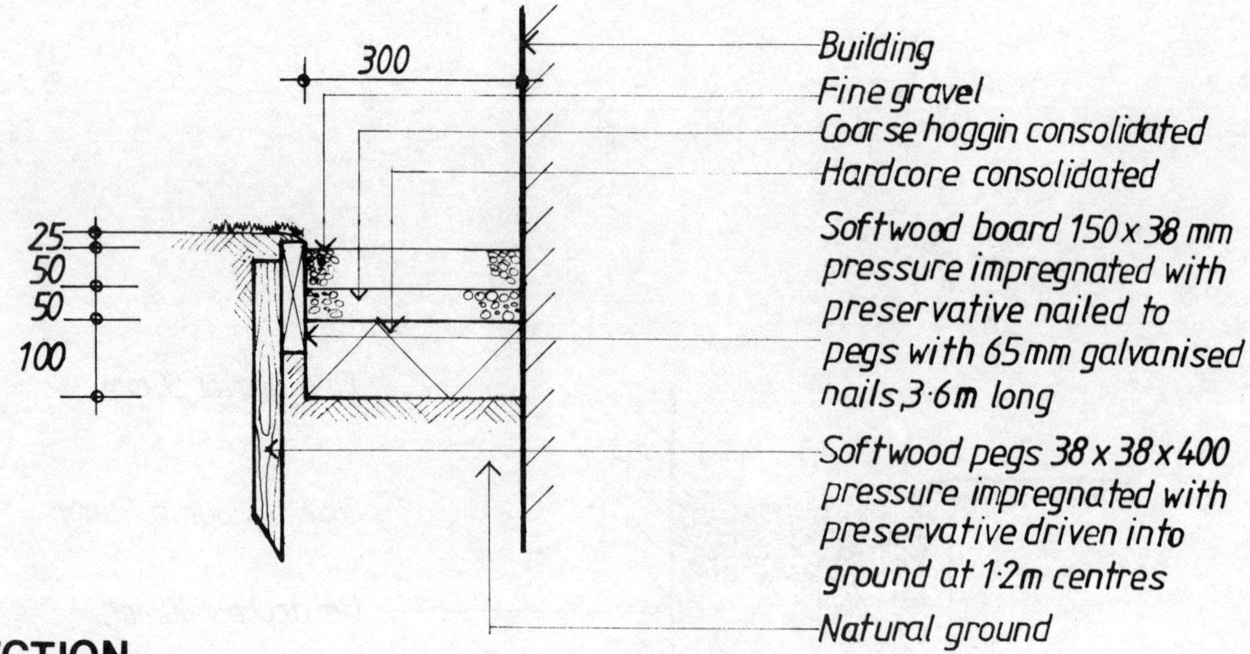

SECTION

Scale 1:10

MARGIN

gravel

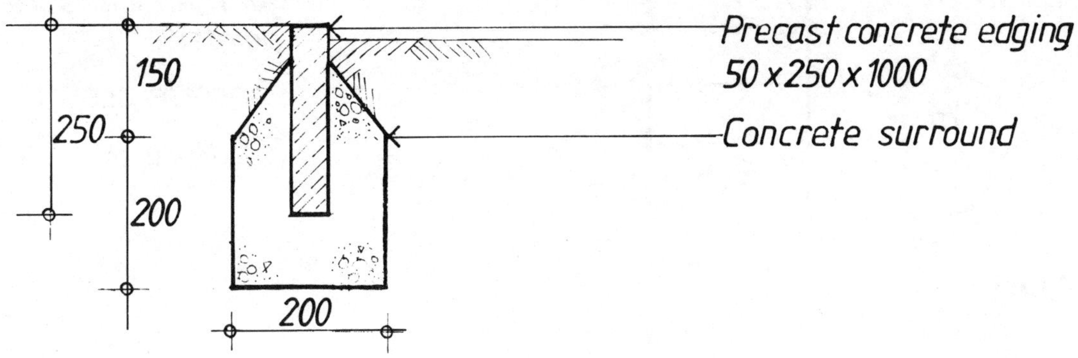

SECTION

Scale 1:10

EDGE
concrete

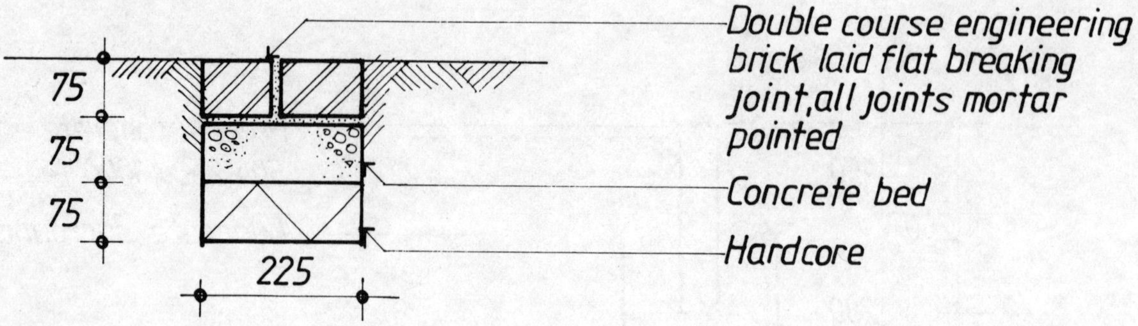

SECTION

Scale 1:10

TRIM
brick

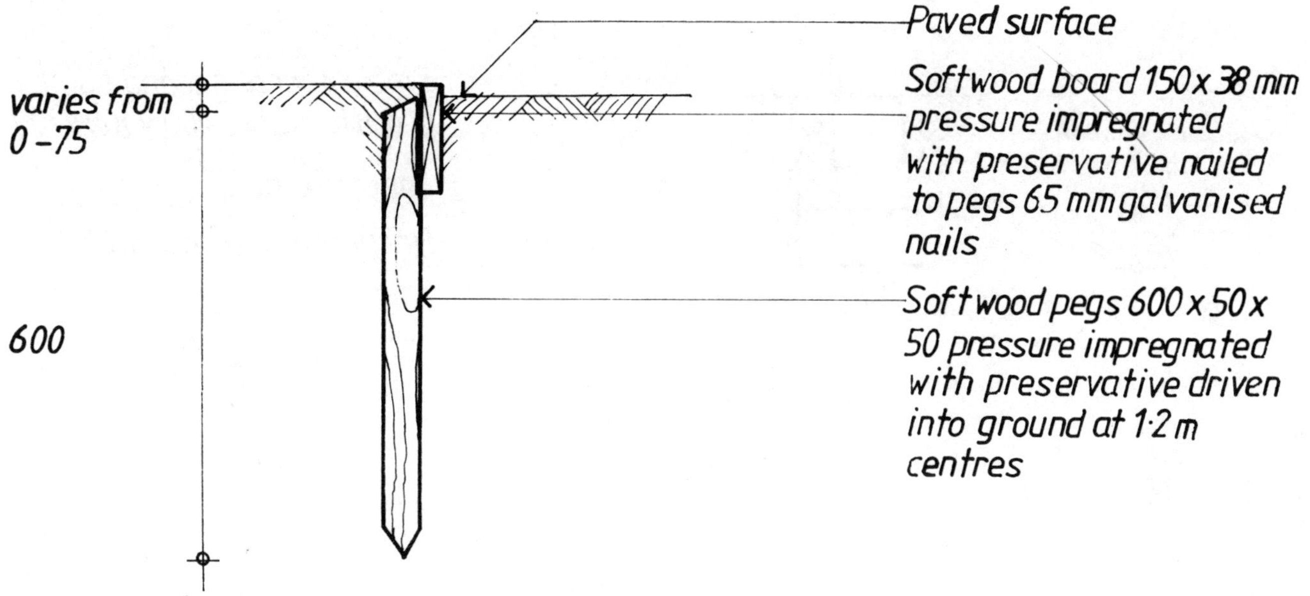

SECTION

Scale 1:10

EDGE

timber board

SECTION

Scale 1:10

TRIM
granite sett

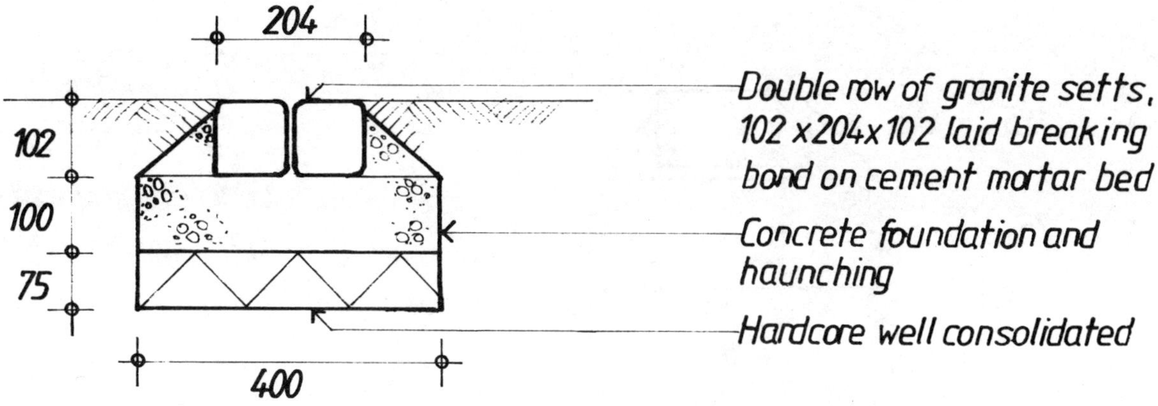

SECTION

Scale 1:10

TRIM

granite sett

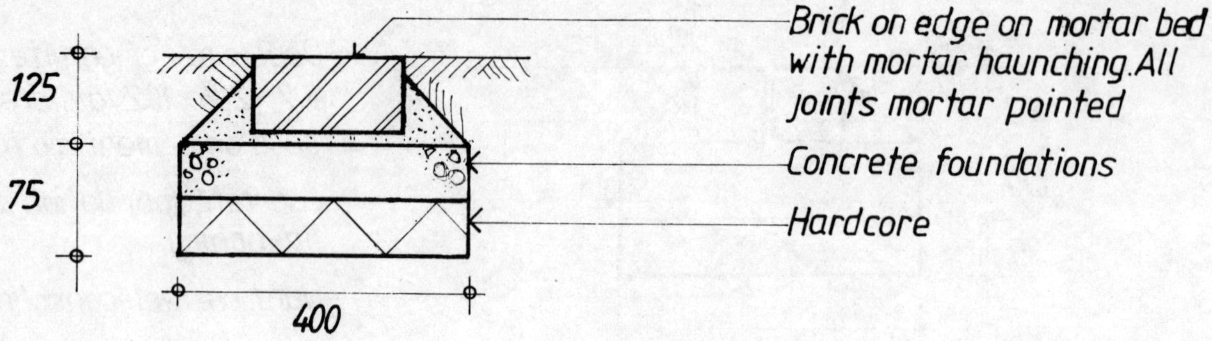

SECTION

Scale 1:10

EDGE
brick

Chapter 11

Kerbs

Kerbs are necessary to prevent the lateral spread of the road, control surface water drainage from the road and to discourage the encroachment of vehicles onto footpaths or grass verges. In certain situations the character of an area could be spoilt by edging its roads with upstanding kerbs, and they can be dangerous where fast-moving traffic is prevalent. In such circumstances flush kerbs (usually of 125 mm – 250 mm pre-cast concrete) are used. There is no reason why other materials or other design approaches should not be considered, particularly where the preservation of a rural area's character is concerned. Any road kerb detail will have to be agreed with the adopting authority

Setting of kerbs

Kerbs should be laid before the base and surfacing of the road and are usually laid on a 100 mm – 150 mm bed of concrete (dry mix of 1 : 3 : 6). The concrete should be well haunched up at the back of the kerb. Joints should be formed with cement and sand mortar (1 : 3). Expansion joints in kerbs to flexible roads should be at 20 metres. With concrete roads the joints should coincide with the joints in the road slab. A filler should be placed between the kerbs as between the road slabs.

References

The Architectural Press Ltd, London
C Tandy
A J Handbook of Urban Landscape, 1972: Information Sheet 35

C C Handisyde
Hard Landscape in Brick, 1976

E Beazley
Design and Detail of the Space between Buildings, 1960

R M Cartwright
The Design of Urban Space, 1980

E and F N Spon
Spon's Landscape Handbook

M F Downing
Landscape Construction, 1977

NBA 'Building' Commodity File, Components File (90) Section 02

British Standards Institute
BS 340 : 1963 Pre-cast concrete kerbs, channels, edgings and quadrants
BS 435 : 1931 Granite and whinstone kerbs, channels and quadrants

Detail sheets

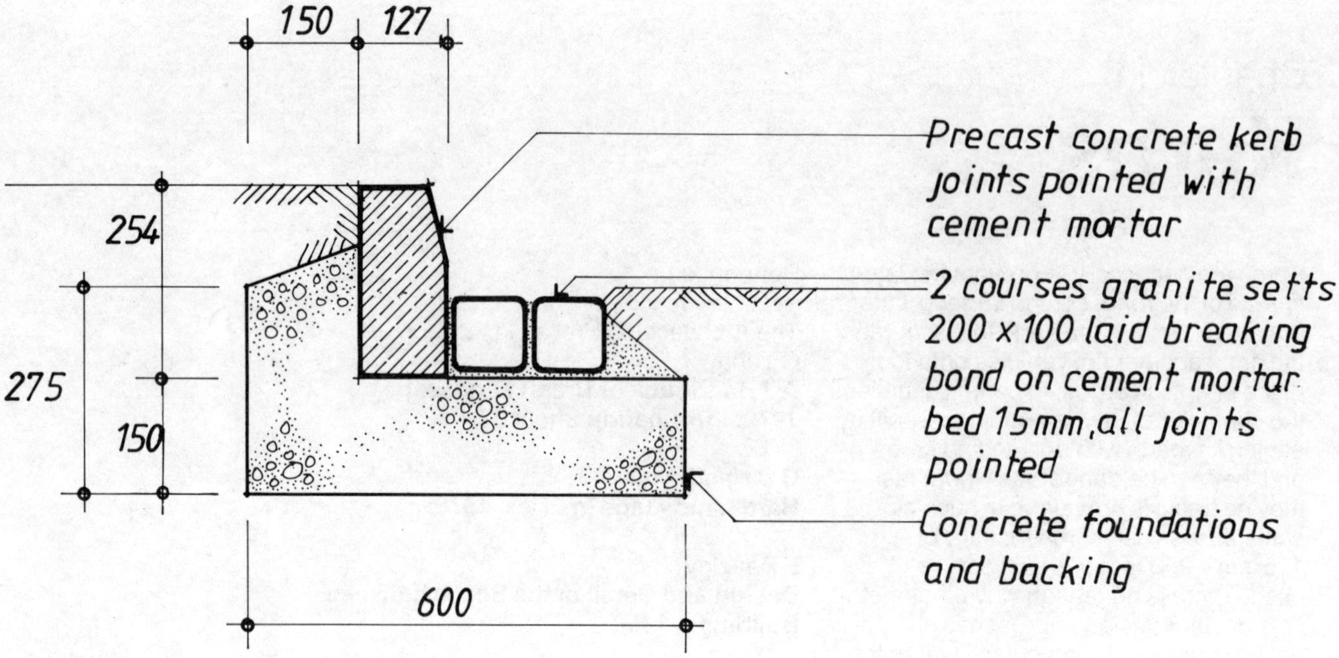

SECTION

Scale 1:10

KERB
granite sett / concrete

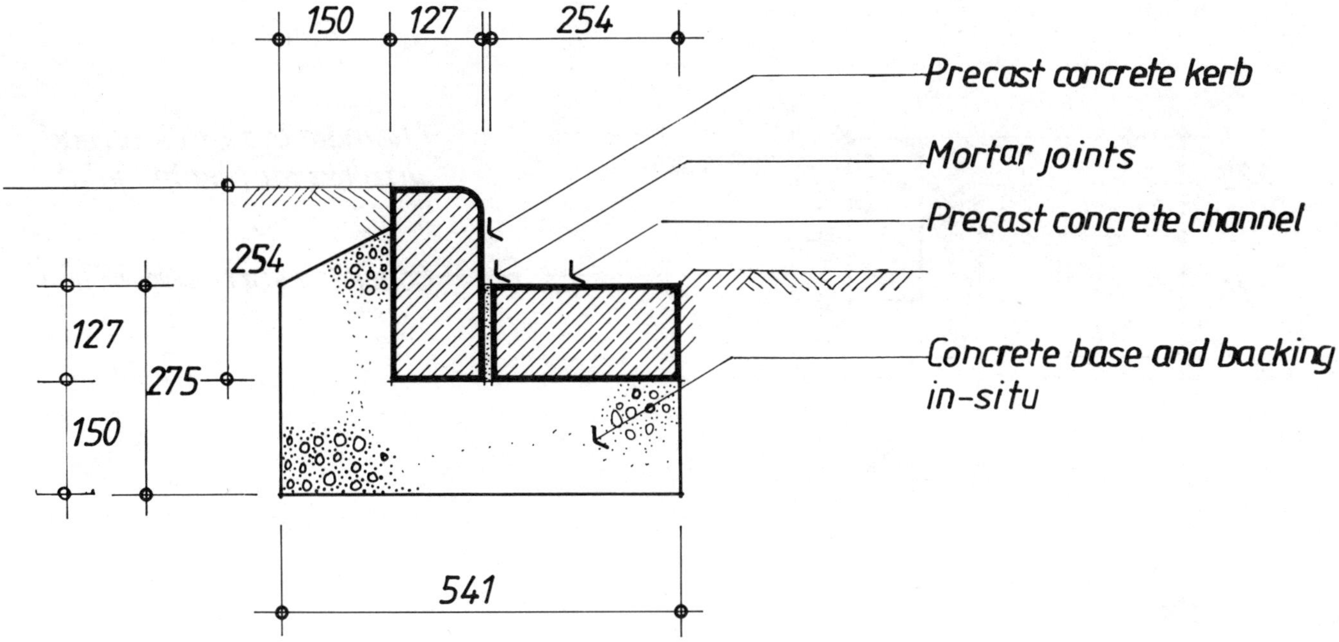

SECTION

Scale 1:10

KERB & CHANNEL

concrete

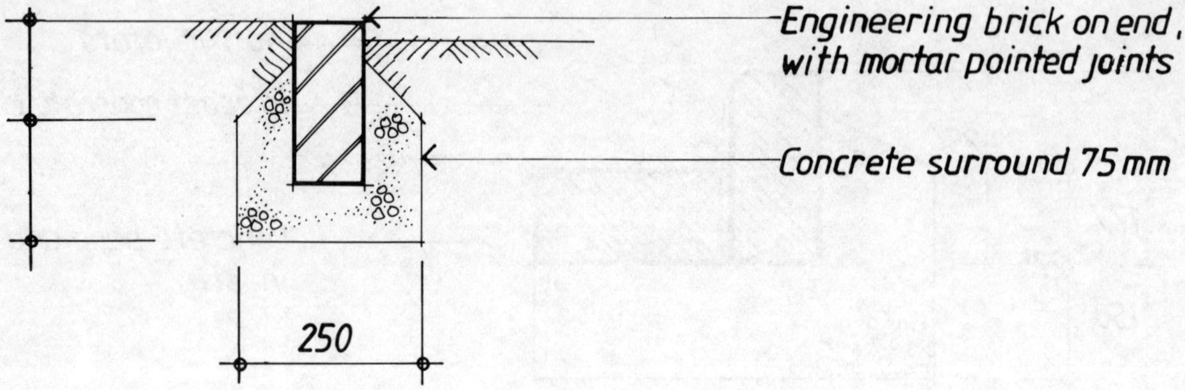

SECTION

Scale 1:10

KERB

brick

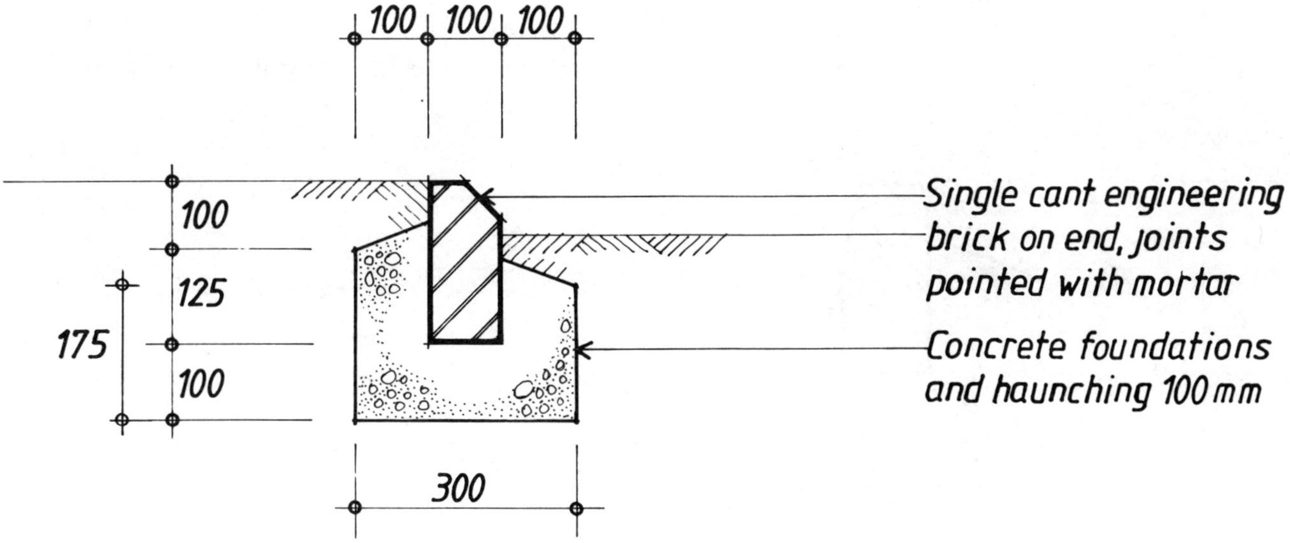

SECTION

Scale 1:10

KERB
brick

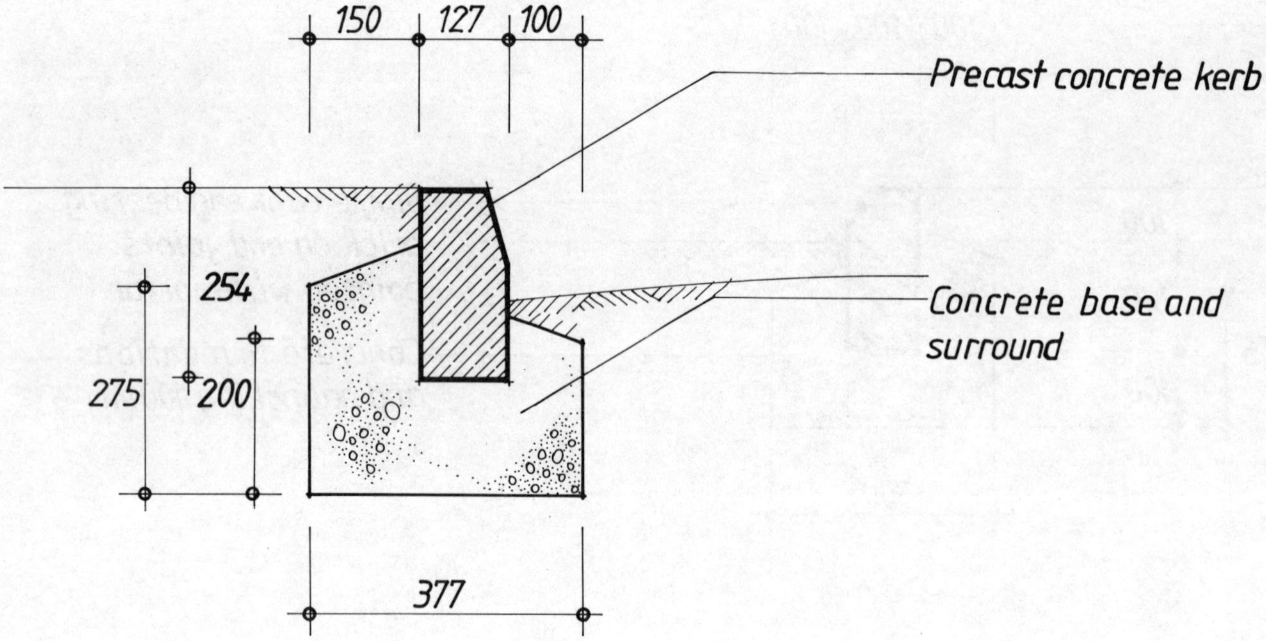

SECTION

Scale 1:10

KERB
concrete

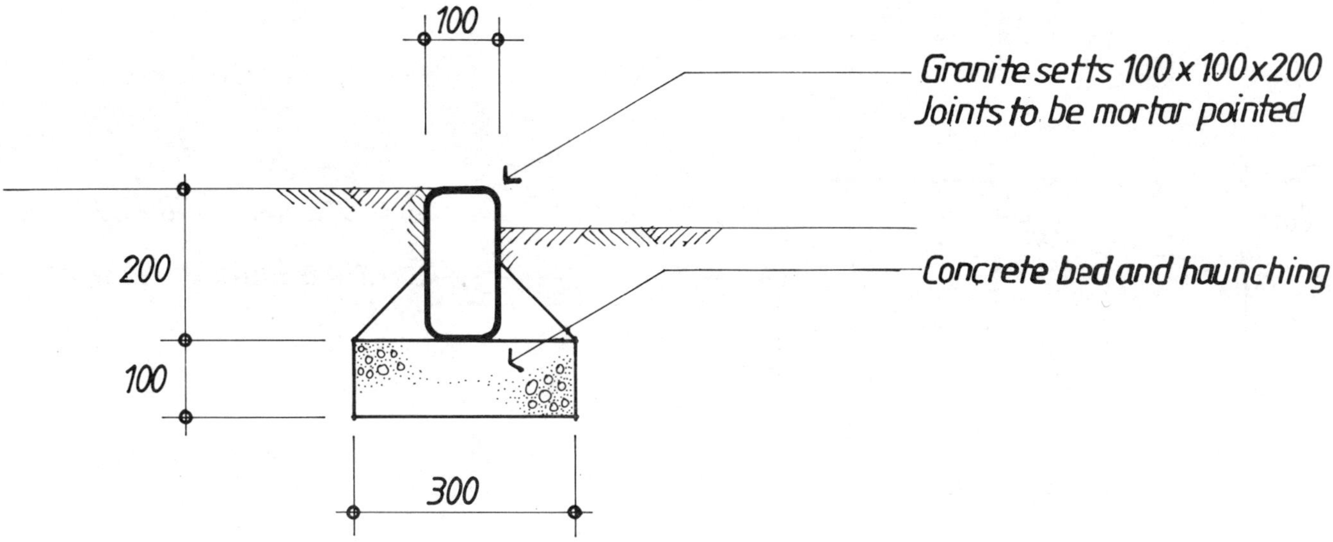

SECTION

Scale 1:10

KERB
granite sett

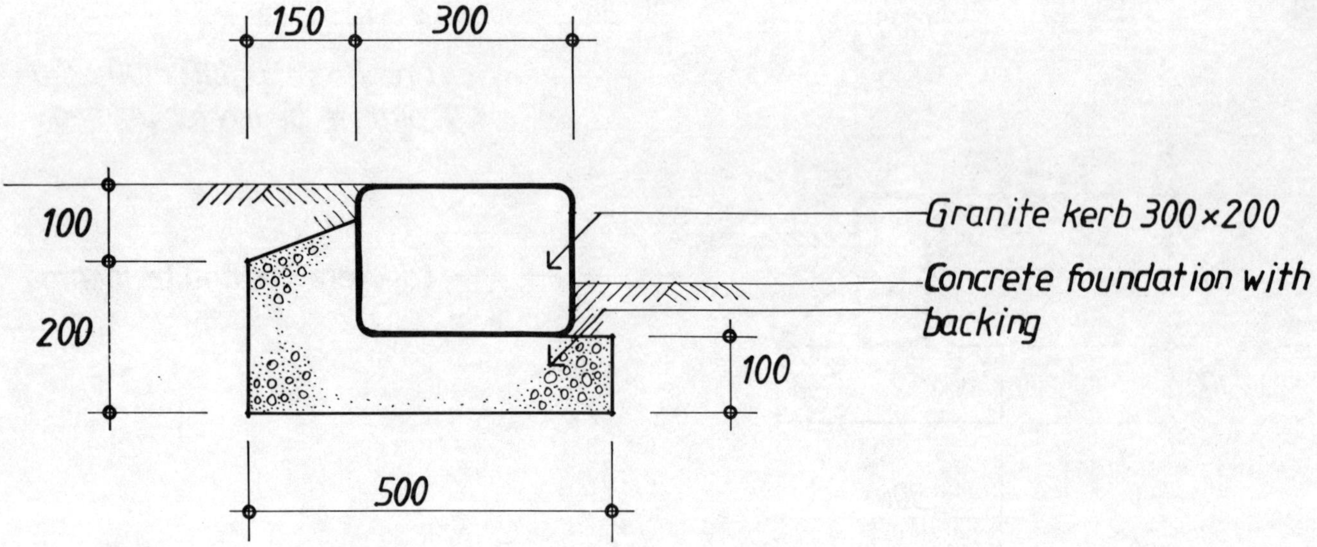

SECTION

Scale 1:10

KERB
granite

Chapter 12

Drainage channels

These are used for draining large areas of paving and ramps or paths contained between walls. The width of the channel must be related to the size of the gully grating. They can also be used alongside roads and driveways, offering an interesting design solution and creating their own character, as can be seen in many Conservation Areas. They should be made part of the paving pattern.

Types

Channels can be dished or flat and can be made of a wide variety of materials. Dished channels are usually of pre-cast concrete or stone; the latter are expensive. Flat channels should have the surface sufficiently shaped to ensure the flow of water to the drainage gully. Falls should be between 1 : 200 for pre-cast concrete materials and 1 : 60 for brick and granite setts. See References for more detailed information.
An alternative to surface channels is the use of a 'safeticurb' section or a glazed half round channel with a cast-iron grating. Both types need a high degree of maintenance to prevent silting up.

References

The Architectural Press Ltd, London
C Tandy
A J Handbook of Urban Landscape, 1972: Information Sheet 35

E Beazley
The Design and Detail of the Space between Buildings, 1960

R M Cartwright
The Design of Urban Space, 1980

E and F N Spon
Spon's Landscape Handbook

M F Downing
Landscape Construction, 1977

British Standards Institute
BS 340 : 1963 Pre-cast concrete kerbs, channels, edgings and quadrants
BS 435 : 1931 Granite and whinstone kerbs, channels and quadrants

Detail sheets

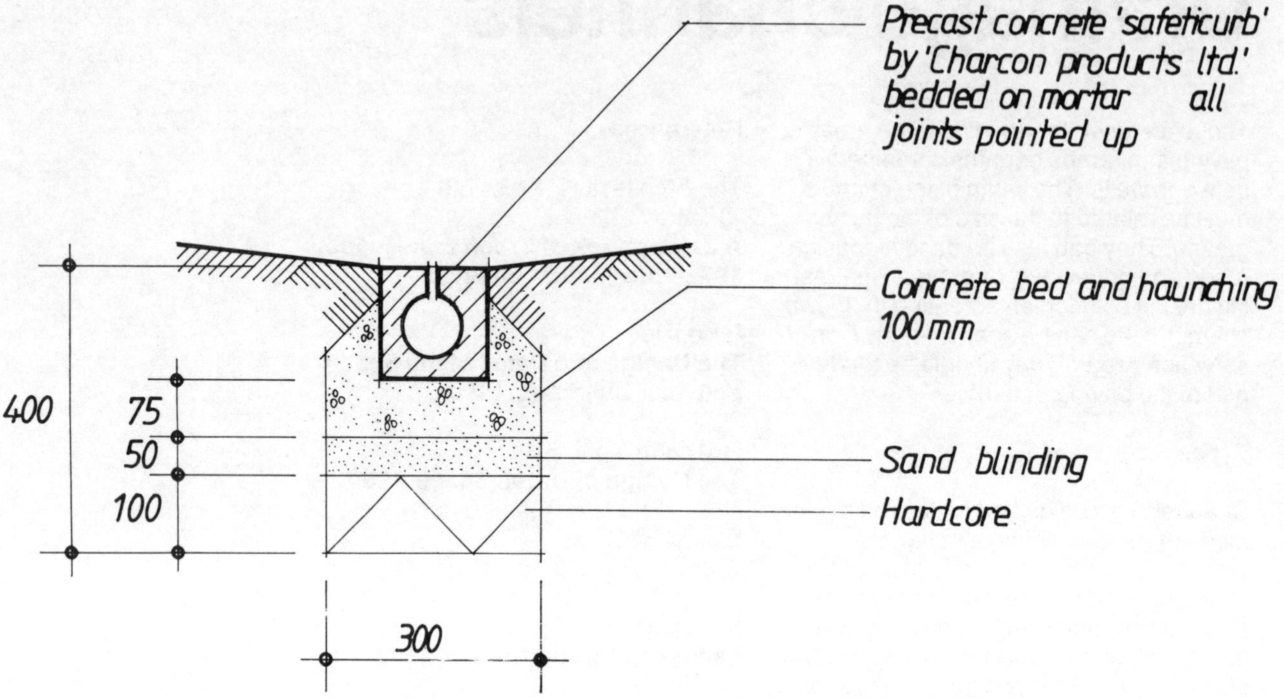

SECTION

Scale 1 : 10

DRAINAGE CHANNEL
Safeticurb

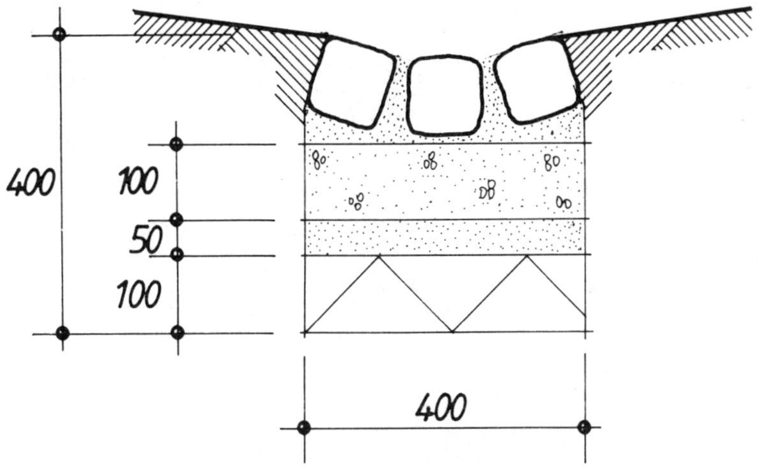

3 courses granite setts laid
to form dished channel
bedded on mortar
all joints pointed

Concrete

Sand blinding

Hardcore

SECTION

Scale 1:10

DRAINAGE CHANNEL
granite setts

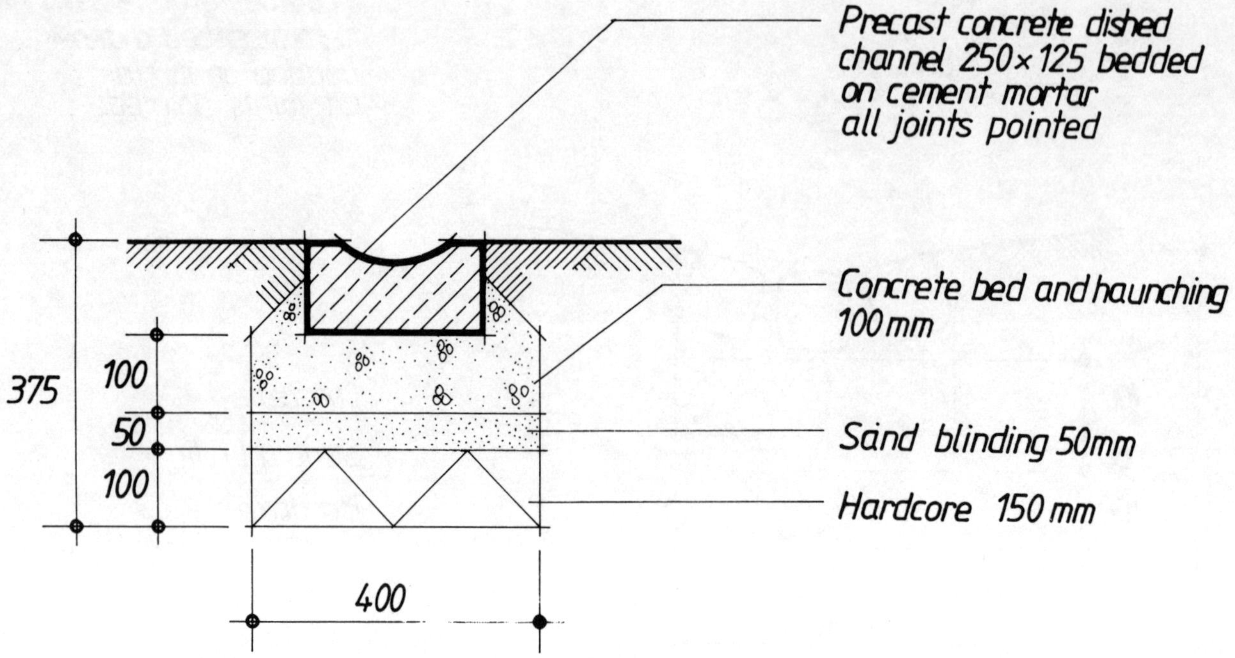

SECTION

Scale 1:10

DRAINAGE CHANNEL
precast concrete

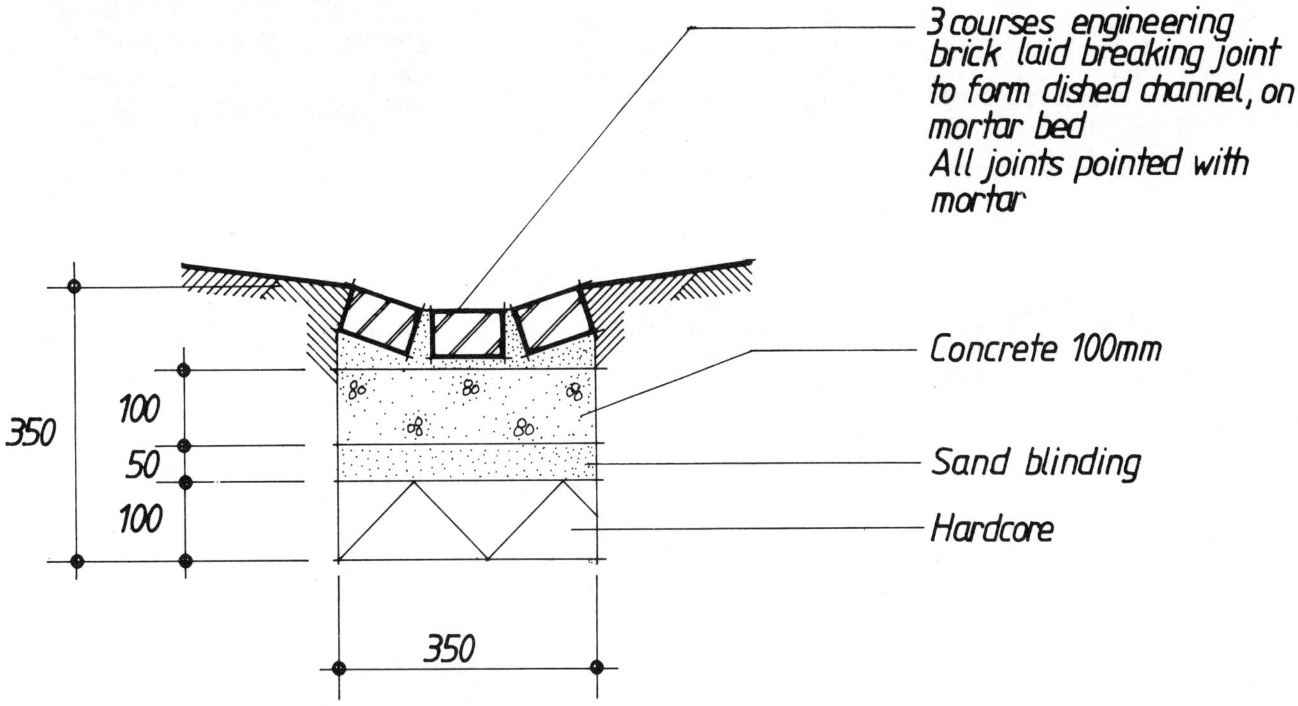

SECTION

Scale 1:10

DRAINAGE CHANNEL
brick

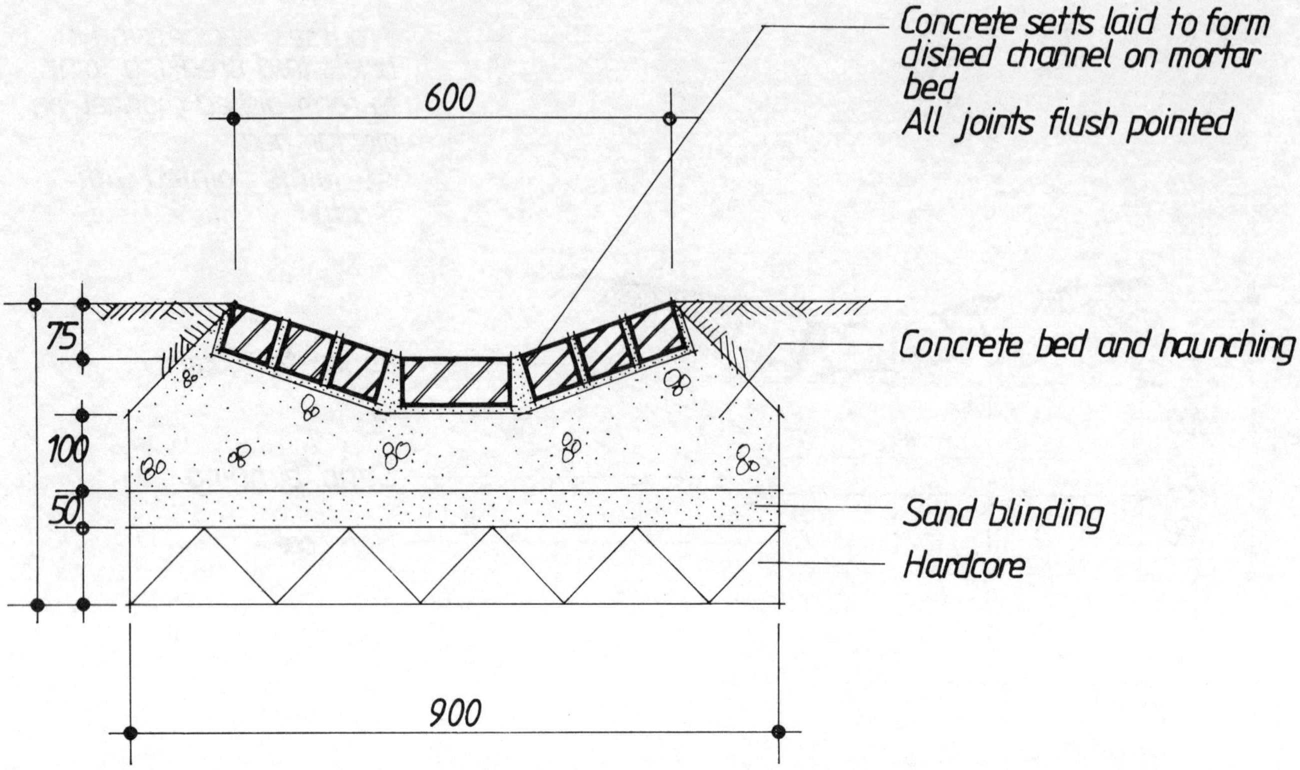

SECTION

Scale 1:10

DRAINAGE CHANNEL
concrete setts

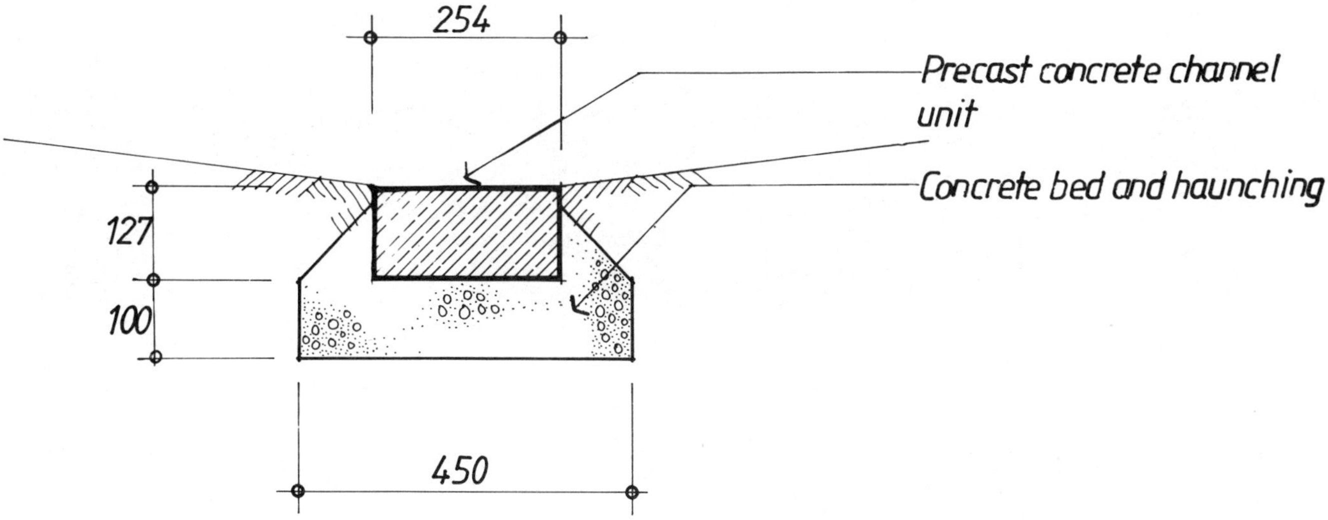

SECTION

Scale 1:10

DRAINAGE CHANNEL
concrete

Chapter 13

Tree surrounds

If trees are incorporated in paved areas, a soil pocket is required around each trunk, and an adequate surface water supply must be able to pass through the soil to the tree's roots. If the earth around the tree is sealed, the tree may dry up and die for lack of water and air. Another important point is that sufficient space be left to allow for the tree's natural growth, including expansion of the trunk.

Choice of surround

There are several methods of detailing tree surrounds.
A radial paving pattern of pre-cast concrete units with drainage holes can be used; or a panel of setts or bricks can be laid around the tree to a radius of approximately 1.5 m – 2.0 m. Tree grids or grilles in concrete or cast iron can be obtained from various manufacturers; or one of the edgings described in the section 'Margins and trims' can be used to retain the paving outside the tree surround, infilled with granular material such as cobblestones or gravel.
A kerb is sometimes misguidedly fitted around a tree to protect it and to edge the paving. This should not be done. It breaks up the horizontal surface and forms a useless miniature flower-bed for collecting litter, while offering only negligible protection to a hardy tree trunk. It could also cause accidents in heavily-used pedestrian areas.

Edging

When working around existing trees care should be taken to choose an edging that will not damage any roots which may be close to the surface. Edgings are usually flush with the surrounding paving to enable the surface run-off to drain into the tree surround.

Infill material

This should be porous so that surface run-off can water the trees. The material should be lightly compacted by hand. With existing trees, the ground should not be excavated at all around the tree, and the infill material should be placed on the hand-compacted topsoil.

Rigid units

These should be bedded on sand, and joints should be either unfilled or filled with sand. When using rigid units as infill, a hole of about 450 mm diameter be left free for the tree trunk.

Grids/grilles

Cast-iron tree grids should be supported off the ground by the edging or can be bedded on sand as paving. Perforated concrete slabs should be bedded on sand.

Note
It is essential that any settlement of the ground under surrounds be made up as quickly as possible to avoid damage or accidents.

References

The Architectural Press Ltd, London

E Beazley
Design and Detail of the Space between Buildings, 1960

R M Cartwright
The Design of Urban Space, 1980

William Heinemann Ltd, London
A E Weddle
Landscape Technique, 1979

E and F N Spon Ltd
Spon's Landscape Handbook

Detail sheets

13.1 Cast iron
13.2 Brick/hoggin
13.3 Mild steel
13.4 Pre-cast concrete units square
13.5 Pre-cast concrete units hexagon
13.6 Concrete block
13.7 Granite setts

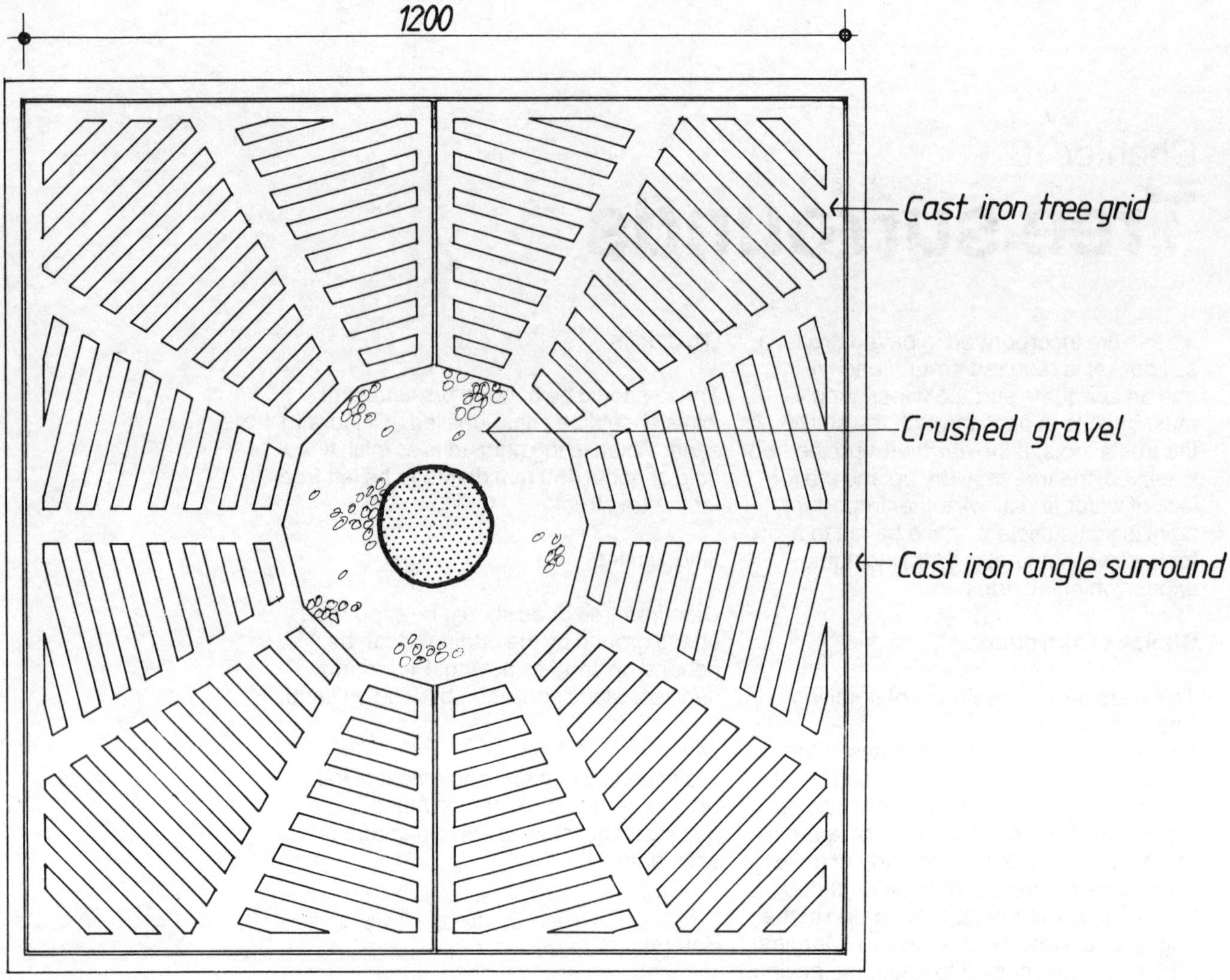
1200
Cast iron tree grid
Crushed gravel
Cast iron angle surround

PLAN

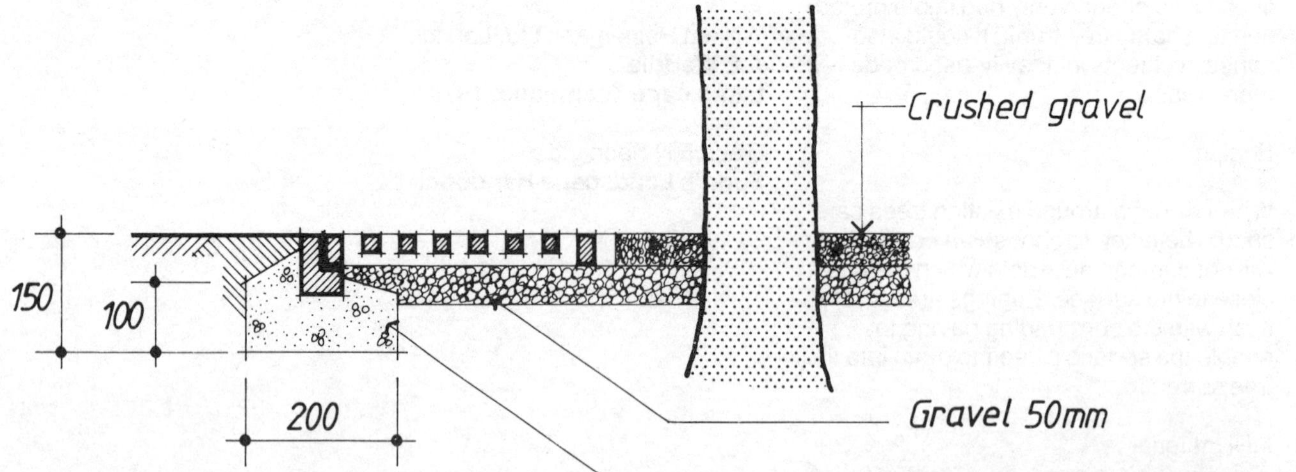
Crushed gravel
150
100
200
Gravel 50mm
Concrete bed and haunching

SECTION

Scale 1 : 10

TREE SURROUND
cast iron

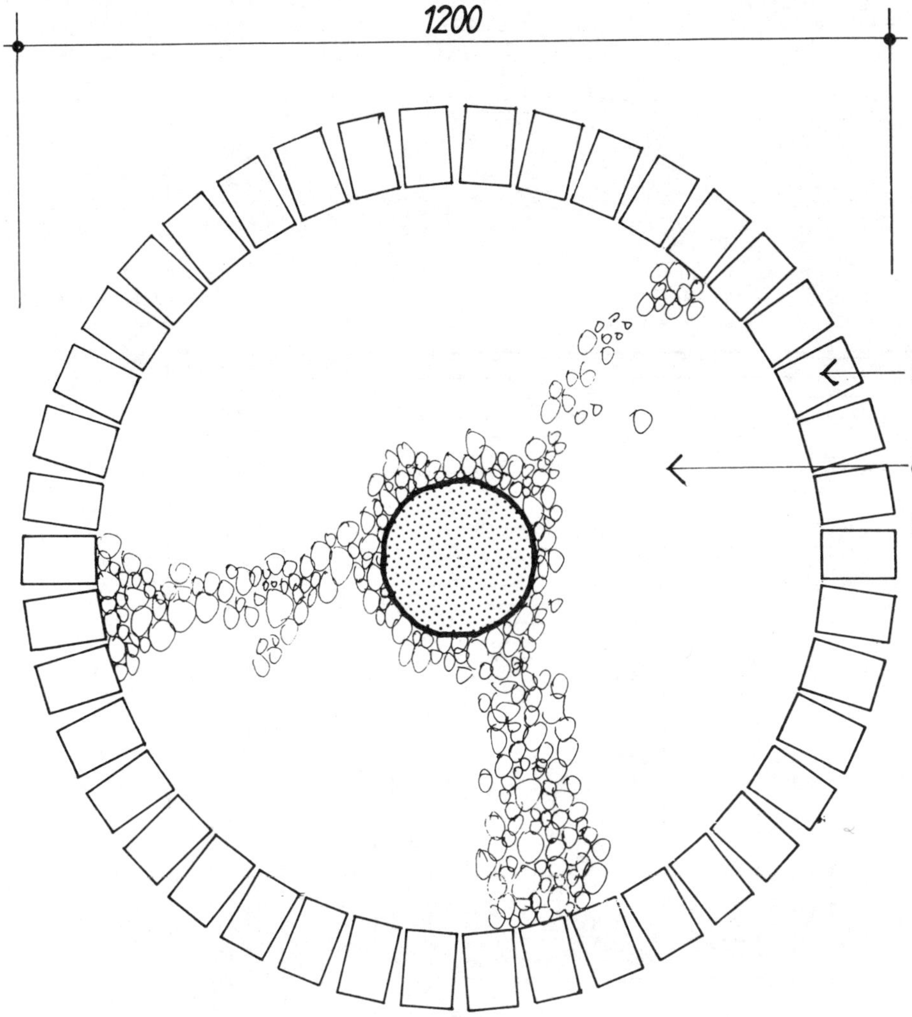

1200
Bricks on end
Crushed gravel
(or planted)

PLAN

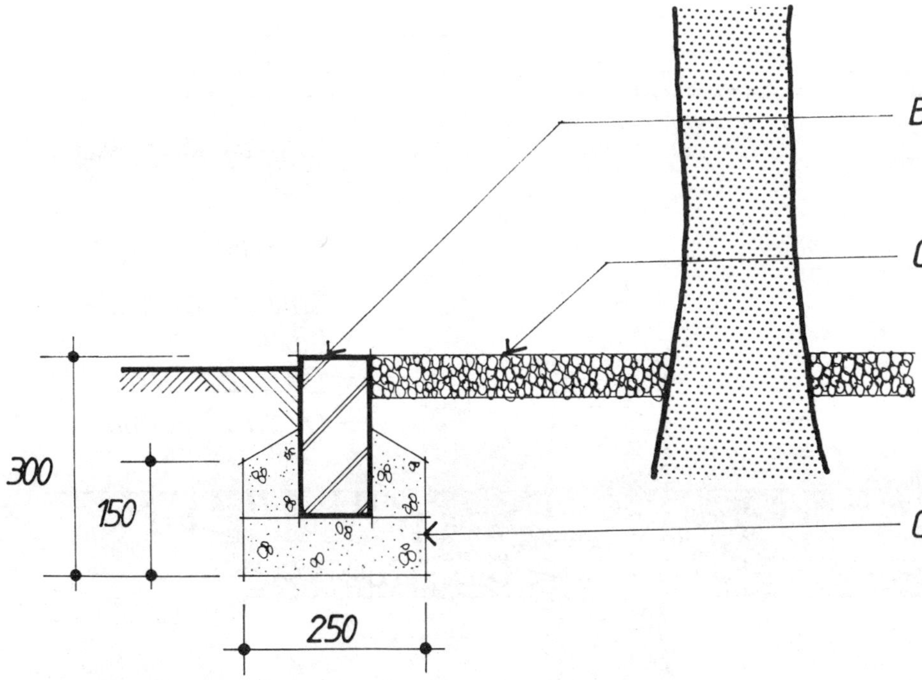

Brick on end surround
Crushed gravel 50mm
300
150
Concrete bed and haunching
250

SECTION

Scale 1 : 10

TREE SURROUND
brick/gravel

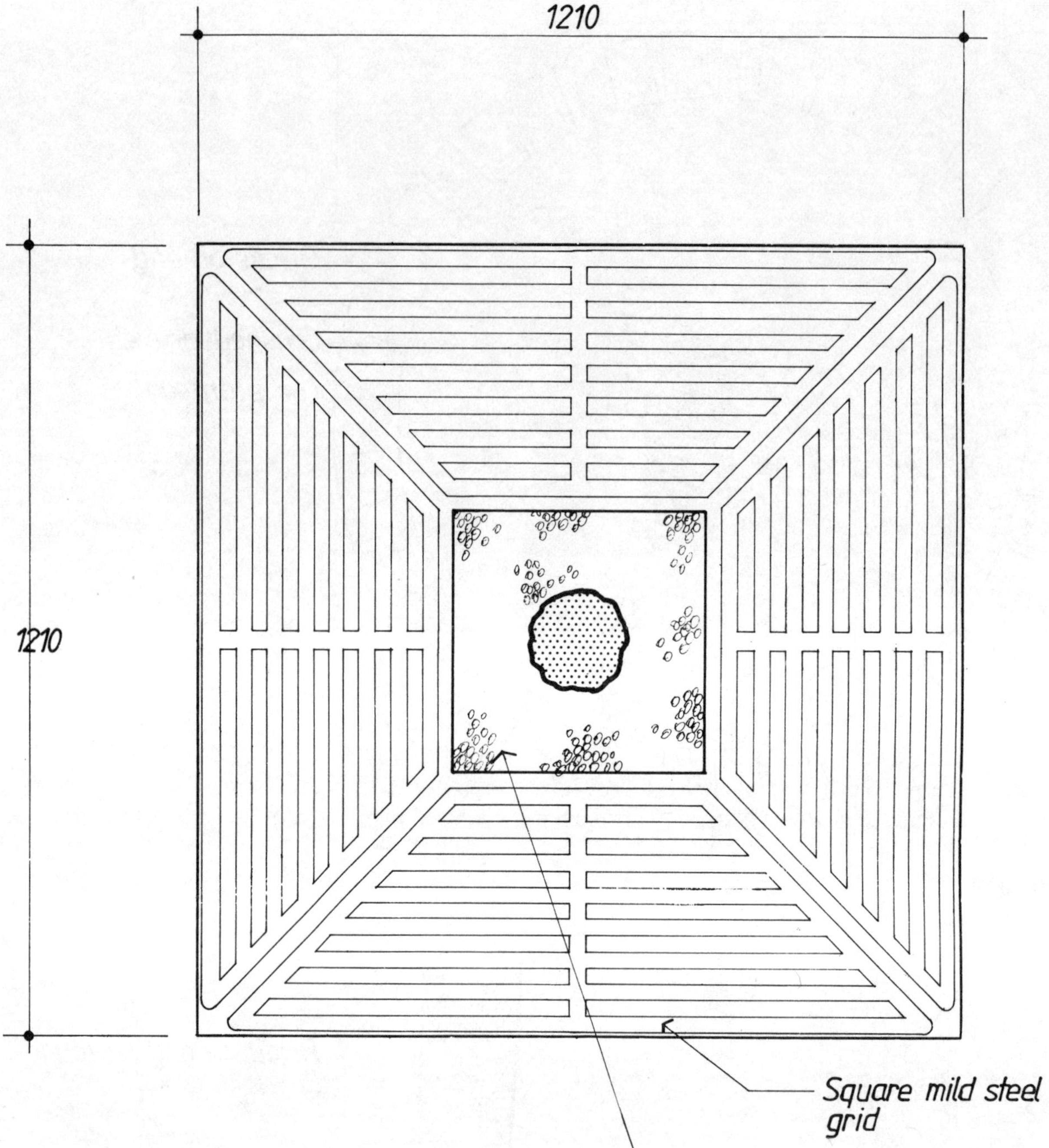
1210
1210
Square mild steel grid
Crushed gravel

PLAN

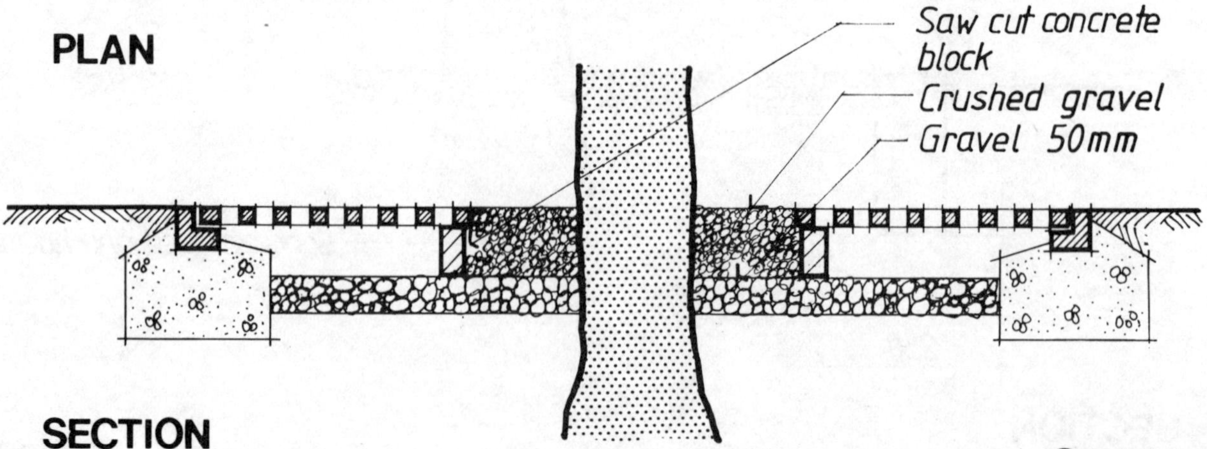
Saw cut concrete block
Crushed gravel
Gravel 50mm

SECTION

Scale 1:10

TREE SURROUND
mild steel

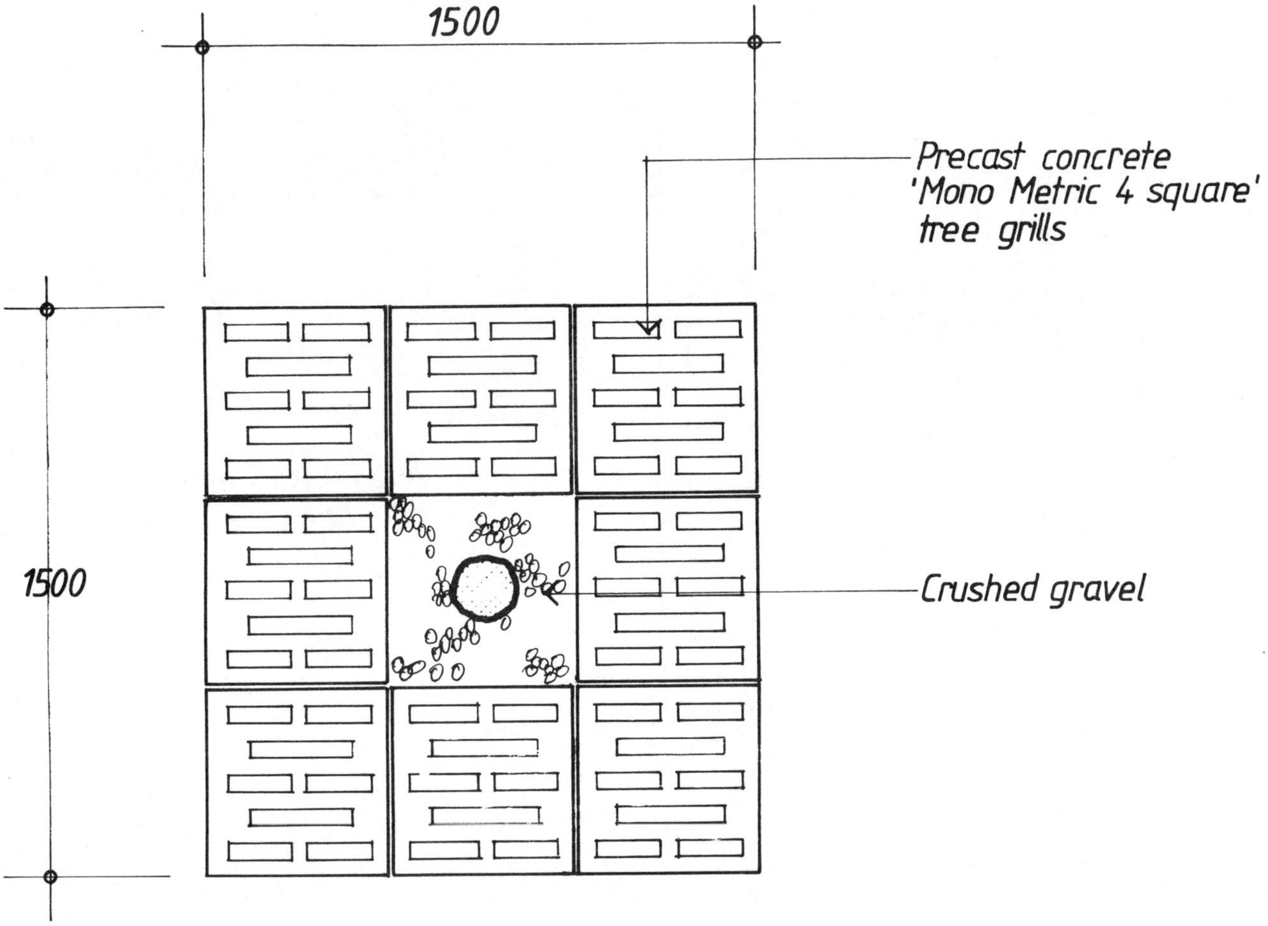

PLAN

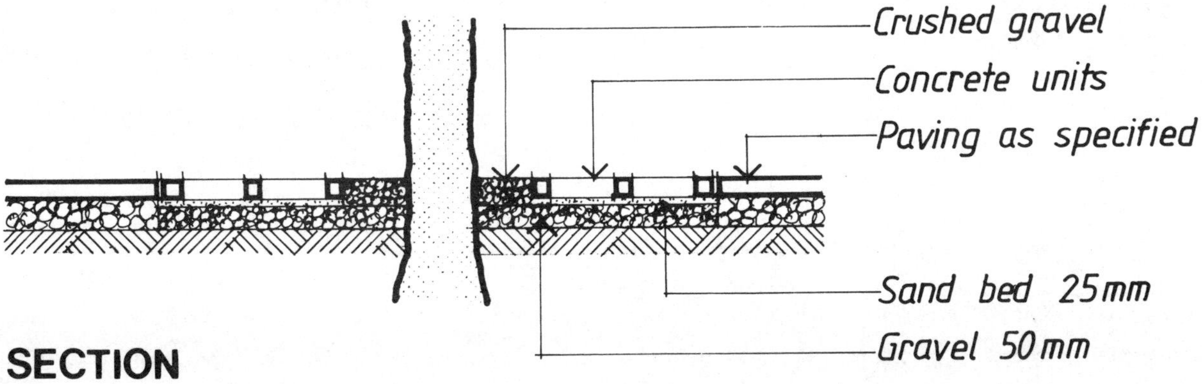

SECTION

Scale 1:20

TREE SURROUND
precast concrete

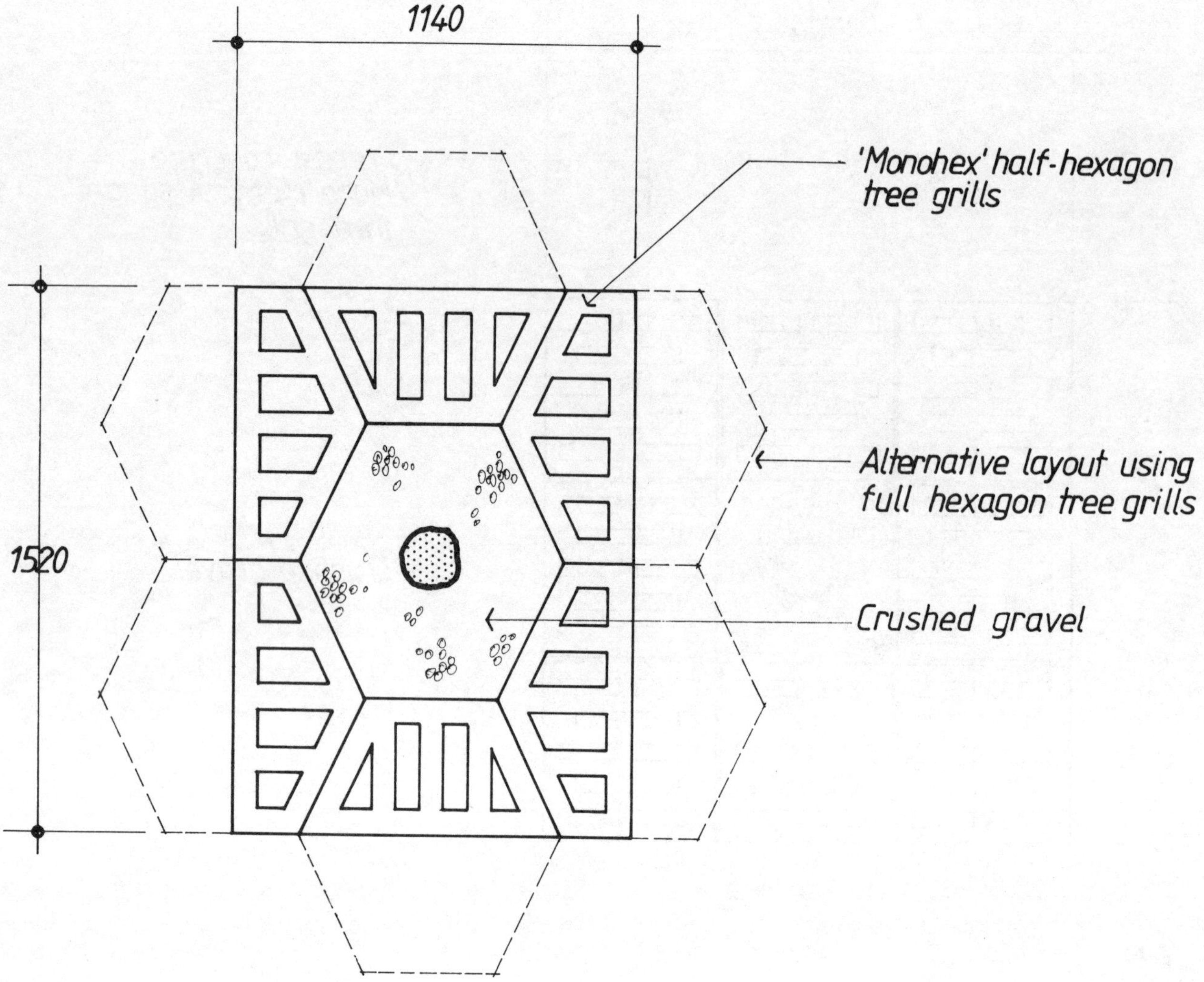
1140
'Monohex' half-hexagon tree grills
Alternative layout using full hexagon tree grills
1520
Crushed gravel

PLAN

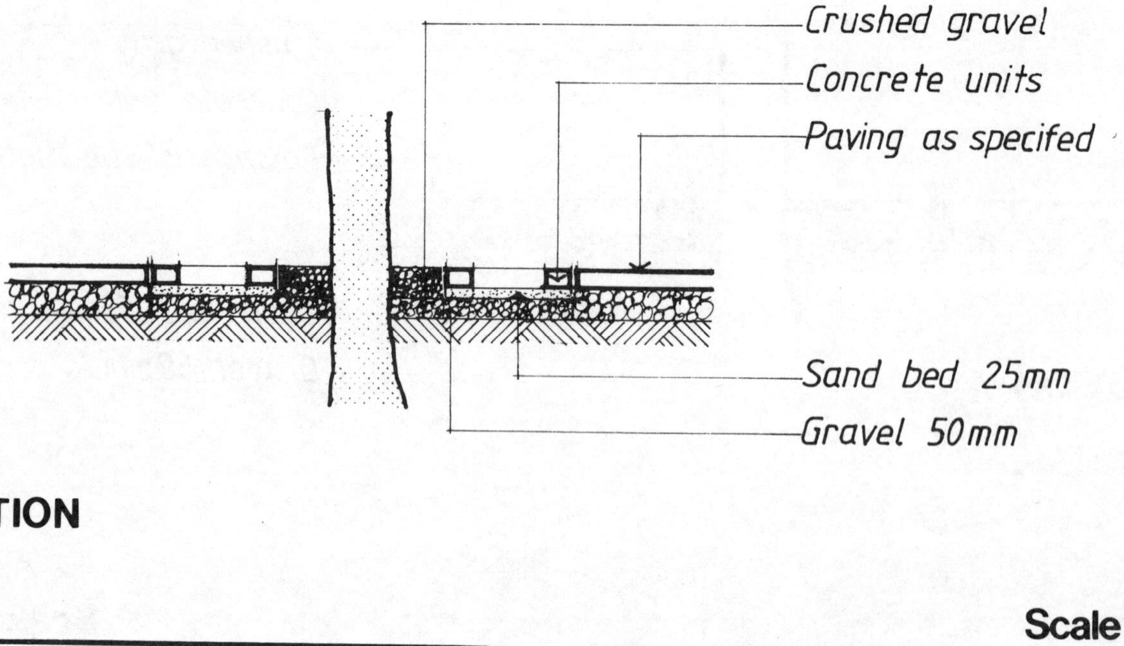
Crushed gravel
Concrete units
Paving as specifed
Sand bed 25mm
Gravel 50mm

SECTION

Scale 1:20

TREE SURROUND
precast concrete

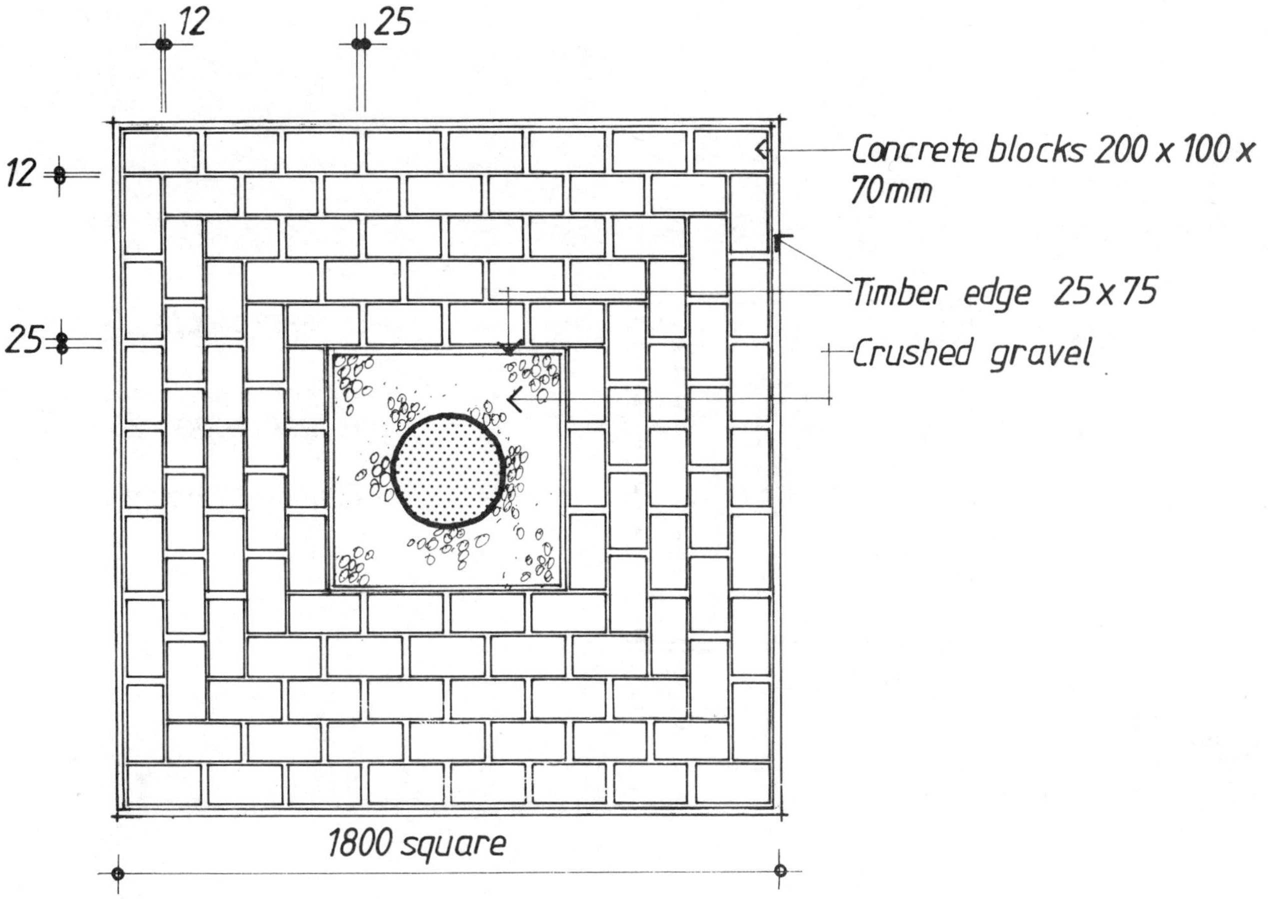
12
25
12
25
Concrete blocks 200 x 100 x 70mm
Timber edge 25 x 75
Crushed gravel
1800 square

PLAN

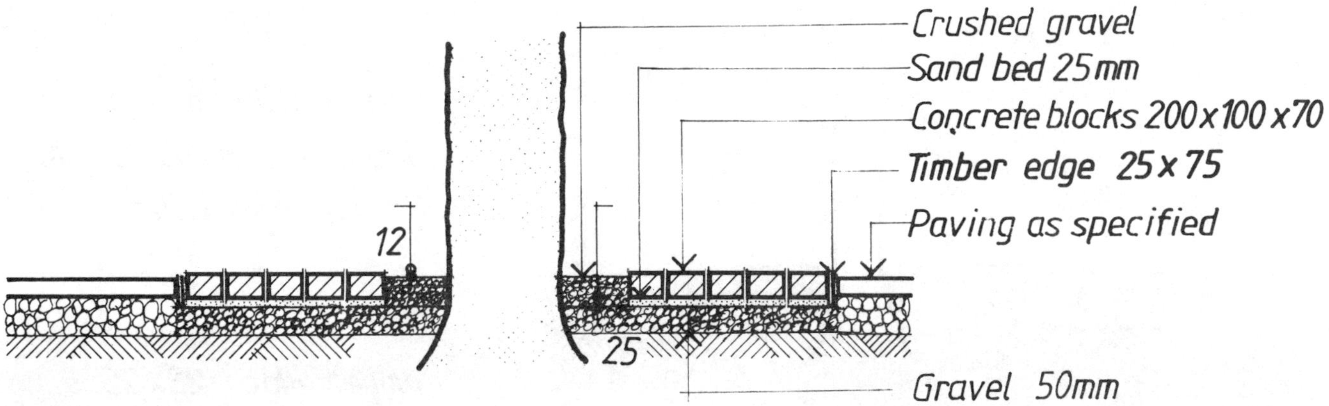
Crushed gravel
Sand bed 25mm
Concrete blocks 200 x 100 x 70
Timber edge 25 x 75
Paving as specified
12
25
Gravel 50mm

SECTION

Scale 1:20

TREE GRILLE

concrete block

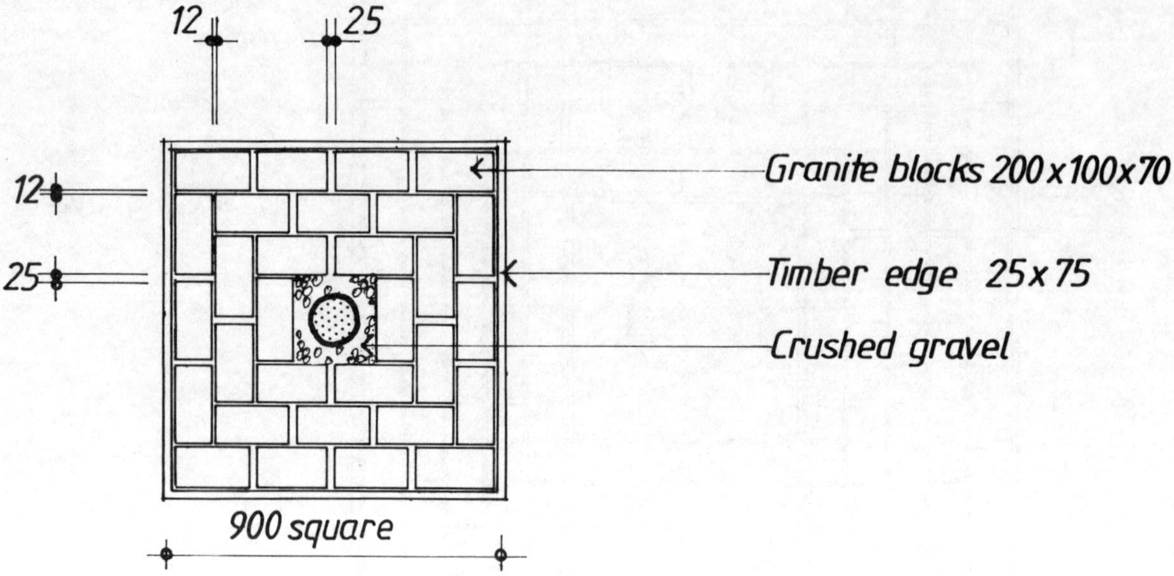

PLAN

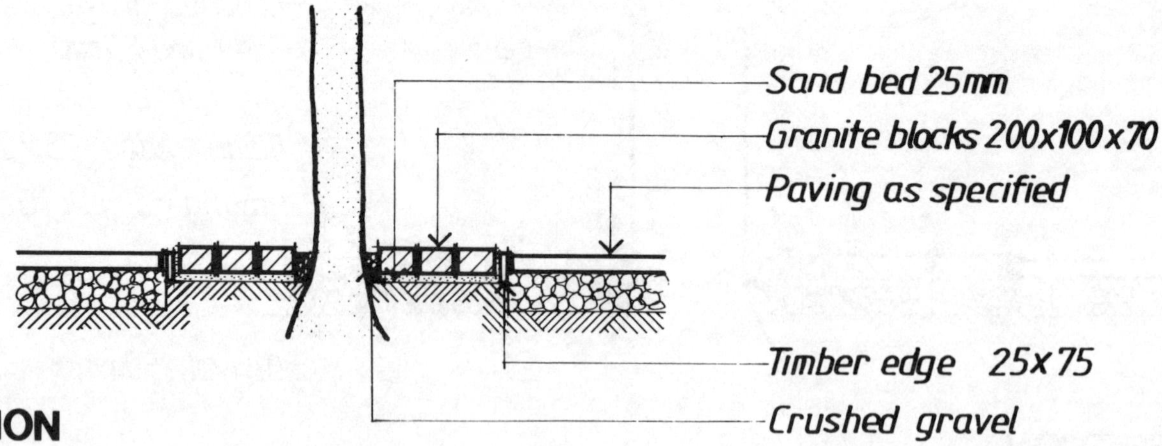

SECTION

Scale1:20

TREE GRILLE

granite setts

Appendix A:

Standards relevant to external works

BS – British Standard
CP – Code of Practice

BS 12 : 1958 **Portland cement (ordinary and rapid hardening)**
BS 65 : 1963 **Glazed vitrified clay drain and sewer pipes**
BS 76 : 1943 **Tars for road purposes**
BS 340 : 1963 **Pre-cast concrete kerbs, channels, edgings and quadrants**
BS 368 : 1956 **Pre-cast concrete flags**
BS 435 : 1931 **Granite and whinstone kerbs, channels, quadrants and setts**
BS 443 : 1969 **Galvanised coatings on wire**
BS 497 : 1952 **Cast manhole covers, road gully gratings and frames for drainage purposes**
BS 539 **Dimensions of drain fittings**
Part 1 : 1951 **Salt-glazed ware and glass (vitreous) enamelled salt-glazed fireclay**
Part 2 : 1951 **Scottish type. Salt-glazed ware and glass (vitreous) enamelled salt-glazed fireclay**
BS 540 : 1964 **Glass (vitreous) enamelled salt-glazed fireclay pipes**
BS 556 : 1955 **Concrete cylindrical pipes and fittings including manholes, inspection chambers and street gullies**
BS 594 : 1961 **Rolled asphalt**
BS 657 : 1950 **Dimensions of common clay building bricks**
BS 659 : 1963 **Light gauge copper tubes for water, gas and sanitation**
BS 706 : 1936 **Sandstone kerbs, channels, quadrants and setts**
BS 729 : 1971 **Hot-dip galvanised coatings on iron and steel articles**
BS 743 : 1970 **Materials for damp proof courses**
BS 802 : 1958 **Tarmacadam with crushed rock or slag aggregate**
BS 804 : 1953 **Capillary and compression fittings of copper and copper alloy for use with copper tube complying with BS 659 and BS 1386**
BS 882, 1201 : 1965 **Concrete aggregates from natural sources for concrete (including granolithic)**
BS 892 : 1954 **Glossary of highway engineering terms**
BS 913 : 1954 **Pressure creosoting of timber**
BS 1010 : 1959 **Draw-off taps and stop valves for water services (screwdown pattern)**
BS 1014 : 1961 **Pigments for cement, magnesium oxy-chloride and concrete**
BS 1185 : 1963 **Guards for underground stop valves**
BS 1194 : 1955 **Concrete porous pipes for under-drainage**
BS 1196 : 1944 **Clayware field drain pipes**
BS 1198-1200 : 1955 **Building sands from natural sources**
BS 1217 : 1945 **Cast stone**
BS 1221 : 1964 **Steel fabric for reinforcement of concrete**
BS 1222 : 1945 **Battery-operated electric fences**
BS 1241 : 1959 **Tarmacadam and tar carpets (gravel aggregate)**
BS 1242 : 1960 **Tarmacadam tarpaving for footpaths, playgrounds and similar works**
BS 1282 : 1959 **Classification of wood preservatives and their methods of application**
BS 1286 : 1945 **Clay tiles for flooring (dimensions and workmanship only)**
BS 1308 : 1970 **Concrete street-lighting columns.**
BS 1324 : 1962 **Asphalt tiles for paving and flooring (natural rock asphalt)**
BS 1377 : 1961 **Methods of testing soils for civil engineering purposes**
BS 1386 : 1957 **Copper tubes to be buried underground**
BS 1446 : 1973 **Mastic asphalt (natural rock asphalt fine aggregate) for roads and footways**
BS 1447 : 1962 **Mastic asphalt (limestone aggregate) for roads and footways**
BS 1485 : 1948 **Galvanised wire netting**
BS 1621 : 1961 **Bitumen macadam with crushed rock or slag aggregate**
BS 1690 : 1962 **Cold asphalt**
BS 1716 : 1963 **Cycle stands**
BS 1722 **Fences**
Part 1 : 1963 **Chain link fences**
Supplement 1 : 1974 **Gates and gateposts used in connection with chain link fences**
Part 2 : 1963 **Woven wire fences**
Part 3 : 1963 **Strained wire fences**
Part 4 : 1963 **Cleft chestnut pale fences**
Par 5 : 1963 **Close-boarded fences including oak pale fences**
Part 6 : 1963 **Wooden palisade fences**
Part 7 : 1963 **Wooden post and rail fences**
Part 8 : 1951 **Mild steel or wrought iron continuous bar fences**
Part 9 : 1963 **Mild steel or wrought iron unclimbable fences with round or square verticals and flat standards and horizontals**
Part 10 : 1963 **Anti-intruder chain link fences**
Part 11 : 1965 **Woven wood fences**
Part 12 : 1979 **Steel palisade fences**
Part 13 : 1978 **Chain link fences for tennis court surrounds**
BS 1831 : 1965 **Recommended common names for pesticides**
BS 1840 : 1960 **Steel columns for street lighting**
BS 1926 : 1962 **Ready-mixed concrete**
BS 1972 : 1961 **Polythene pipe (Type 425) for cold water services**
BS 2040 : 1953 **Bitumn macadam with gravel aggregate**
BS 2468 : 1963 **Glossary of terms relating to agricultural machinery and implements**
BS 2660 : 1955 **Colours for building and decorative paints**
BS 2760 : 1956 **Pitch-impregnated fibre drain and sewer pipes**
BS 2787 : 1956 **Glossary of terms for concrete and reinforced concrete**
BS 2847 : 1957 **Glossary of terms for stone used in building**
BS 3178 **Playground equipment for parks**
Part 1 : 1959 **General requirements**
Part 2A : 1959 **Special requirements for static equipment (except slides)**
Part 2B : 1960 **Special requirements for slides**
Part 3A : 1960 **Special requirements for swinging apparatus. Section A. Pendulum see-saws**
Part 3B : 1962 **Plane swings**
Part 3C : 1964 **Plank swings**

Part 3D : 1964 **Swings**
Part 3E : 1964 **Rocking boats**
Part 3F : 1964 **Rocking horses**
BS 3284 : 1964 **Polythene pipe (Type 710) for cold water services**
BS 3445 : 1961 **Field water troughs**
BS 3470 : 1975 **Field gates and posts**
BS 3505 : 1962 **Unplasticized PVC (Type 1140) for cold water supply**
BS 3589 : 1963 **Glossary of general building terms**
BS 3656 : 1963 **Asbestos cement pipes and fittings for sewerage and drainage**
BS 3690 : 1963 **Bitumen for road purposes**
BS 3798 : 1964 **Coping units (of clayware, unreinforced cast concrete, unreinforced cast stone, natural stone and slate)**
BS 3826 **Silicone-based water repellents for masonry**
Part 1 : 1964 **For clay brickwork**
BS 3854 : 1965 **Farm stock fences**
BS 2028 : 1953 **Pre-cast concrete blocks**
BS 3882 : 1965 **Topsoil**
BS 3810 : 1964 **Colours for specific purposes**
BS 3892 : 1965 **Pulverised fuel ash for use in concrete**
BS 3921 : 1965 **Bricks and blocks of fire brick, earth, clay or shale**
BS 3936 **Nursery stock**
Part 1 : 1965 **Trees and shrubs**
Part 2 : 1966 **Roses**
Part 3 : 1965 **Fruit**
Part 4 : 1966 **Forest trees**
BS 3969 : 1965 **Recommendations for turf**
BS 3975 **Glossary for landscape work**
Part 4 : 1966 **Tree work**
Part 5 : 1969 **Horticultural, arboricultural and forestry practice**
BS 3989 : 1966 **Aluminium street-lighting columns**
BS 3998 : 1966 **Tree work**
BS 4043 : 1966 **Transplanting semi-mature trees**
BS 4092 **Domestic front entrance gates**
Part 1 : 1966 **Metal gates**
Part 2 : 1966 **Wooden gates**
BS 4120 : 1971 **Steel wire for fences**
BS 4156 : 1967 **Peat**
BS 4324 : 1968 **Litter bins**
BS 4428 : 1969 **(1979) Recommendations for general landscape operations (excluding hard surfaces)**
BS 4987 : 1973 **Coated macadam for roads and other paved areas**
BS 5236 : 1975 **Recommendations for the cultivation and planting of trees in the extra-large nursery stock category**
BS 5273 : 1975 **Dense tar surfacing for roads and other paved areas**
BS 5489 : **Code of practice for road lighting**
Part 1 : 1973 **General principles**
Part 2 : 1974 **Lighting for traffic routes (Group A)**
Part 3 : 1977 **Lighting for subsidiary roads (Group B)**
BS 5696 **Play equipment intended for permanent installation outdoors**
Part 2 : 1979 **Recommendations for minimising hazards in equipment**
Part 3 : 1979 **Code of practice for installation and maintenance**
BS 5709 : 1979 **Specification for stiles, bridle gates and kissing-gates**
BS 5837 : 1980 **Code of Practice for trees in relation to construction**
BS 6031 : 1981 **Code of Practice for earthworks**

British Standard Codes of Practice applicable to landscape work
Building
CP 121.101 : 1951 **Brickwork**
CP 121.201 : 1951 **Masonry. Walls ashlared with natural or cast stone**
CP 121.202 : 1951 **Masonry. Rubble walls**
CP 122 : 1952 **Walls and partitions of blocks and slabs**
CP 123.101 : 1951 **Dense concrete walls**
CP 202 :1959 **Tile flooring and slab flooring**
CP 221 : 1960 **External rendered finishes**
CP 231 : 1952 **Painting**
CP 301 : 1950 **Building drainage**
CP 303 : 1952 **Surface water and subsoil drainage**
CP 308 : 1974 **Drainage of roofs and paved areas**
CP 310 : 1965 **Water supply**
CP 325 : 1953 **Farm and horticultural electrical installations**
CP 402.101 : 1952 **Hydrant systems**
CP 2001 : 1957 **Site investigations**

Electrical Engineering
CP 1004 **Street lighting**
Parts 1 and 2 : 1963 **General principles. Lighting for traffic routes**
Part 2A : 1956 **Roads other than traffic routes**

Civil Engineering
CP 2001 : 1957 **Site investigations**
CP 2003 : 1959 **Earthworks**

Index of British Standards

Conversion table

Feet and inches (up to 10ft) to metres and millimetres (to nearest millimetre)

Feet	Inches 0	1	2	3	4	5	6	7	8	9	10	11
	Metres and Millimetres											
0		25	51	76	102	127	152	178	203	229	254	279
1	305	330	356	381	406	432	457	483	508	533	559	584
2	610	635	660	686	711	737	762	787	813	838	864	889
3	914	940	965	991	1·016	1·041	1·067	1·092	1·118	1·143	1·168	1·194
4	1·219	1·245	1·270	1·295	1·321	1·346	1·372	1·397	1·422	1·448	1·473	1·499
5	1·524	1·549	1·575	1·600	1·626	1·651	1·676	1·702	1·727	1·753	1·778	1·803
6	1·829	1·854	1·880	1·905	1·930	1·956	1·981	2·007	2·032	2·057	2·083	2·108
7	2·134	2·159	2·184	2·210	2·235	2·261	2·286	2·311	2·337	2·362	2·388	2·413
8	2·438	2·464	2·489	2·515	2·540	2·565	2·591	2·616	2·642	2·667	2·692	2·718
9	2·743	2·769	2·794	2·819	2·845	2·870	2·896	2·921	2·946	2·972	2·997	3·023
10	3·048	3·073	3·099	3·124	3·150	3·175	3·200	3·226	3·251	3·277	3·302	3·327

Appendix B:

Associations and institutes

Agricultural Development and Advisory Services, Ministry of Agriculture, Fisheries and Food, **Great Westminster House, Horseferry Road, London SW1P 2AE (01-216-6311)**
Arboricultural Advisory and Information Service, Forestry Commission, **Forest Research Station, Alice Holt Lodge, Farnham, Surrey GU10 3LH (0420 22255)**
Arboricultural Association, **Ampfield House, Ampfield, Nr. Romsey, Hants, S05 9PA (0794 68717)**
Arboricultural Association, **Brokerswood House, Brokerswood, Nr. Westbury, Wiltshire (0373 822238)**
Architectural Salvage, **Hutton + Rostron, Netley House, Gomshall, Surrey GU5 9QA (Shere 3221)**
Asphalt and Coated Macadam Association, **25 Lower Belgrave Street, London SW1W 0LS (01 730 0761)**
Association of British Plywood and Veneer Manufacturers, **130 Hackney Road, London E2 7QR (01 739 7654)**
Association of Lightweight Aggregate Manufacturers, **c/o Russlite (Scotland) Ltd, Gartshore Works, Twechar, Kilsyth, Glasgow G65 9TW (0236 822461)**
Brick Development Association, **Woodside House, Wirkfield, Windsor, Berks SL4 2DX (034 47 5651)**
British Aggregate Construction Materials Industries, **25 Lower Belgrave Square, London SW1W 0LS (01 730 0761)**
British Chemical Dampcourse Association, **PO Box 105, Reading, Berks RG3 6NG (0734 24911)**
British Precast Concrete Ltd, **60 Charles Street, Leicester LE1 1FB (0533 28627/8/9)**
British Quarrying and Slag Federation Ltd, **Carolyn House, Dingwall Road, Croydon, CR0 9XF (01 680 7850)**
British Ready Mixed Concrete Association, **Shepperton House, Green Lane, Shepperton, Middx TW17 8DN (Walton-on-Thames 43232)**
British Standards Institution (BSI), **2 Park Street, London W1A 2BS (01 629 9000)**
British Tar Industry Association, **132/135 Sloane Street, London SW1X 9BB (01 730 5212)**
British Water and Effluent Treatment Association, **51 Castle Street, High Wycombe, Bucks HP13 4RN (0494 444544)**
British Wood Preserving Association, **Premier House, 150 Southampton Row, London WC1B 5AL (01 837 8217)**
Building Research Establishment, **Garston, Watford, Herts WD2 7JR (Garston 76612 and 74040)**
Cement And Concrete Association, **Wexham Springs, Slough SL3 6PL (028 16 2727)**
Centre on Environment for the Handicapped, **126 Albert Street, London NW1 7NF (01 482 2247)**
Civic Trust, **17 Carlton House Terrace, London SW1Y 5AW (01 930 0914)**
Council of Forest Industries of British Columbia, **Tileman House, 131-133 Upper Richmond Road, London SW15 2TR (01 788 4446)**
Countryside Commission, **1 Cambridge Gate, London NW1 4JY (01 935 5533)**
Countryside Commission, **John Dower House, Crescent Place, Cheltenham, Glos GL50 3RA (0242 21381)**
Crafts Council, **12 Waterloo Place, London SW1Y 4AU (01 930 4811)**
Design Council, **28 Haymarket, London SW1Y 4SU (01 839 8000)**
The Design Centre Wales, **Y Cyngor Cynllunio, Pearl Assurance House, Greyfriars Road, Cardiff CF1 3JN (0222 395811/2)**
Farm Buildings Information Centre, **National Agricultural Centre, Stoneleigh, Kenilworth, Warwicks CV8 2LG (0203 22345/6)**
Finnish Plywood International (UK), **PO Box 99, Welwyn Garden City, Herts AL6 0HS (043 879 746)**
Forestry Commission, **25 Savile Row, London W1X 2AY (01 734 4251)**
Glass Reinforced Cement Association, **Farthings End, Dukes Ride, Gerrards Cross, Bucks SL9 7LD (Gerrards Cross 82606)**
Institute of Quantity Surveyors, **98 Gloucester Place, London W1H 4AT (01 935 5577)**
Institution of Civil Engineers, **Great George Street, Westminster, London SW1P 3AA (01 222 7722)**
Institution of Highway Engineers, **3 Lygon Place, London SW1 (01 730 5245)**
Institution of Municipal Engineers, **25 Eccleston Square, London SW1V 1NX (01 834 5082)**
Institution of Structural Engineers, **11 Upper Belgrave Street, London SW1 (01 235 4535)**
Interlocking Paving Association, **60 Charles Street, Leicester LE1 1FB (0533 28627)**
Land Decade Educational Council, **9 Queen Anne's Gate, London SW1H 9BY (01 222 4333)**
Landscape Institute, **12 Carlton House Terrace, London SW1Y 5AH (01 839 4044)**
Mastic Asphalt Council and Employers Federation, **Construction House, Paddockhall Road, Haywards Heath, West Sussex RH16 1HE (0444 457786)**
National Association of Master Masons, **Admin House, Market Square, Leighton Buzzard, Beds LU7 7EU (0525 375252)**
National Building Specification Ltd, **Mansion House Chambers, The Close, Newcastle-upon-Tyne NE1 3RE (0632 29594)**
National Trust, **42 Queen Anne's Gate, London SW1 (01 222 9251)**
North Wales Slate Quarries Association, **Bryn Llanllechid, Bangor, Gwynedd, North Wales (0248 600476)**
Road Research Laboratory, **Crowthorne, Berkshire (03446 3131)**
Royal Institute of British Architects, **66 Portland Place, London W1N 4AD (01 580 5533)**
Royal Institution of Chartered Surveyors, **12 Great George Street, London SW1P 3AD (01 222 7000)**
Stone Federation, **82 New Cavendish Street, London W1M 8AD (01 580 5588)**
Timber Research and Development Association, **Stocking Lane, Hughenden Valley, High Wycombe, Bucks HP14 4ND (0240 24 3091)**
Tree Council, **35 Belgrave Square, London SW1X 8QN (01 235 8854)**
Water Research Centre, **Henley Road, Medmenham, PO Box 16, Marlow, Bucks SL7 2HD (049 166 531)**

Appendix C:

Manufacturers and suppliers

1: Fences, railings, gates
2: Walls, pavings, steps, margins

1
Abacus Municipal Ltd.
Sutton-in-Ashfield
Notts NG17 5FT
(0623 511111)

2
Abru Aluminium Ltd.
Building Products Division
Pennygillam Industrial Estate
Launceston
Cornwall PL15 7ED
(0566 3535)

2
ARC Concrete Ltd.
Elms Court
West Way
Botley
Oxford OX2 9LR
(0865 46351)

2
Atlas Stone Company Ltd.
Artillery House
Artillery Row
London SW1P 1RU
(01 222 2091)

1
Blenheim Sawmills
Combe
Oxford
(0993 62344)

1
Braby Group Ltd.
Ashton Gate Works
Bristol BS3 2LQ
(0272 664041)

1
G Brady & Co. Ltd.
Islington Works
Ancoats
Manchester
M60 0BL
(061 205 2797)

2
Brickhouse Dudley Ltd.
Dudley Road West
Tipton
West Midlands DY4 7XD
(021 557 3922)

1
British Aluminium Building Products Ltd.
Norfolk House
St. James's Square
London SW1Y 4JS
(01 839 8888)

2
British Dredging
(Concrete Products) Ltd.
Corporation Road
Newport
Gwent NPT 0WT
(0633 52181)

1
British Gates and Timber Ltd.
Biddenden
Nr Ashford
Kent
(0580 291555)

2
Broads Manufacturing Co. Ltd.
Western Road
Bracknell
Berks
(0344 24545)

1
Brookbrae Ltd.
53 St Leonard's Road
London SW14
(01 876 4370)

2
Brooklyns Westbrick Ltd.
1 Market Close
Poole
Dorset BH15 1NH
(020 13 5751)

1, 2
Broxap and Corby Ltd.
Walker Street
Radcliffe
Manchester
(061 773 7831)

1
Buffalo Fence Ltd.
19 Mill Lane
Benson
Oxford OX9 5SA
(0491 38368)

1
Burt Boulton (Timber) Ltd.
Brettenham House
Lancaster Place
London WC2E 7EN
(01 836 5801)

2
Butterley Building Materials Ltd.
Wellington Street
Ripley
Derby DE5 3DZ
(0773 43661)

2
Cat Castle Quarries Ltd.
Deepdale
Lartington
Barnard Castle
Durham
(0833 50681)

2
Charcon Products Ltd.
Hulland Ward
Derby DE6 3ET
(0332 31262)

2
Concrete (Northern Ireland) Ltd.
Langford Lodge
53 Largy Road
Crumlin
Co. Antrim
Northern Ireland
(02384 52328)

2
Concrete Utilities Ltd.
Great Amwell
Ware
Herts SG12 9TA
(0920 2272/6)

2
Albert Cook and Son (Founders) Ltd.
Wincolmlee
Hull
Yorks HU2 0QF
(0482 20099)

2
J. Delvaux Ltd.
Eastrey Road
Whittlesey
Cambridgeshire
(0733 202566)

1
Dorothea Restoration Engineers Ltd.
Assurance House
Hardwick Street
Buxton
Derbyshire
(0298 3438)

1
Durafencing Ltd.
37 Nightingale Grove
London SE13
(01 318 1215)

2
E. J. Elgood Ltd.
Insulcrete Works
Yeoman Street
London SE8 5DU
(01 237 1144)

1
Ferrous Gate Company
Albion Works
Green-Street-Green Road
Dartford
Kent
(0322 72119)

1
Forest Fencing Ltd.
Stanford Court
Stanford Bridge
Nr Worcester
(08865 451)

2
Furnitubes International Ltd.
90 Royal Hill
Greenwich
London SE10 8RT
(01 691 0019/0)

1
Glynwed Tubes & Structures Ltd.
Queensgate Works
Bilston Road
Wolverhampton WV2 2NJ
(0902 21633)

1
Hopwood Kay Hopwood Ltd.
Tuff-Link House
Chatburn
Lancs
(0200 41666)

2
Ibstock Building Products Ltd.
Ibstock
Leicester LE6 1HS
(0530 60531)

2
Iudex Ltd.
The Manor
East Haddon
Northampton NN6 8BU
(060 125 365)

1
Allan Kennedy Ltd.
Riverside
Stockton-on-Tees
Cleveland
(0642 65464)

1
KUFA Plastics Ltd.
2 Lyon Close
Chantry Estate
Kempston
Bedford MK42 7SB
(0234 854464)

2
S. Marshall & Sons Ltd.
Southowram
Halifax
Yorks HX3 9SY
(0422 22201)

2
Mather & Smith
General Iron Founders
Brunswick Road
Ashford
Kent TN23 1ED
(0233 24911)

2
Mendip Stone and Concrete Co. Ltd.
Leigh on Mendip
Bath
Somerset BA3 5QF
(037 381 396)

1, 2
Marley Building Ltd.
Peasmarsh
Guildford
Surrey
(0483 69922)

2
Minsterstone (Wharf Lane) Ltd.
Ilminster
Somerset
(046 05 2277)

2
Mono Concrete Ltd.
Wettern House
Dingwall Road
Croydon CR9 2NY
(01 686 4311)

1
Non-Corrosive Metal Products Ltd.
(Street Furniture Ltd.)
Horton Road
West Drayton
Middx
(81 42607)

2
The Ockley Brick Co. Ltd.
Smokejacks Brickworks
Walliswood
Nr Ockley
Surrey
(0306 79 481/3)

1
PJP Trading Ltd.
Queensway House
Queensway
Hatfield
Herts AL10 0NP
(30 66726)

2
Pullen Foundries Ltd.
60 Beddington Lane
Croydon
Surrey CR9 4ND
(01 684 1416)

1
Ranalah Gates
Gloucester Road Trading Estate
Malmesbury
Wiltshire
(06 662 3001)

2
Recticel Ltd.
18–22 Summerville Road
Bradford
West Yorks BD7 1PY
(0274 27370/29243)

2
Redland Bricks Ltd.
Redland House
Reigate
Surrey
(07372 49341)

2
Redland Precast Ltd.
PO Box 1
Barrow upon Soar
Loughborough
Leics LE12 8LX
(050 96 2601)

1
Reinforced Concrete Construction Co. Ltd.
Delph Road
Brierley Hill
Staffs DY5 2RW
(0384 78079)

2
Ronacrete Ltd.
296 Ilford Lane
Ilford
Essex 1G1 2SD
(01 553 2096)

2
Sevenoaks Brickworks Ltd.
Greatness
Sevenoaks
Kent TN14 5BP
(0732 59678)

2
Sloan & Davidson Ltd.
Swinnow Lane
Stanningley
Pudsey
West Yorkshire LS28 7XE
(0532 571892)

1
SMP (Landscape) Ltd.
Horton Road
Datchet
Berkshire
(0753 40555)

1
Starkey Gardner Ltd.
Lady Lane Industrial Estate
Hadleigh
Ipswich IP7 9DG
Suffolk
(047 338 2525)

2
Stanton and Staveley Ltd.
PO Box 72
Nr Nottingham NG10 5AA
(060 72 322121)

1
Street Furniture Ltd.
Horton Road
West Drayton
Middlesex UB7 8JE
(0895 42607)

2
Tarmac Roadstone Holdings Ltd.
50 Waterloo Road
Wolverhampton WV1 4RU
(0902 22411)

1
Town and Country Steelcraft Ltd.
Reform Road
Maidenhead
Berks SL6 8DA
(0628 27755)

1, 2
Townscape Products Ltd.
176 Loughborough Road
Leicester LE4 5LF
(0533 65321)

1
Tully Engineering Co. Ltd.
Northern Road
Newark
Notts NG24 2ES
(0636 4496/8)

1
UAC International Ltd.
UAC Timber Division
PO Box 1
UAC House
Blackfriars Road
London SE1 9UG
(01 928 2070)

1
UAC Timber (Wragby)
Wragby
Lincoln LN3 5NE
(067 34 304)

2
Watco (Sales) Ltd.
56 Buckingham Gate
London SW1 6AE
(01 834 5393)

2
Woodscape Ltd.
374 North Road
Preston
Lancs
(0772 57556)

Appendix D
Standard graphic symbols

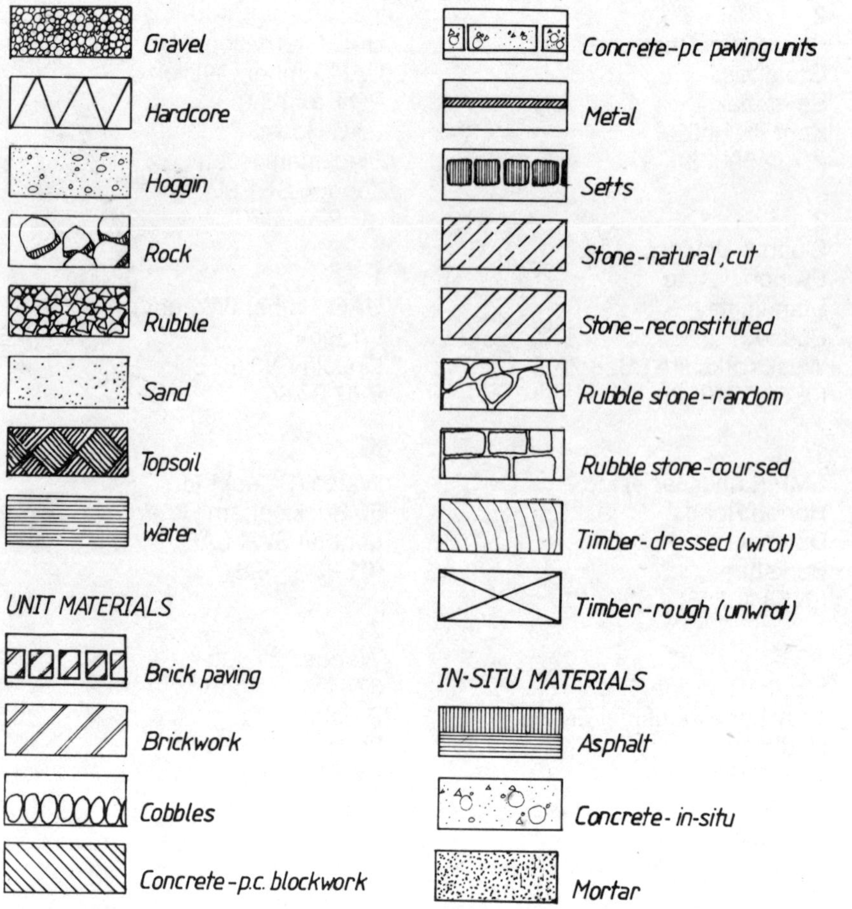

section

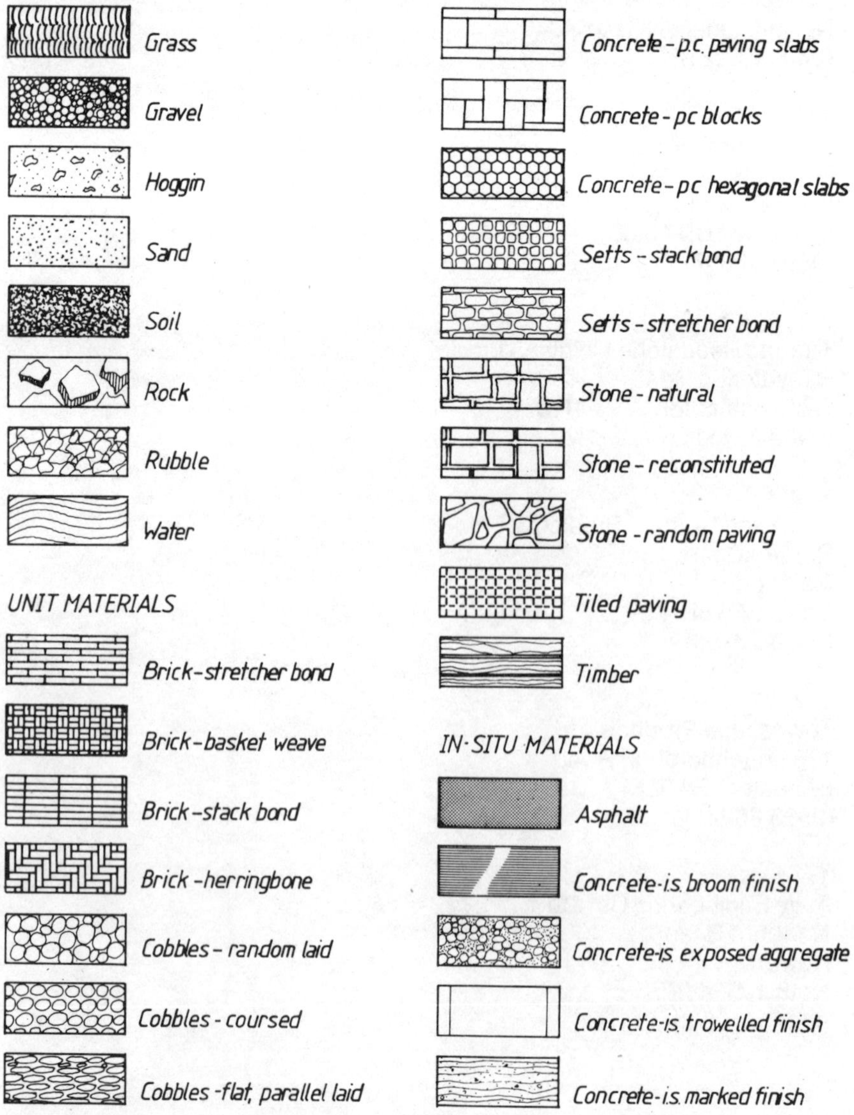

plan